Marginality and Crisis

Marginality and Crisis

Globalization and Identity in Contemporary Africa

Edited by Akanmu G. Adebayo,
Olutayo C. Adesina, and Rasheed O. Olaniyi

LEXINGTON BOOKS
A division of
ROWMAN & LITTLEFIELD PUBLISHERS, INC.
Lanham • Boulder • New York • Toronto • Plymouth, UK

Published by Lexington Books
A division of Rowman & Littlefield Publishers, Inc.
A wholly owned subsidiary of The Rowman & Littlefield Publishing Group, Inc.
4501 Forbes Boulevard, Suite 200, Lanham, Maryland 20706
http://www.lexingtonbooks.com

Estover Road, Plymouth PL6 7PY, United Kingdom

British Library Cataloguing in Publication Information Available

Library of Congress Cataloging-in-Publication Data

Marginality and crisis : globalization and identity in contemporary Africa / edited by Akanmu G. Adebayo, Olutayo C. Adesina, and Rasheed O. Olaniyi.
p. cm.
Includes bibliographical references and index.
ISBN 978-0-7391-4556-2 (alk. paper)
1. Africa—Foreign economic relations. 2. Globalization—Africa. 3. Economic development—Africa. 4. Africa—Economic conditions—1960– I. Adebayo, A. G. (Akanmu Gafari), 1956– II. Adesina, Olutayo C., 1964– III. Olaniyi, Rasheed O., 1971–
HF1611.M37 2010
337.6—dc22 2010006376

™ The paper used in this publication meets the minimum requirements of American National Standard for Information Sciences—Permanence of Paper for Printed Library Materials, ANSI/NISO Z39.48-1992.

Printed in the United States of America

Dedication

To Ireoluwa, Uthman, and Xander:
the hopes for our more equitable and sustainable future

CONTENTS

Figures xi

Tables xiii

Preface xv

Acknowledgments xvii

Section I: Discourse on Globalization

1. Introduction 3
Rasheed O. Olaniyi, Olutayo C. Adesina, and Akanmu G. Adebayo

2. Globalization: The Politics of "We" and "Them" 13
Osita Agbu

3. Origin and Dynamics of Globalization: A Historical Approach 31
Samuel Oluwole Ogundele

4. Compatriotism vs. Cosmopolitanism: Exploring a New Cosmo-Morality of Human Relations from the Yoruba in the Age of Globalization 43
Ronald Olufemi Badru

Section II: Globalization and Culture

5. Kiswahili Language and the Future of East African Integration in the Age of Globalization 61
Mwanakombo Mohammed Noordin

6. The Kabba *Dress: Identity and Modernity in Contemporary Cameroon* 71
Flavius Mayoa Mokake

7. Beyond Memoir: Echoes of Globalization, Identity, and Gender Struggle in Soyinka's Ake: The Years of Childhood 81
Ayo Ogunsiji

8. From the Global to the Local: The Media and Islam in Nigeria, 1979-2007 89
H. O. Danmole

Section III: Marginality: Africa and the Political Economy of Globalization

9. Globalization and the Privatization of State-Owned Enterprises: An Empirical Analysis of the Impact of Privatization on the Nigerian Economy 103
David Omeiza Moveh

10. Contemporary Trade, Investment Practices, and the Challenges of Regionalism and Poverty Alleviation in Africa 117
Aloysius-Michaels Okolie

11. Community-Based Organizations: Household Food and Livelihood Security in Southern Nigeria 133
Stephen Onakuse and Eamon Lenihan

12. Trade Liberalization and Employment in Nigeria 149
Olayinka Idowu Kareem

13. Globalization, Poverty, and the Failure of States in Africa: Is There a Connection? 167
Olalekan Emmanuel Obademi

Section IV: Crisis: Hot Spots and Contestations

14. A Cross-Regional Analysis of African Conflicts in the Age of Globalization 181
Agbo Uchechukwu Johnson

15. Globalization, Identity Politics, and the Escalation of Ife-Modakeke Crisis 197
Olajide O. Akanji

16. The 2001 Tiv-Jukun Ethnic Crisis: The "Indigene-Settler" Factor Reconsidered 209
Moses T. Aluaigba

17. Petroleum, the Environment, and the Economics of Nationalism in the Niger Delta 225
Sheriff Folarin and Henry Okodua

18. Oil Conflict in the Niger Delta: Revisiting the Odi Genocide 239
Andrew Oseloka Sawyer

Section V: Conclusion

19. Conclusion 259
Olutayo C. Adesina, Akanmu G. Adebayo, and Rasheed O. Olaniyi

Index 265

About the Editors 271

About the Contributors 273

FIGURES

Figure 12.1	Unemployment Rate in Nigeria	154
Figure 12.2	Total Foreign Private Capital in Nigeria	155
Figure 12.3	Total Unemployment Rate and Inflow of Foreign Capital	155

TABLES

Table 2.1	Faces of Globalization	19
Table 9.1	U.S. Assistance to Nigeria	105
Table 9.2	Nigeria's Gross Domestic Product and Growth Rate before and after Privatization, 1970-2004	110
Table 9.3	GDP Per Capita Growth Rate in Nigeria before and after Privatization	111
Table 9.4	Inflation Rate in Nigeria before and after Privatization	112
Table 9.5	Incidence of Poverty in Nigeria before and after Privatization	113
Table 10.1	Poverty in the Developing World, 1950-2000	122
Table 10.2	Selected Development Indicators for Major Developing Regions	123
Table 10.3	Tariff Walls in Selected African Countries, 1986-2000	124
Table 10.4	Pattern of Tariff Changes in Africa, 1980-2002	125
Table 12.1	Multiple Regression Result	160
Table 12.2	ADF Test	160
Table 12.3	Phillips-Peron Stationarity Test	161
Table 12.4	Johansen's Cointegration Test	162

Table 12.5	Parsimonious ECM	162
Table 12.6	Pairwise Granger Causality Test	162
Table 13.1	External Debt of Selected Countries	171
Table 13.2	External Debt as Percentage of GNP	172
Table 13.3	Regional Poverty Estimates	172
Table 13.4	People Living on Less Than $2 a Day	173
Table 16.1	Chronology of Events in the 2001 Tiv-Jukun Conflict in Taraba State	214
Table 17.1	Record of Oil Spill Incidents in Nigeria, 1976-2005	229

PREFACE

In an essay published in 2003, Zine Magubane and Paul Zeleza made the following point: "Africa is claimed, with various degrees of glee and gloom, to be marginal and in crisis both in epistemological and economic terms. . . Over the past decade, there have been vigorous debates about the dimensions and dynamics of Africa's alleged marginality and crisis. However, what strikes us . . . is how old these debates are" (Magubane & Zeleza, 2003, p. 165). Zeleza further elaborates on this theme of marginality and what he calls the "unhappy history" of Africa's experience with globalization:

> Africa's purported marginalization from globalization hardly means that the continent is not integrated into the world as such, but that it is integrated in a subordinate position. The degree of this subordination may have changed in recent decades, but its basic structure has not altered fundamentally since the emergence of the modern world system. In a large sense, then, for Africa globalization represents an old problem in new contexts: the hegemony of Northern processes, practices, and perspectives. (Zeleza, 2003, p. 11)

What has changed in the African experience of globalization since these and similar studies? Offered to fill several gaps in the discourse, this book presents current studies on globalization in (and of) contemporary Africa from various disciplinary perspectives. It finds, to a large extent, that not much has changed in the African experience and scholarship vis-à-vis globalization since the beginning of the twenty-first century. This seems to lend credence to the popular expression: the more things change, the more they remain the same.

The chapters in this book were first presented in November 2007 at the international conference on "Globalization: Migration, Citizenship and Identity," held at the University of Ibadan, Ibadan, Nigeria, and organized jointly by the University of Ibadan and Kennesaw State University, Kennesaw, Georgia, United States. Different themes had emanated from the papers presented at the conference. These formed the basis for three publications, two of which have already been published. The first is the special edition of the *Journal of Global Initiatives*, Volume 3, Number 2, 2008 (Guest Editor: Olutayo C. Adesina) subtitled *Globalization and the Unending Frontier*. The second is *Globalization and*

Transnational Migrations (Cambridge Scholars Publishing, 2009) edited by Akanmu G. Adebayo and Olutayo C. Adesina.

This book is divided into five sections. Section I is "Discourse on Globalization." With four chapters, this section presents several studies that evaluate globalization from different disciplinary perspectives. These discourses are followed in Section II by an important exploration in cultural globalization. The section covers everything from religion to mode of dressing. Section III discusses the theme of marginality by exploring the political economy of globalization anchored by the disciplines of political science and economics. Studies in Section IV provide empirical and detailed analyses of Africa's hot spots and terrains of contestations, confirming Zeleza's concept of "crisis." Section V is the conclusion.

In various ways, the studies in this book all affirm the position that globalization has marginalized Africa—in the sense of ensconcing the continent in a subordinate position—and has deepened its crises. The absence of any serious consideration for Africa in extremely popular studies, such as Friedman's *The World Is Flat* (2006), his *Hot, Flat, and Crowded* (2008), or Stiglitz's *Making Globalization Work* (2007), have further demonstrated the extent of this "marginalization and crisis." This study is offered to complement others in the field, to fill the gaps in the literature; to further our understanding of the African experience under globalization; and to present choices and opportunities available to African states, peoples, cultures, economies, and societies especially as the current global economic and financial crises deepen.

References

Friedman, T. (2006). *The world is flat: A brief history of the twenty-first century*. New York: Farrar, Straus and Giroux.

—. (2008). *Hot, flat, and crowded: Why we need a green revolution—And how it can renew America*. New York: Farrar, Straus and Giroux.

Magubane, Z., & Zeleza, P. (2003). Globalization and Africa's intellectual engagements. In M.B. Steger. (Ed.), *Rethinking globalism*, pp. 165-177. Lanham, MD: Rowman & Littlefield Publishers, Inc.

Stiglitz, J. (2007). *Making globalization work*. New York: W.W. Norton Co.

Zeleza, P. (2003). *Rethinking Africa's globalization, volume 1: The intellectual challenges*. Trenton, NJ: Africa World Press.

ACKNOWLEDGMENTS

Many people and organizations helped to make this book possible. We gratefully acknowledge the assistance of the entire staff of the Department of History at the University of Ibadan (UI), and the Institute for Global Initiatives at Kennesaw State University (KSU). We appreciate the support of Dr. Lendley Black, Provost and Vice President for Academic Affairs, KSU; Professor Olufemi Bamiro, FNSE, Vice Chancellor, UI; Professor Adigun Agbaje, Deputy Vice Chancellor (Academic), UI; Professor Labode Popoola, Dean of Postgraduate School, UI; Professor A. L. Oyeleye, the immediate past Dean of the Faculty of Arts, UI; and Dr. C.B.N. Ogbogbo, the current Acting Head of the History Department, UI. We also thank Professor Bolanle Awe, Dr. Dan Paracka, Dr. Nurudeen Akinyemi, Dr. Howard Shealy, Dr. Richard Vengroff, Ms. Vivian Bonilla, Dr. B. A. Mojuetan, Professor A. I. Olayinka, Professor Aduke Grace Adebayo, Professor Dotun Ogundeji, Dr. Babatunde Sofela, Professor Olufemi Omosini, Dr. K. I. Princewill, Mr. Laolu Ogunniyi (Chairman and Managing Director, LOTO Productions), Dr. V.O. Edo, and Mr. Paul Ugboajah.

Several people helped to make the conference and the subsequent editing process go smoothly. We are especially grateful to the following: Mr. Ademola Adebayo, Professor Lai Olurode, Mr. Muritala Monsur Olalekan, Justice Oladejo Akanbi, Mr. Nwachukwu Peace, Ms. Ime Enang, Alhaja Nike Ibraheem, Mr. Wale Adeleke, Mr. Okey and Dr. (Mrs.) Ngozi Anyikwa, Mr. Sola Abioye, Mr. Rasheed Hassan, Dr. Jare Adejuwon, Mr. Folu Ogunbanwo, Engineer Segun and Dr. Foluke Ogunleye, Dr. Sesan and Yinka Fadare, Dr. Bola Udegbe, and Mr. Abimbola Olayemi Oladayo. We also thank the students of the Department of History, University of Ibadan, who acted as foot soldiers during the entire period of the conference.

We use this medium to thank Ms. Betsy Rhame-Minor for copyediting the various chapters. We are also grateful to the editorial staff of Lexington Press, especially Mr. Michael Sisskin, Ms. Lindsey Schauer, Ms. Gwen Kirby, and Ms. Victoria Koulakjian for their professionalism. They made the entire process painless.

Our families provided immense support. We thank Mrs. Tola Adebayo, Mrs. Kemi Adesina, and Mrs. Monsurat Olaniyi for their love and encouragement. Above all, we thank God for His many blessings.

SECTION I

DISCOURSE ON GLOBALIZATION

CHAPTER ONE

INTRODUCTION

RASHEED O. OLANIYI, OLUTAYO C. ADESINA, AND AKANMU G. ADEBAYO

Contemporary challenges of development and interaction need to be conceptualized in terms of global processes and interconnections. This is centrally because everyday life and livelihoods have been re-constituted, re-colonized, or re-westernized. Globalization process has contradictory dynamics and a hierarchical nature that have shaped and respaced modern nation-state, economy, images, cultural forms, commodity flows, and social interaction. It has also re-defined and reshaped people's sense of meaning. The phenomenon could, therefore, be considered the great transformation of our epoch.

The philosophy that undergirds this book is simple enough. Globalization has produced many results for Africa. Two of these are marginalization and crisis. Globalization has caused, promoted, and/or escalated the marginalization and crisis, especially as many Africans (countries, ethnic, religious, and other groupings) negotiate their particular identity vis-à-vis the global identity. The outcome of Africa's structural linkages to the global economy, the marginalization and crises are not acceptable if globalization is expected to be good for all the world. But Africa must be liberated, must get out of the marginality and crisis. The question is how.

Global restructuring of capitalism and turbulent socio-economic transformations are intrinsically interconnected. Globalization's benefits have not reached everyone equally; it is thus highly turbulent, contested, and full of struggles, inequalities, and conflict. The chapters in this volume theoretically and empirically explain new thinking on the historical specificity and peculiarity of globalization, and its prevailing impact in several parts of the African continent, ranging widely from Kenya to Cameroon, and from the Sudan to Nigeria.

The authors examine a wide range of issues including the West and the rest of the world in matters relating to culture, ideology, identity, conflict, literature; global governance, the state, and non-governmental organizations (NGOs); people's understanding and resilience. They pose a wide range of questions: Do the masses of people in the Global South understand the dynamics of globalization? In what ways have they reacted against persistent poverty, food and health crises, environmental degradation, unemployment, influx of foreign cultural and social norms, and other vices? Where is Africa now, and what are the future prospects? While Africa and other developing societies are vulnerable to globalization, the phenomenon has also threatened European, American, and other developed societies, what with the serial collapse of banks, failure of free market ideology, loss of jobs, and homelessness.

With specific reference to the continent of Africa, the corpus of literature on globalization has not significantly taken into account the street situation and struggles, or the citizenship and identity questions playing out in the global age. From Cairo to Kano, Calabar to Casablanca, millions of ordinary Africans have inadequate knowledge of globalization. Discourses on globalization remain formal, elitist, and academic to the exclusion of the masses who bear the pernicious effects. Before the international conference on globalization held at the University of Ibadan in November 2007, the impact of globalization was articulated at several fora and workshops. Such conferences and workshops are still being convened. How do ordinary people conceptualize globalization? How do they feel its effects? How do motion pictures, ATMs, money transfers, reality shows, billboards, mobile phones, cyber cafes and the Internet, rap music, wigs, fast food joints, and other manifestations of globalization influence their everyday life?

Given that globalization involves invisible political calculations and expediencies, it is difficult for the masses to react to unseen forces that affect their everyday lives. In the industrial capitalist countries, American citizens may not think of outsourcing in the context of globalization but would rage against Mexicans, Somalis, and other immigrants pushing them out of the labor market. Similarly, in other parts of the world, the ambiguities and uncertainties spurred by globalization could be perceived as local, attributable to bad governance, corruption, nepotism, and witchcraft. Most African leaders and other parts of the Global South are historically disconnected from the needs and aspirations of their masses. This lack of understanding of the social struggles of the masses constitutes profound challenges to development.

Religion and spirituality have usually had a prominent role in African worldview, power of judgment, and cosmology. Since nation-states appear to be an inadequate structure under globalization, faith-based organizations and informal associations have had overwhelming control over the masses. This increases religious space and the process of seeking spiritual remedies to the challenges of living. Religiosity also affects state-citizen relations. Even though some clerics do criticize government officials and policies, religious institutions expect the peasants to be content with their leaders no matter the level of corruption. The masses are expected to address their socio-economic challenges through fasting, vigils, and prayers at domestic as well as workplaces. Struggles against bad governance and corruption continue to be affected by religious doctrines and dogma. *Boko Haram,* a recent Islamic movement in northern Nigeria, preached against Western education and launched attacks on security officials and outposts of the state. It took the combined security forces of Nigeria several weeks to crush the spontaneous uprisings of *Boko Haram* adherents in many parts of northeast and northwest Nigeria. Challenges posed by globalization were considered as repercussions of sins or machinations of the enemy. This notion has compounded domestic disputes, rivalries in the marketplace, conflicts over water supply in the neighborhoods, and so on. These are issues that confront not just the masses of the people but also today's intellectuals and other members of the middle class.

It is amazing that responses to neo-liberalism and globalization have enthroned the capitalist idiom of individualism by eroding African communal ethos. Individualist approaches are now adopted in order to survive the effects of globalization. In Nigeria, it has become popular to see low- and middle-income earners buying "generators" to provide power supply in the absence of electricity from government sources, or sending their children to private schools due to the collapse of public schools. In this equation, some gain but others (the majority) lose. Among those who profit from the chaos are importers of generators and, by extension, makers of cheap generators in China, Taiwan, India, and other (mostly Asian) countries. On the other hand, the declining capacity of the state invariably triggers solidarity along ethnic and religious lines among people whose security and livelihoods are threatened.

In spite of its overarching influences, globalization remains basically an intellectual concept and ideological commodity. Despite the presence of anti-globalization movements, popular discourses about the phenomenon is almost lacking in Africa. Samuel Ogundele in chapter 4 of this book adopts a non-esoteric approach to analyze globalization. According to Ogundele, globalization research should not be conceptualized as a mere academic engagement that makes scholars get lost in verbiage or verbosity to the detriment of comprehensibility by a broad spectrum of people.

The disruption of the Seattle meeting of the World Trade Organization (WTO) in December 1999, that of mass rally in Quebec in Canada; demonstration in Gothenburg in Sweden and the mass rally against the World Bank Conference in Oslo, Norway, in 2000, had no parallel elsewhere in the Southern Hemisphere. Anti-globalization sentiment as developed in the West has no equivalent in the South. In Africa, popular musicians and the new Pentecostal elites found globalization as an opportunity for growth and expansion of their trades. In these masses-oriented spaces, globalization is glorified and celebrated.

Since the early 1990s, left-wing student unionism and scholarship has virtually disappeared from several ivory towers. Prior to the 1990s, these groups, coupled with vibrant civil society, had fought military dictatorship, human rights violations, and abuse of power. Many activists were hounded into exile, incarcerated, or silenced through state-sponsored assassination. This process had emasculated popular movements, and had denied the masses the opportunity of radical mobilization against the forces of globalization. Compared to the global South, anti-globalization in the North was mediated through the Internet. Local struggles in the South continue to deepen but are also disconnected from the global struggle due to ideological differences, identity politics, and most significantly, technological backwardness. Indeed, the victims of globalization have been manipulated and remain too fragmented to unite against globalization. For example, the Ogoni struggle for self-determination in the oil-rich Niger Delta developed no linkage with the religious protests in some parts of northern Nigeria against American occupation of Iraq and Afghanistan.

In capitalist countries, the Internet and other means of communication were used to organize mass resistance to the institutions of capitalist globalization. Oppositional politics used new technologies to intervene in the global restructuring of capitalism in order to promote democratic and anti-capitalist social movements aiming at radical structural transformation.

Africa and the larger parts of the global South are firmly integrated into the dominant global trends of institutional change. According to Bangura, the continent of Africa is tightly locked into the processes of global economic policy making as directed by the Bretton Woods institutions. Institutional changes and reforms in Africa involve technocratic capacities, economic policies, market reforms, and budgeting crafted and enforced in order to send credible signals to investors and donors. In essence, institutional reforms in the public are investor driven with little regard for the struggling masses. Indeed, despite the democratization process, there has been reduction in social accountability. Governments are less able and unwilling to control their own economic destinies. It is no longer an assumption that the state power of economic policy making and budgeting has been ceded to international financial institutions and multilateral agencies.

Following the withdrawal of the state from social welfare, the international NGOs have been providing social support to civil society organizations, women's and farmers' groups. These international agencies funded and organized workshops on human rights, gender equality, poverty alleviation programs, HIV/AIDS campaigns, and peace-building and conflict resolution. Funding from donor agencies deepens the culture of dependency. Some communities consider NGO intervention as a form of cultural imperialism, the "modern missionaries" on "civilizing mission." In northern Nigeria, the resistance against polio vaccines was partly borne out of cultural and religious sentiments, despite untold health consequences for children and women.

These soft anti-poverty packages take inequalities for granted and merely address the symptoms of underdevelopment. Contemporaneously, African states are under pressure for budget cuts in agriculture, education, and health, which has a correlation with taxing the poor more. The redistributive capacity of the state declined, and global governance emerged to deal with global problems such as poverty, women's rights, conflicts, and environmental issues. Globalization engenders unequal development and perpetuation of poverty on an unprecedented world scale in the southern hemisphere.

In chapter 15 of this book, Akanji suggests that globalization has overwhelmingly contributed to the escalation of local conflicts. Akanji's study of the hydra-headed Ife-Modakeke crisis in Nigeria shows that the volatility of the recent phase of the crisis (1997-2000) could be explained by the supply of weapons and resource mobilization by the diaspora hometown associations. Aluaigba in chapter 16 similarly makes allusion to this fact in the case of the Tiv-Jukun ethnic crisis. Even though the ethnic conflict was one of the most prolonged and violent crises in Nigeria, the free flow of weapons into Nigeria from neighboring countries aggravated the conflict. The unaccountable forces of globalization, especially the cross-border flow of arms, are largely beyond the control of effective state regulation (Mittelman, 1994, p. 439). Sandbrook and Romano (2004) further contend that globalization has a general tendency that generates conditions which are conducive to the emergence of extremist movements, instability, and conflict. According to Sandbrook and Romano, the ascendance in tensions and grievances, combined with an increasingly ineffective and unpopular regime, provide an opening for violent protest movements and conflicts. In this context, Johnson in chapter 14 demonstrates that due to the marginalization of Africa in the process of globalization, identity has become a tool for competition in the desire to gain undue advantage by one group against another. This chapter, focusing on the Mano River area, Darfur, and Rwanda, explores the identity context and marginality inherent in the conflicts.

The poor are notoriously non-ideological actors in the globalization debate and the concomitant inequitable workings of free market. The donor agencies, as "secular missionaries," are guided by preconceptions and notions that exclude the poor in the bargaining and income-distribution processes. In addition, many donor agencies promote patronage, corruption, and clientelism by bending to the interests of the ruling elites. Invariably, donor regime sustains the inequalities of income and power and the processes that undermine the livelihoods of the poor. In the developing world, only a small fraction of NGOs focus on global economy and global issues. Most NGOs focus on issues ranging from women's rights and democratization, to eliminating female circumcision as a barbaric relic of the past (Bhagwati, 2007, p. 37).

Since the 1990s, the deepening process of globalization reconstitutes and redefines the development process in Africa. Under the aegis of globalization, developing nations in Asia, Latin America, and Africa remain peripheral, rural, and non-industrial parts of the global system. Some of these issues have received the attention of scholars in this volume.

The globalization process has strongly affected the African economy. So also is the expansion of global capital and Information and Communication Technologies (ICT). The penetration of these forces has significantly influenced African culture and self-understanding. Acculturation processes and socialization have been spurred by foreign culture, social values, lifestyle, dressing, music and dance, consumerist culture, and eating and drinking habits. In the aftermath of these, Akin Fadahunsi suggests that, "the prospect for promoting authentic and sustainable indigenous culture will remain dim as long as Africa cannot access ICT facilities for use in the learning of local African languages. The slow death of the languages may emasculate the various African identities and loss of dignity by the African" (2002, p. 6).

Most countries in the developing world are strong states that jealously guard their strength and sovereignty and suppress threat to their powers. As the case of the Niger Delta imbroglio shows, the state in the age of globalization intervenes to protect global capital. Globalization represents the triumph of capital over all social classes. The protracted conflicts in the Niger Delta, even though domestic, have pandered to the global value of oil, with all its devastating consequences for the U.S. economy and elsewhere in the industrial world. Sawyer analyses the oil conflict in the Niger Delta and the Odi genocide. He argues in chapter 18 that official handling of conflicts in Nigeria has been characterized by inadequacies and questionable methods. The iron fist and militaristic approaches remain endemic in Nigeria's conflict management.

The Nigerian state protected transnational oil companies in an attempt to expropriate the revenue from oil while the local communities remained impoverished. The soaring oil production intensified the centrality of the state as the locus of the struggle for resources for personal aggrandizement and group security, especially in a prebendal system. Clientelism, patron-system, and clusters became crucial elements in the governmental process. Since independence in 1960, Nigeria has never had a stable state power, except in an environment of prebendal politics. In essence, the prevailing prebendal system and clientelism advance global capital and power of the local elite while the poor citizens bear the brunt. Against this background, Sawyer adopts an advocacy approach in assessing the actions of the soldiers sent to destroy Odi.

In chapter 17, Folarin and Okodua demonstrate how the Niger Delta conflict came into the global limelight. For decades, the people of the Niger Delta agitated over the sordid acts of ecocide by the oil multinationals in the process of oil exploration and without the expected economic vantages and physical development.

How have communities confronted and challenged globalization? How are community-based organizations (CBOs) organizing and mobilizing the poor in the Global South? Onakuse and Lenihan in chapter 11 analyze the relationship between household food security and CBOs in rural villages in the southern states of Nigeria. Through empirical research, Onakuse and Lenihan demonstrate that rural CBOs are strategic in the process of livelihood security.

From the evidence adduced, it is unclear whether the African political elite can reassume responsibility for designing socio-economic development. Many leaders from the developing world consider globalization as a conspiracy against their countries. They portray globalization as exploitation since "free trade" forces on developing countries the options of integration or the severe conditions of marginalization and stagnation. For Thandika Mkandawire, "The tragedy of Africa's policy-making and policy implementation in the last several years is the complete surrender of national policies to the ever-changing ideas of international experts" (1999, p.1). In this scenario, dependency syndrome stifles imagination, local knowledge, and initiative. Thus, hegemonic forces, sabotaging development in Africa, are not primarily external to the global south. The "comprador elite" reproduce and entrench the colonial exploitative structure. African leaders exploited the liberalization process to commercialize their politics. Moveh in chapter 9 builds on the suggestion that privatization of public enterprises aggravates the disarticulation of the economy and inequalities.

Kareem, in chapter 12, discusses the impact of globalization by measuring the effects of trade liberalization on employment generation in Nigeria. He demonstrates that the openness of the economy and liberalization of custom and excise duties on the one hand seems to enhance job creation. On the other hand, the liberalization of exchange rate and import duties enhance the level of unemployment through high cost of exports.

Furthermore, it seems economic recovery can hardly occur without local initiative and historical experiences that are required for development. In chapter 2, Osita Agbu traces the historical trajectory and philosophical moorings of globalization as well as its practical manifestations in relation to the inequalities between the advanced industrialized nations and countries of the South. Every nation and culture is a product of borrowings, appropriation, and adoption of different cultural influences and diversities. Globalization illuminates that cultures co-create and coexist. The way in which globalization influenced popular culture could be perceived as a new means of modernity, leading to naïve illusions, false expectations, and false consciousness. This is in spite of the fact that cultural globalization threatened local languages and cultures. Globalization makes the poor feel ashamed of their poverty most especially when they encounter products of new technology they cannot consume.

In chapter 5, Noordin argues that the expansion of the East African Community (EAC) immediately posed the fundamental question of the role of Kiswahili in relation to other languages in the process of identity formation in the EAC. Noordin analyzes discourses surrounding language, migration, and citizenship in Kenya in order to enhance the understanding of the role of language in public conception and what it means to be an East African; and she explores how Kiswahili competes with English and French (spoken largely in Rwanda and Burundi) to retain and expand its influence in the cultural and economic space of East Africa.

Ake is a narration of the childhood experience of Wole Soyinka. In chapter 7, Ogunsiji's postmodern reading of Soyinka's *Ake* reveals that the text contains echoes of globalization. Some indicators of the new world order in the text include the references to a transistor radio and a gramophone, the soldiers and Hitler to produce echoes of the world wars, photography and fashion designing, magicians who "train in India," confectionaries and provisions, cosmetics, snacks and European food, e.g., hamburgers, sausage-rolls. As shown in the text, all these not only modify the life of Ake community but also highlight the salient features of a world in motion.

The power of clothing to mediate notions of self and society, consumer desire, culture, and identity shows the importance of globalization from the margins. In chapter 6, Flavius Mokake describes the multiple functions of *Kabba* over the years and how modernization provided the dress a national character which justifies the need for its canonization as a national attire for women and a marketable cultural artifact in a globalizing world.

In chapter 8, Danmole explores the litigious relations between the media and Islam in Nigeria. Danmole posits that through the media, Nigerian Muslims have been able to achieve a greater participation on global issues particularly when such issues are a matter of concern over their religion. Through constant contacts with Muslims in other parts of the world through new media technologies—Internet, cell phones, e-mails—Islamic cultural values have continued to be transformed. Global media outpourings have not only influenced religious harmony but more often triggered violent religious protests and uprisings against what Nigerian Muslims considered political marginalization, Western dominance, and blasphemous images or imprints.

Ronald Badru's argument in chapter 4 suggests that the ontology of globalization is a commitment to the ultimate institution of a global village where common human values are promoted. Contrary to this, compatriotism and cosmopolitanism constitute a problem in the ethic of care.

In chapter 10, Okolie focuses on the incidence of poverty and the possibilities of eradicating or reducing the poverty level within the context of "fair trade regime and re-defined investment practices." Building on this, Emmanuel in chapter 13 demonstrates that unlike in China, India, and Malaysia, globalization has deepened the fragility and failure of the state in Africa in terms of poverty reduction.

The book goes further to explain new forms of contestations, power relations, citizenship, and politics engendered by globalization. There are cleavages and conflicts within and among religions, ethnic groups, states, regions, continents, and hemispheres. It is argued that the world is divided against itself posing great challenges to the achievement of equity and justice.

References

Adejumobi, S. (2002, August). Perspectives on globalization: From WTO to NEPAD. Paper presented to the 2002 Damina School, Research Methodology Workshop on Globalization and Democracy (CRD), Kano, Nigeria.

Alao, A. (2007). *Natural resources and conflict in Africa: The tragedy of endowment.* Rochester, NY: University of Rochester Press.

Alemika, E.O., & Okoye, F. (2002). *Ethno-religious conflicts and democracy in Nigeria: Challenges*. Kaduna, Nigeria: Human Rights Monitor.

Alubo, O. (2002, August). The social impact of globalization. Paper presented to the 2002 Damina School, Research Methodology Workshop on Globalization and Democracy (CRD), Kano, Nigeria.
Bangura, Y. (2001, May). Globalization and African development. Lecture delivered at the seminar "Africa in the New Millennium" of the Nordic Africa Institute and African Heads of Mission, Stockholm, Sweden.
Barber, B.R. (2001). *Jihad vs. McWorld.* New York: Ballantine Books.
Bhagwati, J. (2007). *In defense of globalization.* Oxford: Oxford University Press.
De Soto, H. (2000). *The mystery of capital: Why capitalism triumphs in the West and fails everywhere else.* New York: Basic Books.
Fadahunsi, A. (2002). The political economy of globalization. *African Forum for Development Dialogue.* Ibadan, Nigeria, Unpublished paper.
Huntington, S.P. (1996). The clash of civilizations? In *The Clash of Civilizations? The Debate.* New York: Council on Foreign Relations, pp. 1-25.
Kellner, D. (2003). Globalization, technopolitics, and revolution. In J. Foran (Ed.), *The future of revolutions, rethinking radical change in the age of globalization*, pp. 180-194. London: Zed Books.
Magubane, Z., & Zeleza, P. (2003). Globalization and Africa's intellectual engagements. In M.B. Steger (Ed). *Rethinking globalism*, pp. 165-177. Lanham, MD: Rowman & Littlefield Publishers, Inc.
Mittelman, J.H. (September, 1994). The globalization challenge: Surviving at the margins. *Third World Quarterly*, 15(3), pp. 427-443.
Mkandawire, T. (1999). International policies, African realities. In T. Mkandawire & C. Soludo (Eds.), *Our continent, our future: African perspective on structural adjustment.* Trenton, NJ: Africa World Press.
Obi, C.I. (1997). Globalization and local resistance: The case of the Ogoni versus Shell. *New Political Economy*, 2(1), pp. 137-148.
Obi, C.I. (2001). Global, state, and local intersections: Power, authority, and conflict in the Niger Delta. In T. Callaghy, R. Kassimir, & R. Latham (Eds.), *Intervention and transnationalism in Africa.* Cambridge: Cambridge University Press, pp. 173-193.
Sandbrook, R., & Romano, D. (2004). Globalization, extremism and violence in poor countries. *Third World Quarterly*, 25(6), pp. 1007-1030.
Schuftan, C. (1998). *Beyond maldevelopment praxis in Africa.* Dakar: CODESRIA Monograph, vol. 1.
Singer, P. (2002). *One world: The ethics of globalization.* New Haven, CT and London: Yale University Press.
Zeleza, P. (2003). *Rethinking Africa's globalization, volume 1: The intellectual challenges.* Trenton, NJ: Africa World Press.

CHAPTER TWO

GLOBALIZATION: THE POLITICS OF "WE" AND "THEM"

OSITA AGBU

It is our conception of development and societal goals that determine the veracity or otherwise that globalization is either positive or negative. In short, viewed from the simple criteria of physical well-being, self-actualization, and societal cohesion, globalization has been a destructive force of immense dimensions for Africa.

"What is needed is not globalization of world economy but globalization of development." (Iman Ill-Haque, 1999)

Introduction

Let us begin by clarifying what "We" and "Them" mean, though this appears obvious in the context of the globalization discourse. By "We," is meant the developing countries, the poorer countries of the South; while "Them," stands for the advanced industrialized countries, the rich countries of the North. Globalization and its meaning could be taken for granted considering the avalanche of literature that exists in this field of study. However, this will be a mistake, as globalization is such an overarching and multi-dimensional concept that it simply cannot be taken for granted.

This chapter, therefore, approaches this enquiry with caution, even as it tries to understand, assimilate, and proffer suggestions for addressing the problematic of this phenomenon. The historical trajectory and philosophical moorings of globalization as well as its practical manifestations as they relate to the inequalities existing between the advanced industrialized nations and countries of the South are explored in this chapter. The central argument here is that globalization creates a dichotomy between "We" and "Them," or the "poor" and the "rich," or the "North" and "South," a dichotomy that could feed the embers of marginalization, distrust, and insecurity in the world. Implicit in the arguments in this chapter is that globalization is not necessarily powered by the invisible hand of the market, but rather, by forces behind the scene, by political calculations and expediencies, and by interests that do not hesitate to use political instruments and institutions to attain their goals. It is no secret that globalization is today impacting almost all areas of human activity. Apart from the issue of poverty and its discontents, cultural and social formations are being assaulted at an unprecedented rate under the onslaught of finance capital and one-sided global information dissemination architecture. In short, though globalization may have its positive side, depending on one's capacity to exploit, in the main, it generates marginality and crisis, and creates a platform that forces people to negotiate and re-negotiate their identities in the global arena. The objective of this inquiry, therefore, is to assist us in better understanding the phenomenon, the dynamics of the dichotomy or asymmetry that is created and replicated, and probable ways of checkmating the undesirable aspects of globalization on disadvantaged societies.

The plethora of literature about globalization that has been churned out tends to confuse rather than explicate the different dimensions of this phenomenon. The discussion about globalization has, in fact, mystified the concept to a degree that is unhealthy. However, the fact also remains that whether we do understand globalization or not, it definitely impacts on quality of life, the peace and stability of the environment, and one's relevance in the twenty-first century (Utomi, 2000). In the main, without necessarily rehashing the literature, the globalization debate has raged between those who see in it opportunities for economic growth and more efficient markets, and those who see a disadvantage for the late starters mainly of the developing world. Many also see economic and corporate globalization as eroding state powers with serious implications for weak developing states (Utomi, 2000). It suffices to state that globalization is a major site of contestation with supporters (Ohmae, 1995; Scholte, 1996; Axtmann, 1998) and opposers (South Centre, 1996; Khor, 2001; Stiglitz, 2003).

From the literature, globalization is assumed to have played a very important role in increasing economic growth and reducing absolute poverty in developing countries of the South. To this end, proponents of globalization argue that it has led to better products, lower costs, job opportunities, increased productivity, and improvement in global quality of life and welfare. Indeed, some believe that globalization has enriched the world scientifically and culturally, and has benefited a greater part of the people economically. However, Berberoglu (1997) was of the view that globalization actually accentuates class, regional, national, and local inequalities and that it increases disparities in wealth, resources, and power. Dare (2001) had shown in his article how transnational corporations (TNCs) with the support of global structures had, in collaboration with rogue governments in Africa, plundered the rich resources of the continent. That globalization reflects the increasing contradictions between capital and labor, and the logic of accumulation between the local and the international cannot be overemphasized.

Indeed, ongoing discussions indicate that the global financial crisis has further exposed the underbelly of globalization. Apart from the crisis highlighting the deep but unhealthy degree of interdependence today, the situation calls for a rethink of current global governance structures, being alert to increased threats of protectionism, climate change, and generally being mindful of the social dimension of globalization.

Historical Trajectory in the Growth of Globalization

Globalization is neither a new concept nor a new phenomenon. It is simply a particular (but critical) moment in the expansion of capital. It could be argued that globalization is a logical stage that could be traced to the slave trade, through to colonialism and imperialism, and to the present stage in the expansion of capitalism, especially finance capital propelled by new technologies. Ordinarily, this should not be a problem; however, for capitalism to grow, there must be some exploitation of either human or material resources. And this is what has happened. In fact, Tandon (2000, p. 56) equates globalization in its broadest sense with the movement of history. The larger movement of history he also considers as the movement of civilization itself, which comes with both positive and negative effects.

The roots of globalization date back to the time of European exploration and eventual colonization of other parts of the world. It is believed that the first great expansion of European capitalism took place in the sixteenth century following the first circumnavigation of the earth between 1519 and 1521, and at the early phases of the slave trade (Institute of Ethics and Developmental Studies, 2002). The salient features were characterized by the search for markets, raw materials, and cheap labor. There was an extensive market in Africa where slave trade was the first sign of globalization. Africa, it appears, was inducted into globalization quite early. It could be said that the second phase of Africa's integration into the global system was that of the colonial period. In both instances, Africa was at a disadvantage for several reasons, the most important being its technological weakness.

However, the process of integration became more global in the nineteenth century as capital moved from Europe to North America and Australia, to open up the areas with the building of railroad systems and agriculture that would be central to the expansion of capital (Akindele et al., 2002). The arrival of joint-stock companies and developments in the acts of banking, industrial capital, and technology enabled the scramble for and partition of Africa in 1884. Though interrupted by the Cold War between the United States and the USSR, globalization was to reassert itself with the effective end of the Cold War in 1990. With this, there was no need this time around for the West to compromise its ideology of globalized trade and culture on account of Communism. Capitalism had seemingly triumphed.

Capitalism—with its dogmas of promoting private initiatives regulated mainly by the market forces, free trade, and limited governmental intervention in public policy formulation and implementation, and also of individual or multinational accumulation of surplus, and its supportive procedural democracy—became the most important institution around which social progress or social change was articulated in contemporary times (Lumumba-Kasongo, 2001, p. 3). Marx had espoused the nature of capitalism in his three-volume *Das Kapital* amidst other writings, noting the importance of the profit motive in the expansion of capital and in its undoing. From Marx's writings, no region of the world was too remote for the penetration of capital. However, the end of bi-polarism (itself a product of globalization) could be the *nunc dimittis* of capitalism as it creates neo-bipolarism (between the haves and have-nots), and therefore between the North and South in novel ways (Olurode, 2003).

It had been observed for instance that significant in the new imperialism was the emergence of several empires in competition, and the predominance of finance capital over mercantile capital (Hobson, 1938; Magdoff, 1978). Jinadu (2007, p. 3) also observes that the accelerated and more aggressive push of the scramble between 1880 and 1900 was partly and strategically impelled by the imperative cardinal foreign policy objectives of the European countries in order to maintain a balance of power in Europe. Many therefore view contemporary globalization as the continuation of the historical and structural processes of capitalist and imperialist domination on a world scale and of the global diffusion or replication of its economic substructures and cultural and political superstructures. According to Jinadu (2007, p. 5), globalization has not only led to the marginalization of Africa but also denied it the possibility of auto-centered development by regarding African countries as follower-societies in the image of the globalizing and hegemonizing West.

The point, therefore, is that there is nothing really new about globalization as a motive force. The forces had been at work from the onset of the industrial revolution (Economides & Wilson, 2001, p. 9). Like the old imperialism, Jinadu (2007, p. 6), reiterates that the new one is anchored and reinforced by a number of universalizing cultural, legal, political, and social factors that constitute its ideology.

Theoretical and Conceptual Issues

The perspective through which this enquiry examines globalization in modern times is through the prism of the Marxist tradition, which invariably entails the dependency explanation of the nature of globalization and its impact on disadvantaged societies of the world. The Marxist tradition over the years has given birth to other strands that tried to explain social change in different societies. Some of these include the dependency theory, world systems theory, radical Marxist political economy, and Neo-Marxism. Though Marx did not have a theory of imperialism *per se*, which is fundamental to understanding globalization, he did have a theory of history in which capitalism played a big role. This is sometimes called historical materialism, and its basic assumption is that history is a product of social forces of production and the contradictions generated by these forces. Virtually all theories of imperialism are attempts to explain international political occurrences, mainly from the economic perspective. For Marxists, globalization is viewed as a new age of imperialism where national, regional, and global asymmetries characterized by social injustice and unequal exchanges are much more pronounced and pernicious than was the case before (Institute of Ethics and Developmental Studies, 2002).

From this perspective, the internal contradictions of feudalism for instance, led to its downfall and the establishment of capitalism (MacRae, 1969). Each stage was a necessary precursor to the next. The conditions for capitalism were established by feudalism and the conditions for socialism were established by capitalism. The historical role of capitalism was particularly important to Marx. Unlike other modes of production, it succeeded because of its dynamic nature. It expanded to every corner of the globe through its own internal logic and dynamics. In doing so, backward, pre-capitalist modes of production and their attendant customs and habits, myths, and superstitions were dismantled, and the world united for the first time under a single socio-economic system. Subsequently, capitalism would give rise to the formation of a world-wide urban proletariat, revolutionary class consciousness, and the conditions for realization of socialism. According to Economides and Wilson (2001, p. 55), capitalism is thus not only a disturbing, dislocating, destructive force, but also a progressive one with the vital historical task of shepherding the destruction of backward social formations. This paradox, that capitalism is at the same time destructive and progressive, which was also central to Marx's thesis, is one that later Marxists have found difficult to assimilate.

It was Lenin, however, who dramatically illustrated the internal political implications of Marx's analysis of capitalism. Lenin, in his *Imperialism: The Highest Stage of Capitalism* (1917), famously defined imperialism not as the possession of overseas territories, but as a stage in the evolution of capitalism. Half a century later, social theorist Johan Galtung, in his *A Structural Theory of Imperialism* (1971), expanded the concept even further by equating it with any form of international inequality.

Not all theories of imperialism are Marxist in orientation. In 1902, the English liberal economist and social theorist, J.A. Hobson published *Imperialism: A Study*. The work opined that fundamental contradictions in the structure of advanced capitalist economies in Europe led to the need to export capital overseas and hence the rise of imperialism. There is the "realist" theory of imperialism that gave primacy to the struggle for power (Morgenthau, 1973, pp. 48-76).

Globalization is thus a historical process of change that has been with humanity for a long time. It is a system that generates domination and disempowerment, and impacts differently and often detrimentally on individuals, social groups, and political entities, especially of the South. The present character of imperialism denotes less explicit control, influence, domination, and even covert colonization. It can take the character of unequal bargaining power, enabling an economically powerful state to determine the economic policies of another, much weaker state.

Often analyzed at the level of the global economy as the unit of analysis (Biersteker, 1998; Madunagu, 1999), globalization is empowered by an international division of labor broadly characterized by dichotomy between high and low skill intensity of production between the advanced and developing countries respectively. While the South provided the bulk of the raw materials, the North employed superior technology in converting these and exported back to Africa. Indeed, today there is the added dimension of offshoring and production relocations from the North to the South as a way of maximizing economies of scale. This is possible as a result of liberalization – a critical component of globalization (Akindele et al., 2002). So the history of production and reproduction is important in the ability of a society to change and in determining its strengths and weaknesses (Lumumba-Kasongo, 2001, p. 5).

There is little doubt that the economic factor is important in the process of change. Globalization is a process of economic change with implications for social, cultural, and political relations. Perhaps, we could conceive of globalization as the Marxists have done, as a dialectical process of thesis and antithesis that may then produce a synthesis (Olurode, 2003). The two faces of globalization described below clearly highlight its disjuncture. These are by no means exhaustive.

Therefore, it is reasonable to opine that globalization generates contradictions, which further generate other contradictions with implications for all, more so those that are disadvantaged. The reconciliation of these contradictions has fundamental implications for the global economy and global governance, and these contradictions are played out at the various sites of contestation and within global governance structures.

Sites of Contestation

Globalization has many sites of contestation that are not bereft of politics and other overt and covert mechanisms and strategies for protecting the interests of the advantaged over the disadvantaged. The sites of contestation include, for example, institutions and fora relating to issues of trade and investment, Information and Communication Technologies (ICT), finance capital, immigration, national policy formulation, poverty reduction, knowledge and technology, culture and regions, democratization and reforms, and global governance. These sites are by no means exhaustive, but embody issues of critical analysis in this enquiry (see Table 2.1 for a simple list of positive and negative aspects of globalization).

Table 2.1: Faces of Globalization

Positive Expectations	Negative Realities
• Market driven	• Tariff walls on products from developing countries
• World without borders	• Borderless only for capital and technology
• Increased interdependence	• Competition has killed businesses in the South
• Opportunities for economic growth	• Growth hampered by low technology evolution and lack of capital in developing countries
• Reduces inefficiency	• Creates unemployment, local businesses and traditional societies threatened with extinction
• Provides technology	• Has facilitated moral decline
• Enhances concerted global responses	• Increased capacity of external actors to intervene in local governance.

Source: Adapted from I. Ill-Haque, *The Human Development Report*, 1999.

For instance, matters of international trade have become the high politics of the twenty-first century (Economides & Wilson, 2001, p. 84). Questions are being asked about how fair the international trade architecture is. Competition and market accessibility do not seem to favor the developing countries. Take the issue of coffee for instance. During the first decade of the twenty-first century, the price of raw coffee beans has been on a free fall, while the price of processed coffee continues to rise. Failures of developing countries to gain from the World Trade Organization (WTO), lack of market access, and protectionism all point to deteriorating and not improving international trade for the developing world. In Africa, local enterprises are daily being destroyed as a result of globalization, thereby halting creativity and innovation. While this destructive process is going on, the preeminence of transnational corporations (TNCs) continue to grow. Chishti (2002) counted 63,000 parent firms and around 690,000 foreign affiliates of TNCs, and a plethora of inter-firm arrangements that span virtually all countries. Whereas over sixty countries in the developing world have a GNP of less than U.S. $10 billion, about 135 TNCs have sales in excess of U.S. $10 billion (Economides & Wilson, 2001, p. 189). This shows the impact of globalization and likely reach and influence of the TNCs.

In the past two decades or so, efforts at addressing lopsided trade relations have not been fruitful. The Structural Adjustment Programme (SAP) has proved to be a failure. It was characterized by constraining economic measures and conditionalities that further pauperized the masses of Africa (Gibbon & Olukoshi, 1996, p. 57-58). It suffices to state that politics of fair or unfair trade is being played out within the ambit of the WTO and the EU-ACP (Africa, Caribbean, and Pacific) arrangements. While countries of the developing world strive for capacity and access to markets of the richer countries, the rich countries devise measures to protect their interests and ensure continued dominance of trade and markets.

On finance capital, the speed at which capital flows take place today constitutes both an advantage and a disadvantage. The movement of finance capital, a key messenger of capitalism, is almost uncontrollable. While many countries in the South compete amongst themselves for access to Foreign Direct Investment (FDI), the investments that come do not necessarily go to areas relevant to the needs of the local peoples, but to those areas of interest to the investors. In Nigeria, for example, while investments are needed in the agricultural sector and infrastructure development, they rather go to the oil and gas industry. These are resources that constitute the engine of capitalist production and its survival. The ICT sector is one of the major forces that propel the globalization process. The convergence of three streams of technology—computing, telecommunications, and broadcasting—ensured that the once far-fetched, almost science fiction, "global village" became a reality (Utomi, 2000, p. 64). Information technology has made it easier for the entire world to be within the reach of global investors. With trade barriers down, ensured by the Uruguay Round of General Agreement on Trade and Tariffs (GATT) and WTO, the economies of less efficient countries have suffered, resulting in de-industrialization. In addition, cultural imperialism is now aided by control of ICT infrastructure by the advanced industrialized countries to the detriment of the South.

Another major site of contestation is the increasing incidence of poverty around the world and efforts being made at reducing or curbing it. While one-half of income worldwide is generated by trade among nations, 1.3 billion people live on less than one dollar a day and 3 billion people, or half the population of the world, live on less than two dollars a day (Utomi, 2000). A situation in which the assets of the top three billionaires in the West are more than the GNP of all least developed countries and their 600 million people is most alarming and unacceptable, in spite of whatever positive impact globalization has had. This situation is scandalous, as experience suggests that it is possible to provide and eradicate poverty through right policy choices.

In addition, the globalization of policy making has resulted in the national polices of individual countries being compromised with implications for poverty reduction. According to Khor (2001, p. 11), national policies, including the economic, social, cultural, and technological, that until recently were under the jurisdiction of states and peoples have increasingly come under the influence of international agencies and processes of big private corporations and economic/financial players. While globalization creates a revolution of rising expectations, it at the same time, reduces state capacity with respect to economic and social policy options.

Clearly visible in the march of globalization in the twenty-first century are the contradictions generated by this phenomenon (Olaniyi, 2009). While it requires qualified but cheap labor from countries of the South, it at the same time imposes strict immigration measures to check the movement of labor, which has been a key feature of capitalism. Still, it is estimated that each year, between two and three million people immigrate to the developed countries. The beginning of the twenty-first century saw more than 130 million people living outside their native countries, and the number has continued to rise by about 2 percent per annum (World Bank, 2000).

There is no gainsaying that globalization has therefore enhanced brain drain from Africa. Prospects for retaining highly skilled individuals are daunting, as the richer countries of the world snatch up these individuals with better offers. This has given rise to the perspective that, even if FDIs and related technologies are eventually obtained in Africa, there is no guarantee that the relevant manpower would be available since the most qualified hands are sojourning in foreign lands. Even at this, restrictions on labor mobility as evident in tougher immigration laws in the United States and Europe continue unabated. The import of this is that economic globalization is really about capital rather than labor, and focused on global accumulation rather than income re-distribution.

Globalization through commission or omission also has a cultural and civilizational dimension as a site of contestation. That globalization is impacting fundamentally on the organization and evolution of traditional societies is not in doubt. The worrisome dimension is that whereas the advanced industrialized societies have almost already attained the post-industrial era, globalization is threatening to erode the last vestiges of traditional culture and traditional political organization existing in many developing countries. Some of the values associated with capitalism and globalization are definitely not the best to emulate. It is agreed that human societies must go through the process of social change through cultural diffusion and that the imported material and immaterial aspects are substantial; this does not, however, imply that there should be no resistance or options as to what changes are desirable and those that are not. Increasingly, countries like Japan, India, and China are showing that there is a choice in determining the rate and type of cultural diffusion. The developing countries should learn from this. Though culture is the totality of a people's way of life, and there is no culture that is closed to influence, however, one should have the freedom and choice of determining the speed and character of the changes that are occurring. History indicates that borrowing ideas and material culture through diffusion is inevitable, and this has been largely facilitated through migration over long distances, a process that is now abridged in time because of transportation and the revolution in communication technology (Olurode, 2003). Therefore, conscious effort should be made to monitor and control the speed and spread of undesirable cultural influences associated with globalization.

The situation today is that young people in developing countries are undergoing uncontrolled acculturation, and are under the tremendous influence of Western culture in music, dress style, food, and behavior. This situation breeds confusion and disorientation in the youth, making them difficult to shape into law-abiding adults. The point being made is that when we consider the centrality of culture to human development, globalization in its present form is undoubtedly undermining the future of young people in Africa and the developing world in general. There is consciously or unconsciously media imperialism perpetrated by the media networks of the advanced or rich countries of the world. For example, reportage on Africa is biased and unbalanced. It is either nature programs, implying that Africa is still at the level of food gathering, or it is conflict, showing wars and starvation. This indeed is imperialism of a particular kind. Footages of the beautiful infrastructure at Abuja, Nigeria, or the clean environment of Accra and civility of Ghanaians are never shown. Included also is the non-recognition of Africans and peoples of the developing world that have made giant strides in science, technology, and the arts. The increase in uncensored consumption of information detrimental to the morals and values of traditional societies, such as pornography and unsavory TV shows, has also become worrisome. This is a site of contestation between negative change and positive change. The spheres of culture and popular education are also under pressure from globalization, and these have implications for local languages, consumption patterns, and production relations. While there is a need to retain positive aspects of one's culture, respect cultural differences, and share a common sense of commitment about the world, it is also imperative for the developing world needs in the present era to be selective as a matter of urgency and necessity. They can think globally, but must act locally.

Let us at this juncture examine the issue of religion and civilizational differences in the age of globalization. Globalization took on a different interpretation after the September 11, 2001, attacks in the United States. Generally condemned as inhuman and unacceptable, the attacks appeared to be a re-statement of the ideological differences between the West and the Muslim world. The West led by the United States became sufficiently alarmed to unleash offensives against individuals, forces, and nations perceived as bearers of international terrorism and enemies of the West. Iraq, Afghanistan, Pakistan, and the Palestinian Territory became theaters of conflict. Many innocent lives were lost, and limbs and property were also lost in a war on terror that appeared to have no code of conduct or rules of engagement. The crisis in the Middle East therefore took on a new dimension, and Arab fundamentalism and the Muslim vanguard clashed with this amorphous offensive. It was Huntington who had previously written that in the immediate post-Cold War global political order, the dominating source of conflict will be "cultural," and that the principal conflict of global politics will occur between nations and groups of different civilizations (Codesria, 2004). Perhaps, this prompted Mahmood Mamdani to write the book *Good*

Muslim, Bad Muslim, as a way of showcasing the current trend of contradictions between the West and other parts of the world.

Here, there is definitely a focus on religion as the carrier of evil, and by implication a site for the clash of civilizational differences. It appears to be the case that Islam has disapproved of and denounced Western civilization and the capitalist economic systems as exploitative and evil, as it is predicated on the exploitation of man by man, and creating social imbalances. From Islamic perspectives, capitalism is seen as decadent, highly materialistic and fanatically secular. This view is shared by many Arab Muslims. It is therefore not surprising that it is from the Middle East that the greatest opposition to capital in its modern form, and Western civilization is coming; this could indeed be the beginning of the clash of civilizations (Codesria, 2004). The fact remains that Islam with its elaborate belief system on the provision of welfare finds itself in opposition to economic globalization.

Contestation is also being played out in the field of knowledge and technology. While traditional societies are desirous of protecting their indigenous knowledge, globalization is making this difficult. Meanwhile, the technological gap between the developed and developing countries continues to worsen. The Organization for Economic Cooperation and Development (OECD) countries with 19 percent of the global population has 91 percent of Internet users, for example. In addition, tighter Intellectual Property Rights have raised the price of technology transfer, blocking developing countries from the dynamic knowledge sector. This exclusivity is creating parallel worlds of "haves" and "have nots" in the field of science and technology. Developing countries therefore have little option but to steal, borrow, purchase, or embark on a long-term program of producing scientists and technologists in order to bridge a gap that is increasingly widening.

The political dimension to the current globalization comes in the form of the export of democracy as of capital. So, democratization and reforms embodied in liberalization and decentralization presently constitute mantras of globalization. States under a one-party system were required to open up the political space to admit competition and political liberalism with a view to making the state more stable and to minimize political contestations from ethnic and religious groups (Olurode, 2003). This in itself is nothing bad, but what is worrisome is the fact that liberalization of the political space empowered hitherto amorphous groups and suppressed forces (Agbu, 2004) that went on to challenge the sovereignty of states built on shaky foundations of European partition and scramble. In addition, under democratization and the current global economic crisis, the liberal democratic state is supposed to have been rolled back in preference for private capital. However, the reverse is the case as the modern state is now relied upon to bail out shaky neo-liberal, democratic, and capitalist states and their businesses like the auto industry in the United States. Democratization comes with expectations, which in many cases African states have been unable to meet, resulting in social and political crises. In recent times, we now hear of "choiceless democracies" in countries like Benin, Zambia, Malawi, and even Nigeria.

Globalization also breeds contestation at the level of global governance. This is because global governance has become an important issue in the twenty-first century. Since politics is inherent in all human activity including governance structures, it is only logical that it is also found at the level of global governance. Politics here entails who takes the ultimate decisions and in whose interest. The North has increasingly arrogated to itself the right to interfere at will in all structures of global governance, often, in complete disregard for the interests of others and the basic premises of the U.N. Charter. It is therefore, not surprising that development no longer features as a central issue or a priority in the list of topical issues on the global agenda. While there is the real need for new and improved global rules and regulatory arrangements to provide for public goods, protect the global environment, manage global financial risks, and discourage anti-competitive processes, global rules have now tended to reflect the interests of the rich rather than give voice or votes to poorer countries and people (Center for Global Development, 2007). As expected, the South has risen up in opposition to the composition and workings of global governance institutions like the U.N., WTO, and World Bank with a view to having better representation and protecting their interests.

Responses from the South

A lot has been written about the magnitude and nature of the responses of the countries of the South to globalization (Ake, 1995; Khor, 2001; Aina, 1997; South Centre, 2003). It suffices to note that it is not as if globalization has had a free run. As observed by the call for proposal of the "Joint International Conference on Globalization: Migration, Citizenship and Identity" in 2007 by Kennesaw State University, Georgia, and the University of Ibadan, globalization by its character has attracted opposition; everywhere, mobility, identity, and citizenship are generating increasing tensions.

Indeed, beginning from the 1970s, as inequalities between the North and South increased, developing states have called for a radical overhaul of the international economic system, involving the regulation and relegation of the market, and the introduction of radical redistributive mechanisms. This gave rise to the North-South debate, in which the New International Economic Order (NIEO) became one of the most important issues on the international agenda (Economides & Wilson, 2001, p. 10). By 2001, Starr (2001) was able to identify at least 200 organizations that had anti-corporate, anti-capitalist, and anti-globalization political programs and agendas. The resistance centered on contestation and reforms with respect to SAP, grassroots resistance to the impact of globalization, and delinking, relocalization, and saving localities from the ravages of globalization.

In recent times, there has been a better-coordinated opposition to globalization through protests from South countries. Anti-globalization protests have greeted meetings of the World Bank, IMF, WTO, and the Group of Eight industrialized countries (G8), and other institutions that serve as support bases for globalization. The protests during the WTO meetings in Doha, Seattle, and Cancun in 2003 indicated that there was something wrong in the way globalization was evolving. In Davos, there were protests against the Trilateral Commission, the World Economic Forum, while in Washington it was against the World Bank and IMF. These were surprisingly not anticipated at all (Chachage & Annan-Yao, 2004, p. 330).

Re-Negotiating Participation in the Process

That globalization has positive elements is not in doubt (see Table 2.1), but because its negative impact is deeply destructive, it behooves states, individually and collectively, to respond to globalization by re-negotiating participation in the process. This has to be done because sharp contrasts exist between the economic gains of globalization and the social and political problems it has generated (Utomi, 2000). Abraham (2006) had noted that the international system is driven by an unequal power structure, which has created an imbalance that is destroying the economies of developing countries. There is no doubt that the approach taken in negotiating the consequences of globalization will induce a modification in the process.

Though globalization has been likened to a runaway train that the developing countries must get control of, there is a sense in which this train could be blocked or diverted. To begin with, each developing and disadvantaged country must define its own destination, or do so in concert with the other developing countries to determine the route of diversion, in order to achieve national objectives. On the other hand, countries of the developing world should also learn to live with capitalism, and engage with it constructively (Chachage, 2004). This approach is necessary as globalization's ideology of free-market liberalism and political, economic, and cultural imperialism are made possible through the exploitation of weaker partners—the developing countries (Tandon, 1998). Underlying the domination and exploitation is the inequality inherent in the distribution of power at the global level. In other words, globalization has been largely driven by the interests and needs of the developed world (Grieco & Holmes, 1999). Though supposedly market-driven, it is not actually driven by the invisible hand of the market, rather benefits and losses are managed by undemocratic, opaque, and supremacist forces which defy rational dialogue on most items in the various agreements of international organizations, such as the WTO.

In subsequent negotiations, developing countries should begin to attack and strive to alter the conditions that gave undue advantages to the rich countries. Where do these advantages lie? They lie in the possession of economic, military, and political leverages, off-shoots of power. According to E.H. Carr, three main elements constitute political power—military power, economic power, and power over public opinion (Razeen, 1998). The possession of considerable economic power is implicit in the notion of "hegemony" and domination. Therefore, developing countries will do well to begin to accumulate those elements of power relating to military prowess (if not actual, potential), economic power, and the necessary information technology to counter media imperialism and acculturation. Nigeria recently launched an observatory satellite into space *(NIGCOMSAT I)*, and was expected to launch a communications satellite in 2009 *(NIGCOMSAT II)* and another *(NIGCOMSAT X)* in no distant future. Its national television station (NTA) has gone international helping to tell the story of Nigeria, Nigerians in diaspora, and Africa to the world from an African perspective. This is the type of engagement and re-negotiation that the South requires to counter the negative aspects of globalization that relates to information flow.

In addition, economic power could relate to industrial strength, size, and skill of population, degree of technological advancement, and food security. It could also relate to extensive international influence as a result of financial power, production power, and market power. These are areas that developing countries need to pay attention to in their contestation with globalization.

Finally, developing countries should also seek to possess "structural" strength and advantages to determine agenda and shape the context and environment in which decisions affecting them are taken. The WTO, World Bank, and IMF readily come to mind as institutions that not only set agenda but seek to perpetuate ideas that intersect with the interest of the developed world. Therefore, being able to have a voice in the decision-making process and global governance structures will help reduce the penchant of the richer countries riding roughshod over the interests of the South.

Conclusion

In this chapter, effort has been made to identify those areas that require attention, and how countries of the South should redress their predicament. The developing world must reorient and renegotiate their participation in the global political economy for them to be able to achieve meaningful and sustainable development. This is because there is gross inequality and inequity in the allocation of the benefits of globalization. But then, how possible is it to promote one's interests in a system that is already designed against one? Can salvation come through the emergence of a parallel system? For now, especially for Africa, it is important to recognize that a critical component of reconstructing the continent and achieving effective renegotiation is the development of capacity to identify and exploit its own resources in a way that adds value to its products before export.

The point had earlier been made about the need for all to shift emphasis from the "globalization of world economy, to globalization of development."

For the West, this should be a more practical philosophy for assisting in addressing underdevelopment in the South. The wealthier parts of the world should realize that the scourge of underdevelopment can increase the dialectics of capitalism and shake the very foundations of the global economy as presently constituted. With the alienation of vast masses of the world's peoples, "petty national interests" should give way to "global developmental needs" for the stability of the international system. The West should also realize that the sociology of economic life in Africa, for instance, is not all about the economic rationale, but about community welfare. Indeed, there is a sense in which communalism is a higher civilization than capitalism with its individualistic character.

In summary, globalization does not mean that there should not be national controls at all; rather, it challenges countries to be more vigilant and proactive, and to readapt their national strategies to survive in a challenging and exploitative global political and economic system. In this quest for survival, Asia and South America must meet Africa and together devise and execute a grand alliance and strategy for confronting unbridled capitalism embodied in globalization.

References

Abraham, K. (2006). The marginalization of Africa and globalization. Retrieved August 24, 2007, from *Ethiopian Online Newsletter*, http://www.dekialula.com/articles/K_abrahim_feb_ 11_2006.html.

Agbu, O. (2004). *Ethnic militias and the threat to democracy in post-transition Nigeria*. Uppsala: Nordiska Afrikainstitutet.

Agbu, O. (2006). Globalization and Nigeria's economy. *Nigerian Journal of International Affairs*, 32(1), p. 29.

Aina, A.T. (1997). *Globalization and social policy in Africa*. Working Report Series, Dakar: CODESRIA

Ake, C. (1995). The new world order: The view from Africa. In H.H. Holm & G. Sorensen. (Eds.), *Whose world order: Uneven globalization and the end of the Cold War*. London: Westview Press.

Akindele et al. (2002). *Globalization, its implications and consequences for Africa*. Retrieved March 26, 2007 from http://www.globalization.icanp.org/content/v2.1/01akindele_etal.html

Axtmann, R. (1998). Globalization, Europe and the state: Introductory reflection. In Axtmann, R. (Ed.), *Globalization and Europe: Theoretical and empirical investigations*. London: Mansel.

Berberoglu, B. (1997). Globalization and its impacts on the Third World: A comparative historical analysis. *Development and Social Economic Progress*, 10(69).

Biersteker, T.J. (1998). Globalization and the models of operation of major institutional actors. *Oxford Development Studies*, 20 (1).

Center for Global Development. (2007). Retrieved August 24, 2007, from http://www.cgdev.org/doc/commentary/ birdsall/WIDERlecture_inequality.pdf.

Chachage, S.L., & Annan-Yao, E. (2004). Conclusion – Future agenda: Beyond globalization. In T.A. Aina et al. (Eds.), *Globalization and social policy in Africa*. Working Report Series, Dakar: CODESRIA.

Chishti, S. (2002). Globalization, international economic relations and the developing countries. *International Studies*, 39(3), p. 228.

Codesria Bulletin. (2004). *Terrorism and globalism*, 3 & 4. Dakar: CODESRIA.

Dare, S. (2001). A continent in crisis: Africa and globalization, *Third World Traveller*, Retrieved July 2001 from http:www.thirdworldtraveller.com/Africa/Continent_crisis.html.

Economides, S., & Wilson, P. (2001). (Eds.). *The economic factor in international relations*. London: I.B. Tauris.

Eze, O. (2007, April). Globalization and the dynamics of external interests in Africa. Paper presented at the *Conference on the New Scramble for Africa*, Abuja, Nigeria.

Galtung, J. (1971). A structural theory of imperialism. *Journal of Peace Research*, 13(2)

Gibbon, P., & Olukoshi, A. (1996). Structural adjustment and socio-economic change in Sub-Saharan Africa. *Research Report*, No.102. Uppsala: Nordiska Afrikainstitutet.

Grieco, M., & Holmes, L. (1999). Tele options for community business: An opportunity for economic growth in Africa. *Africa Notes*. October, pp.1-3.

Hobson, J.A. (1938). *Imperialism: A study*. London: Allen and Unwin.

Ill-Haque, I. (1999). *The human development report*. United Nations: Geneva.

Institute of Ethics and Development Studies. (2002). Globalization is a reverse gear for Africa. Retrieved October 4, 2007 from Inter University Seminar, http://www.fiuc.org/esap/MAKER/MAKER2/General/globalization?

Jinadu, A. (2007, April). Conceptual and theoretical issues in the scramble for Africa. Paper presented at the international conference on the New Scramble for Africa, organized by The Presidency and Ministry of Foreign Affairs, Abuja, Nigeria.

Khor, M. (2001). *Rethinking globalization*. London: Zed Books.

Lenin, V.I. (1917, 1963). *Imperialism: The highest stage of capitalism*. Peking: Foreign Language Press, (Original work published 1917).

Lumumba-Kasongo, T. (2001). Globalization, capitalism, liberal democracy and the search for new development paradigms in Africa. AAPS Occasional Paper Series, 5(1).

MacRae, D. (1969). Karl Marx. In T. Raison (Ed.). *The founding fathers of social science*. Harmondsworth: Penguin.

Madunagu, E. (1999). Globalization and its victims. *The Guardian*.

Magdoff, H. (1978). *Imperialism: From colonial age to the present*. New York: Monthly Review Press.

Mamdani, M. (2004). *Good Muslim, bad Muslim*. Dakar: CODESRIA.

Morgenthau, H. (1973). *Politics among nations*, 5th ed. New York: Knopf.

Ohmae, K. (1995). *The end of the nation state: The rise of regional economies*. London: Zed Books.

Olaniyi, R. (2009). "We asked for workers but human beings came": A critical assessment of immigration policies on human trafficking in the European Union. In A.G. Adebayo & O.C. Adesina. (Eds.), *Globalization and transnational migrations: Africa and Africans in the contemporary global system*, pp. 140-161. Newcastle Upon Tyne: Cambridge Scholars Publishing.

Olurode, L. (2003). Gender, globalization and marginalization in Africa. *Africa Development*, Vol. XXVIII, Nos. 3 & 4, 2003, pp. 67-88.

Razeen, S. (1998). *Classical liberalism and international economic order*. London: Routledge.

Scholte, J.A. (1996). Beyond the buzzword: Toward a critical theory of globalization. In E. Kofman & G. Young (Eds.), *Globalization: Theory and practice*. London: Routledge.
South Centre. (1996). *Liberalization and globalization: Drawing conclusions for development*. Geneva: Atar.
South Centre. (2003). Challenging hegemonic globalization: Voices from the South. *South Letter*, Issue 39.
Starr, A. (2001). Naming the enemy—Anti-corporate movements confront globalization. Retrieved March 20, 2008, from http://www.bad.server.org/ reviews/2001/2001-10-12-8,48AM.
Stiglitz, J. (2003). Do as the U.S. says, not as it does. *South Letter*, 39.
Tandon, Y. (1998). Globalization and Africa's options (Part One). *AAPS News Letter*. Harare, 3(1), p. 56.
Tandon, Y. (2000). Globalization and Africa's options. In D.W. Nabudere (Ed.), *Globalization and the post-colonial African state*. Harare: AAPS.
Utomi, P. (2000). *Critical perspectives on Nigerian political economy and management*. Ibadan: Spectrum Books.
World Bank. (2000). *Entering the 21st century: World development report, 1999-2000*. New Delhi: Oxford University Press.

CHAPTER THREE

ORIGIN AND DYNAMICS OF GLOBALIZATION: A HISTORICAL APPROACH

SAMUEL OLUWOLE OGUNDELE

This chapter attempts a critical examination of the origins and dynamics of globalization with particular reference to Africa. This is done with a view to deepening our understanding and appreciation of its character, scope, and relevance to contemporary life and living. In this context, globalization is defined as a human phenomenon enshrined in flows and interconnections at different points in time and space. It is a process of villagizing the world in which we live, and this goes beyond the domains of economic consideration. However, globalization is not an innocent intellectual discourse. This accounts for its numerous definitions and methods of approach, arising from the diversity of racial/cultural and disciplinary backgrounds of scholars. Globalization, in its simplest form, started during the Stone Age period when some members of *Homo erectus* began to migrate from Africa to Europe and Asia about one million years ago.

Introduction

The globalization discourse should not be construed as a mere academic exercise that has no bearing to reality. Similarly, it is not about "knowledge for knowledge's sake" or an exercise in obscurantism. Since globalization is about people, its discourse must necessarily be relatively simple to follow and digested by all and sundry. It is against this background, that a non-esoteric approach has been adopted in this work.

Our contemporary world is a more delicate and more tangled web of political, social, economic, demographic, and ecological relationships that cuts across national, regional, and continental boundaries. Although the globalization discourse is not innocent and therefore occasionally evokes emotions, it remains the sturdy fabric of global peace, harmony, understanding, economic progress, and oneness of humanity. This underscores the centrality of a deep historical excursion (through the lenses of archaeology and anthropology) to the subject of globalization.

Suffice it to say that the present did not just emerge out of nothing overnight. As a matter of fact, globalization, contrary to popular thinking or belief, began at least in a very simple way during the Stone Age period (about one million years ago). The trends continue up till now, with considerable rapidity and sophistication, in the face of advanced information technologies and greater partnerships among other factors.

There is abundant archaeological, anthropological, and art historical evidence in support of this development (Ogundele, 2001; Bentley & Ziegler 2003). Biological and social exchanges have always been an important feature of history. Thus for example, peoples, animals, plants, and cultural traditions were migrating and/or diffusing from one corner of the globe to another. Such a development underscores the emergence of new forms of human society among other things. For example, the culinary cultures of several parts of the world, particularly Nigeria, Togo, Benin, Ghana, Kenya, Brazil, and Chile, were significantly modified. But despite the seemingly simple character of these developments as well as their occurrences in many literary works, much is yet to be done with respect to the translation of knowledge into wisdom—that is, applying the knowledge to contemporary issues and problems bordering on food, security of lives and property, and urban violence, among others. These are issues, problems, and challenges all deeply rooted in globalism. Therefore, this chapter attempts to fill in some of the existing lacunae in this regard.

Periodizing Globalization

It seems that globalization as a complex human experience cannot be properly understood and appreciated without situating it within a deep historical framework (Zeleza, 2003). This is because of the fact that humans as early as about one million years ago had started migrating from one location to another. This development is known in palaeoanthropology as the *Homo erectine* level of hominization—a process that began in Africa. Some members of this early form of mankind went to "colonize" parts of Europe and Asia, having developed a better kind of technology called "Acheulian." This is in addition to the discovery of fire as a resource for conquering the physical environment. These early hominids or humans were a seafaring lot. Consequently, they were able to occupy many islands including remote archipelagos (Hilton-Barber & Berger, 2002).

Biological and social exchanges continued during the *Homo sapiens* stage of evolution over 100,000 years ago in Africa. *Homo sapiens sapiens* (anatomically modern humans) first emerged in Africa and, from there, many members of these hominids began some great adventure into the hitherto uninhabited parts of the world such as the Americas and Australia. These flows and interconnections about 30,000 years ago were possible because around this period, much of the waters from the earth's oceans froze into glaciers as well as ice fields. Consequently, the area of submerged land joining northern Asia to North America was exposed. This land link made it possible for the globe-trotters to move on foot into the New World. It is most highly probable that this *Homo sapiens* group got to Australia through a series of voyages using simple dug-out canoes.

Some evidence of the phenomenon of flows and interconnections has emerged from historical, cultural, anthropological, and linguistic researches in Egypt (Champion & Ucko, 2003). To a large degree, Egypt was the center of the ancient world where peoples from different regions went to acquire enormous training and education. This is with particular reference to such human endeavours as philosophy, mathematics, engineering, and medicine. Egyptian pyramids and temples were a great example of the successful translation of the knowledge of ancient science, especially mathematics, into wisdom for the betterment of the society—that is, the application of scientific knowledge to some of the practical as well as vital issues of life and living.

In this regard, numerous non-Africans such as the Greeks and Romans studied for several years (up to two decades in certain instances) under the Egyptian gurus in the sanctuaries of the numerous temples. Two of the world-famous philosophers who went to school in ancient Egypt were Aristotle and Plato. Similarly, one of the local Egyptian gurus was Imhotep, who was the first author of a book on mathematics. This was about 4,000 years ago. It is up till now the oldest known mathematics textbook in the world.

Medicine usually practiced within the framework of mysticism (at least at the initial stage of its evolution) also started in Egypt. Numerous members of the global village beyond the confines of Africa benefited tremendously from the ancient medical practices of the Egyptians. In this respect, although Hippocrates remains up till now the undisputed father of modern medicine (Peebles, 1996), Egypt at that point in time was the hub of the entire globe. That is to say that Egypt was the center of the world, while Europe and America among other regions constituted the peripheries or margins. But it would be totally erroneous to think that this form of globalization made Egypt a predator, frightening off the rest of the global village. It was not a relationship characterized by over-dependence and economic exploitation. The concept of "borderlessness" at this period of human history was based on mutuality of respect. This kind of globalization is a common-sense necessity for the promotion of local, regional, and world peace and progress.

Around 5,000 years ago or thereabout, humans started the process of food production or agriculture in West Africa. Human migrations led to the diffusion of crops and techniques of agricultural production from one region to another.

Thus for example, some Southeast Asians introduced such crops as cocoyam or taro (*Colocasia esculenta*), water yam (*Discorea alata*), some varieties of bananas (*Musa sapientum*), and Asian rice (*Oryza sativa*) to West Africa during the late pre-colonial period. Oil palm (*Elaeis* guineensis), a West African tree crop, diffused from the sub-region and reached as far afield as Malaysia.

Similarly, cassava (*Manihot esculenta*) and maize (*Zea mays*) got to West Africa from South America. Some Portuguese explorers and traders brought these crops to such West African coastal settlements as Lagos, Lome, and Accra after 1500 A.D. (Ogundele, 2004; Osae & Nwabara, 1982). All the above crops, among others, were successfully adapted to the West African subregion. They remain a major component part of the local diet and culinary delights of West Africans. By about 1800 A.D., maize had become a well-established secondary crop in most parts of West Africa. Indeed, today, the consumption of maize is almost (if not exactly) at par with yam in several areas of the sub-region, especially Nigeria, Togo, Benin, and Ghana (Ogundele, 2007). The list of the uses of maize among such ethnic groups as Yoruba, Igbo, Asante, and Ewe is a very long one, although most present-day West Africans are oblivious of its history. Maize can be processed into flour and pap among the Yoruba of southwestern Nigeria. Pap is a soft and almost liquid food for babies and adults alike. *Kenke* is a popular dish prepared from maize among the various ethnic groups in Ghana (Nii Kortey, 2007). Maize can also be processed into local liquor called *pito* or *sekete* in Yoruba land. The preparation involves fermentation—an exercise that embraces a chemical change because of the action of yeast or bacteria, often changing sugar into alcohol (Ogundele, 2004). The history and spread of maize and cassava, among other crops, is basically about inter-group relations at the regional and global levels. For example, the diffusion of crops and techniques of agricultural production from different regions of the world could not have taken place in isolation of other cultural traits such as language and mode of dressing. These are no doubt exchanges rooted in globalization.

The spread of cassava was much slower than that of maize in West Africa. This is because cassava tubers have a high toxic content and so certain relatively rigorous techniques are needed to convert them into edible food items. Some Portuguese, having mastered the art of cassava processing (that is, how to remove the poison, among other things) from the American Indians, started teaching the West Africans upon reaching the coastal parts after about 1500 A.D. Fluid and sap that contain the poison are systematically removed from cassava after grating the tubers. This takes two or three days to actualize, after which the spongy mass of cassava in a sack is broken up and sieved gradually with the aid of a wire, plastic, or fiber net attached to a ring or square-like frame. By so doing, smaller pieces go to the bottom of a receiver leaving behind lumps.

This stage is followed by frying into a kind of flour called *gari*. *Gari* is a pan-West African staple, usually prepared into a bulky paste by stirring in a bowl or pot of very hot water. This paste is called *eba* among the Yoruba of southwestern Nigeria and as far afield as the southern parts of the Republics of Benin and Togo. *Eba* is normally eaten with a tasty sauce prepared with fish, beef, and/or game meat. The Portuguese had successfully trained a lot of West Africans on the coasts how to prepare *gari* flour as early as 1700 A.D. Indeed, by this time, *gari* processing had become very popular in such settlements of considerable Portuguese influence as Porto Novo, Sao Tome, Fernando Po, Whydah, and Warri.

In Dahomey (now Benin Republic), F. F. de Sousa, an ex-slave trader of great repute taught a lot of people how to process cassava into *gari* flour using the King's palaces as his training centers (Flint, 1974; Ogundele, 2004). In addition, African returnees from Brazil and Cuba among other places in South America played a key role in training the local West Africans the techniques of *gari* production after about 1800 A.D. These ex-slaves otherwise known as Afro-Brazilians or *Aguda* were already well used to *gari* as a food item during their period of servitude abroad. They showed keen interest in popularizing what had become their staple food item in the aftermath of the Trans-Atlantic slave trade that lasted for about 300 years (Osae & Nwabara, 1982). There is another food item from cassava called *lafun* or *elubo* among the Yoruba. Processing cassava into this kind of food item involves a different set of techniques.

During the period of slavery in the Americas, the Africans especially the Yoruba of Nigeria contributed enormously to the evolution of the socio-cultural landscape. The entanglement of African peoples generally in the evolution and development of cultures and societies outside the shores of the continent, is a testimony to the considerable antiquity of globalization. Indeed, no critical analysis and reconstruction of the realities of the vibrant colors and evolution of the diverse cultural heritages of the New World and, to a lesser degree, the southern part of the United States of America can be made without giving pride of place to Africa. Exhuming these realities in order to create a new world characterized by peace, progress, and social justice, is possible through the lenses of a determined consciousness of a wide range of people. In this regard, globalization discourse is capable of combining knowledge with wisdom.

Despite the numerous physical and psychological difficulties and/or hardships the African slaves working in the European plantations went through, they succeeded in achieving some degree of regularity and predictability with respect to their indigenous social life and living (Uya, 2003). The African slaves adapted some Euro-American and American socio-cultural values to their indigenous ways of life in order to produce a formidable synthesis. Elements of this development can be seen up to now, in such places as Cuba, Trinidad, Chile, Haiti, Brazil, Argentina, and the southern parts of the United States of America. Two of the most prominent African peoples in this connection are the Yoruba of Nigeria and the Ewe of Ghana.

The emergence of these new forms of life in the Diaspora following the slave trade experience can be better appreciated against the background of religion, music, and food culture. For example, Santeria has its origins in the Yoruba religious practice and, to a lesser degree, the Spanish folk Catholic faith (Uya, 2003; Oguntoyinbo-Atere, 2002).

Santeria, the worship of saints or deities (Gonzalez-Wippler, 1994), is a syncretism of Yoruba religion rooted in the belief in gods and goddesses otherwise known as *Orisas*. Some of these *Orisas* are *Ogun* (god of metals and warfare); *Sango* (god of thunder and lightning); *Osoosi* (god of hunting); *Osun* (goddess of the river waters, love, and marriage); *Orisa Oko* (goddess of agriculture); *Yemoja* (goddess of the sea) and *Obatala* (god of peace and father of all deities); and *Obaluaye* (god of diseases especially small pox). The devotees believe that all these *Orisas* (deities) are comparable in several respects to such Christian saints as St. Peter and St. Lazarus.

Although the spellings of the names of these *Orisas* have changed with the passage of time in the New World, it would be erroneous to think that these deities are exclusively for religious purposes in the Euro-American sense. On the contrary the *Orisas* play a major role among the Yoruba both at home and in the Diaspora, in addressing the issue of disease and illness. In this connection, Santeria is a component part of the ethno-medicine of a lot of people in Chile, Cuba, Brazil, and Argentina among other places around the globe. Here, the priest who also doubles as the diviner (comparable to the Ifa diviner in Southwestern Nigeria) is highly respected by all the devotees.

Music and dance occupy a conspicuous position in this religion (Santeria). Music involving the playing of *samba* (especially among the Brazilians) must be appreciated beyond the domains of mere entertainment. Indeed, it is a major instrument for engendering group solidarity and political consciousness among the Cubans, Brazilians, and Argentines of African extraction. This is a commonsense necessity in the face of social injustice and oppression (Ruperez, 2005; Ogundele, 2007; Gonzalez-Wippler, 1994). In the area of food culture, the influence of Nigeria cannot be over-emphasized. For example, *akara*—a popular snack made from ground beans—is a delicacy in many parts of the New World, particularly Brazil. Ground beans mixed with water and ingredients like pepper, onion, and salt are fried bit by bit in a large metal bowl of vegetable oil (Ogundele, 2007). The nomenclature has, however, changed through time in the New World from *akara* to *akaraje* (Gonzalez-Wippler, 1994).

The ex-slaves that returned to Nigeria in the nineteenth century also brought home a lot of cultural traits from the New World. One of these was Brazilian architecture. The style of architecture has to do mainly with arched windows and plastered surfaces with ornamental details. This baroque style usually has a garret in the upper part of the house with a small window (Duro-Emanuel, 1989). This is a unique building heritage that started gaining ground in Lagos and its environs from the late nineteenth century. From here, Brazilian architecture began to spread to the hinterland of Nigeria, particularly the Southwestern part. This shows that the Trans-Atlantic slave trade experience, despite its ugliness in several senses, remains an issue too important to be studied from a simplistic perspective. This ugliness can be understood against the background of human oppression, disturbance of the equilibrium of the local African economies and social lives, as well as erosion of the people's confidence through uncritical assimilation of Western values and education in general. All these problems constitute an anathema to human development on a sustainable scale in Nigeria as well as other parts of Africa. But these difficulties notwithstanding, Africans showed great courage and resilience. For example, the slaves, especially those who left for the New World from Nigeria, had played a key role in rebuilding the form and content of the grammar of human existence in their new locations. This is in addition to their home countries like Nigeria, Benin, and Ghana after regaining their freedom in the nineteenth century.

Aside from the above, the evolution of African languages has benefited from contacts with other parts of the global village at different points in time. For example, the people of the southwestern region of Nigeria speak the Yoruba language with several dialects like the Ekiti, Ijesa, Oyo, Egba, Ijebu, Yewa, and Ikale. This language is not entirely pure in terms of its origins and subsequent development. Such words as *alafia* (peace) and *alubosa* (onion) are of Arabic origins. Similarly, *idoti* that appears so frequently in Yoruba language today etymologically derived from "dirty" in English. All these, among others, have been neatly embedded in the Yoruba language with the passage of time (Ogundele, 2004). Such a development is a reflection of both human and physical movements and socio-cultural diffusion at different time periods. At the local level, some similarities in such words as *oju* and *eju* (meaning "eye" in the Yoruba and Igala languages in southwest and central Nigeria respectively) could be suggestive of a common remote ancestry. This might also explain the broad similarity in *eti* and *nti* ("ear") among the Yoruba and Igbo ethnicities. Even as far afield as Ghana, there are similar words and expressions among the Asante and Yoruba. For example, melon seeds are called *agusi* in southern Ghana, while the Yoruba of Nigeria refer to this soup ingredient as *egusi*. The Yoruba also call welcome *ekuabo* or *ekaabo*, while the Asante people of Ghana say *akwaaba*. The above examples are a confirmation of the considerable antiquity of the concept of "borderlessness" or trans-national interconnections in Africa vis-à-vis the rest of the world.

The above experience shows that no language and, by extension, culture are totally pure or isolated from the cross-currents of regional and/or global history and civilization (Ogundele, 2007; Southgate, 1974). Similarly, English is indebted to a number of cultures or languages, in the course of its evolution and development into an international communication system. The language benefited from the cultures of Denmark and France among others. All these are elements of globalization, which cannot be reduced only to the contemporary economic and political maneuvering of the African nations and other weaker groups around the world by the powerful West. In other words, globalization also has a deep historical dimension, and this must be neatly incorporated into any meaningful discourse on the subject.

Contemporary Globalization: A Discourse

As noted earlier in this chapter, globalization is a good idea that today's world cannot wish away. It is obvious that what affects one country has socio-economic, political, health, and demographic implications for her neighbors as well as the rest of the globe. This development did not start today. It is enshrined in the domain of ancient historical and archaeological record. Contrary to popular thinking, the concept of borderlessness of our world is not new after all, although its (borderlessness) degree has gone up considerably in the face of better and more efficient communication systems.

But unfortunately, globalization as a human endeavor is now being misused and abused to the detriment of justice, peace, and progress (on a sustainable scale) especially of the weaker nations and peoples of the world by the developed world. The level of this misapplication and misdirection has increased tremendously in the last two decades.

The twentieth century witnessed a radical change in the conceptualization of globalization as a human phenomenon rooted in mutuality of respect. The technologically advanced nations such as the United States, the United Kingdom, and France as well as international finance capital constructed some structures to this effect. These included the International Monetary Fund (IMF) and World Trade Organization (WTO). These structures were supposed to help manage and give direction to the economies of the weaker nations, but unfortunately, these remained at the level of mere rhetoric. These supranational bodies or organizations claimed (on paper) to promote international fiscal cooperation as well as facilitate international trade (Ajayi, 2005). It is increasingly obvious, however, that arising from the activities of these organizations there is a dire need to promote an open exchange of ideas and information on a global scale (Ajayi, 2005).

On the surface, the idea of free trade championed by these organizations (IMF, World Bank, WTO) is good, but a thorough examination shows that contrary to the outward philosophy of the stakeholders, it is neither free nor fair in several respects. The free market system and other related policies are far from being socially and/or politically innocent. They are not value-free, except one is economical with the truth. The idea of free trade is one-sided, and this continues to promote the monopoly of the West, as opposed to competitiveness and sustainable economic development of the African nations among others. In rolling out economic policies for the entire world, particularly Africa, the Western nations through these bodies consistently negate the principles of democracy and fairness.

African nations who are puppets (as opposed to real or respected member states) in WTO and IMF, do not have any active role to play with regard to decision making. This is with respect to the formulation and implementation of economic policies that directly affect them. Therefore, it is not an overstatement to claim here that Africa remains a great pawn on the chessboard of Euro-American neo-colonialism and imperialism (Ogundele, 2001).

The idea that globalization is rooted in "inclusiveness" of the weaker nations of the world is a big ruse. Indeed, the so-called free trade or free market system is an anathema to competitiveness, technological development, and productivity in many respects. Globalization today as a concept is full of contradictions largely because it has no regard, among other things, for the development of local socio-political and economic initiative or conditions. As a matter of fact, the free market system destroys African capacity to effectively combat such serious problems as large-scale unemployment, abject poverty, and political instability including urban violence.

It is incontestable that while Euro-American and, to a lesser degree, Asian goods and services continue to enter the African markets freely, the reverse is the case for the Western world. Local African goods, especially agricultural products, cannot compete effectively with those from countries like the United Kingdom, the United States, France, Germany, Japan, and China. This is because of the high production costs arising largely from a drastic reduction or a total lack of subsidies by the African government. The IMF dictates to African governments the amount of subsidies to be given to farmers under the guise of one-world macroeconomic policy. It even occasionally "advises" them not to give subsidies to their farmers at all.

But to the chagrin of socio-economic analysts, the same Western nations who are in fact the architects of IMF and WTO still give out subsidies to their farmers in order to reduce production costs. Again, such cheaper and better packaged goods like frozen chickens, enter the African market freely to compete with, and indeed, cripple the poorly packaged and highly expensive local goods or items. Not surprisingly, the former stifles the local African market. This is one illustration of how the technologically advanced nations and multinational corporations use the instrumentality of IMF and WTO to engage in the objectification as well as pauperization of the African peoples.

Modern globalization is therefore a new form of socio-political and economic enslavement of Africans. It amounts to some interference in the internal affairs of the African world by the Western nations. The recent global information revolution, despite its several benefits to all and sundry, is increasingly becoming an instrument of economic, political, and intellectual imperialism. That is to say that they are to a large extent a cover for espionage and economic exploitation. By this token, globalization has become a dreadful monster that walks freely on all fours on the African socio-cultural landscape. This situation reminds us of the fact that Africa's independence is merely on paper and that its (Africa) real sovereignty is no doubt very fragile.

It is a commonsense necessity for Africa to reject the current but wrong conceptualization of globalization that connotes over-dependence of the continent on the Euro-American world. This is a negation of the principles of justice and sustainable development. Globalization is naturally a process of flows and interconnections embedded in mutual respect. This is opposed to a form of subservience to the Western world that continues to heap indignities on the weaker nations through its numerous toxic economic policies.

Taming and broadening the concept of globalization are a great challenge for contemporary African political leaders. These are indeed a task that must be done! Political leaders in the Western world must begin to appreciate the philosophy of genuine partnership with the African nations. Abject poverty, unemployment, and political instability in Africa have serious socio-political, economic, and demographic implications for the rest of the global village, particularly Europe and North America. This can be understood against the background of the fact that our contemporary world is becoming more borderless on a daily basis.

Summary and Conclusion

Globalization is certainly a multi-faceted intellectual discourse involving a deep understanding and appreciation of such variables as ancient history, geography, and exchange networks. Globalization is an age-long concept that can be stretched as far back in time as the *Homo erectine* stage of hominization, going back to at least one million years ago in Africa. Similarly, the ancient Egyptians were pioneers in several facets of human endeavors like mathematics, philosophy, medicine, and engineering. Greek scholars such as Aristotle and Plato received their education and training in some of the sanctuaries of the Egyptian temples. Indeed, the first textbook on mathematics was written by Imhotep about 4,000 years ago. Many members of the global village in antiquity benefited tremendously from the Egyptian civilization or education. But this was based on mutual respect as opposed to what has been happening as from the late nineteenth century A.D.

The phenomenon of flows and interconnections continues up to the present day. It is unending. The physical human movęments or migrations and the subsequent spread of ideas of agriculture from Southeast Asia (during the late Stone Age period) to West Africa have become an unforgettable experience with respect to the construction of the form and content of the lexicon of modern African culinary history and geography. The African Diaspora, especially the enslaved Nigerians in the Atlantic Slave Trade, contributed to the development of a new culture in such countries as Brazil, Cuba, Chile, Trinidad, Puerto Rico, and Argentina. Santeria (the worship of saints) was a religious form that arose from the mixture of the Yoruba traditional worship and the Catholic faith. Today, Santeria devotees are numerous in the New World, particularly Brazil.

The phenomenon of globalization from the twentieth century to date is full of contradictions. Thus, for example, the formulation and implementation of the free market system is a testimony to the Western form of hypocrisy emanating from an insatiable appetite for African natural resources. However, the African market is open to all kinds of goods from the West. It also confirms the current unbridled immorality and indescribable degree of insincerity in international politics.

Such bodies as IMF and WTO were established by the Western nations in the twentieth century to "promote" international monetary cooperation and "facilitate" international trade. This development drastically changed the age-old conception of globalization. A close examination of the activities of these bodies or organizations shows that they (IMF and WTO) are agencies for the promotion of greater economic domination in post-colonial Africa.

Africans and other technologically weaker peoples of the world must cage, tame, and broaden the concept of globalization as a basis for getting out of the woods. This is achievable only within the framework of collective solidarity and self-discipline by African political leaders who (with a few exceptions) continue to play to the gallery because of their unfettered gluttony.

References

Ajayi, O.O. (2005). Globalisation and the politics of marginality. In O. Vaughan et al. (Eds.), *Globalization and marginality*. Ibadan: Sefer Books Ltd.

Bentley, J.H., & Ziegler, H.F. (2003). *Traditions and encounters: A global perspective on the past. Vol. 11: From 1500 to the present*. Boston: McGraw Hill.

Champion, T., & Ucko, P. (2003). Introduction: Egypt, ancient and modern. In P. Ucko & T. Champion (Eds.), *The wisdom of Egypt: Changing visions through the ages*, pp. 1-5. London: UCL Press.

Duro-Emanuel, T.L. (1989). The origins and persistence of Afro-Brazilianism in the Brazilian quarters of Lagos island. Unpublished B.A. Long Essay, University of Ibadan, Ibadan, Nigeria.

Flint, J.E. (1974). Economic change in West Africa in the 19th century. In J.F.A. Ajayi & M. Crowder (Eds.), *History of West Africa, Vol. 2*, pp. 380-401. London: Longman Group Ltd.

Gonzalez-Wippler, M. (1994). *Legends of Santeria*. St. Paul Minnesota: Llewellyn Publications.

Hilton-Barber, B. & Berger, L. (2002). *The official field guide to the cradle of humankind (Sterkfontein, Swartkrans, Kromdraai & Environs World Heritage Site)*. Cape Town: Struik Publishers

Nii Kortey, O. (2007), January 15. Personal communication.

Ogundele, S.O. (2001). *Human origins: A critical perspective*. Ibadan: John Archers Ltd.

Ogundele, S.O. (2004). *Rethinking West African archaeology*. Ibadan: John Archers Ltd.

Ogundele, S.O. (2007). Understanding aspects of Yoruba gastronomic culture. *Indian Journal of Traditional Knowledge*, 6(1), pp. 50-56.

Oguntoyinbo-Atere, M. (2002). An exhibition of Yoruba religion, arts and culture among the Cubans: A visitation. In E. Ifie (Ed.), *Papers in honour of Tekena Tamuno at 70*. Ibadan: Oputoru Books.

Osae, T.A., & Nwabara, S.N. (1982). *A short history of West Africa, A.D. 1000–1800*. London: Hodder and Stoughton.

Peebles, J.W. (1996). Preface. In C.H. Felder (Ed.), *The original African heritage study Bible*, pp. 20-53. Nashville: The James C. Winston Publishing Company.

Ruperez, E.L. (2005). *Puerto-Rico: Cultural and natural heritage*. Barcelona: Anman Grafiques del Vallas.

Southgate, G.W. (1974). *A textbook of modern European history (1789–1960)*.

London: J.M. Dent and Sons Ltd.

Uya, E.O. (2003). *Contemporary issues on slavery and the black world.* Calabar: Clear Lines Publications.

Vaughan, O. (2005). Introduction. In O. Vaughan et al. (Eds.), *Globalization and marginality*. Ibadan: Sefer Books Ltd.

Zeleza, P.T. (2003). *Rethinking Africa's globalization, Vol. 1: The intellectual challenges*. Trenton, NJ: Africa World Press.

CHAPTER FOUR

COMPATRIOTISM VS. COSMOPOLITANISM: EXPLORING A NEW COSMO-MORALITY OF HUMAN RELATIONS FROM THE YORUBA IN THE AGE OF GLOBALIZATION

RONALD OLUFEMI BADRU

The chapter explores a new morality of relations among nation-states and peoples. Ontologically, the current globalization process moves towards the ultimate institution of a global sphere of common human values. However, compatriotism and cosmopolitanism are opposed ethical thinking that negate the institution of the speculated global sphere. To reconcile and transcend the seeming difference between the forms of ethical thinking, the study recommends the institution of *alajobi* thinking, which espouses common descent of humankind, and thus the morality of self-other complementarity in human interaction. Establishing the globalization process on this ethical thinking leads to a truly moral global village.

Introduction

In the contemporary age, one of the core issues dominating the central space of intellectual discourse is that of globalization, a subject that seems to be reverberating from every corner of the perceptible world. Really, the concept of globalization has become some sort of buzzword (see Scholte, 1996, pp. 43-57). According to Chase-Dunn, the discourse on globalization has become a flood (1999, p. 187) which seems to have transformed into a phenomenon heralding both qualitative and quantitative changes to the life of the average person as a being in the world. The reality of the changes becomes more perceptible when we remember that the globalization process has ecological, cultural, communication, economic, and political dimensions and implications (See Chase-Dunn, 1999, pp. 191-193; also Sklair, 1999, pp. 148-159).

Although existing literature reveals that there are multifarious conceptions of the phenomenon of globalization, a critical analysis shows that at the core of the phenomenon of globalization, in the moral sense, lies the moral ideal of instituting a global sphere where common human values are respected and promoted. However, the realization of the moral ideal is threatened by two diametric forms of ethical thinking: compatriotism and cosmopolitanism. While compatriotism emphasizes that the whole issue of morality truly makes sense within the notion of a bounded society of socio-historically related people, cosmopolitanism reverts to the thinking that morality ought to be transcultural, that moral obligations ought to be founded on the universal ethic of equal value of life. Against the foregoing background, the primary focus of the chapter is a critical examination of the two forms of ethical thinking, with a view to reconciling and transcending the seeming divergence by the institution of *alajobi* thinking from Yoruba cosmology. This thinking is founded on common descent of humankind (the cosmological aspect) and this invariably generates a moral norm of self-other complementarity (the moral aspect) in human association and interaction. Thus, it is apposite to make the lexical conjugation, cosmo-morality. Founding the globalization process on this ethical thinking leads to a truly moral global village.

The chapter is divided into five parts. Following the introductory section, the second section engages in some preliminary ontological analysis; the third section examines morality, compatriotism, and cosmopolitanism as well as their relative strengths and weaknesses; the fourth section explores a new morality of human relations founded on *alajobi* thinking; and the final section is the conclusion of the chapter.

Preliminary Ontological Analysis of Globalization

In accord with the earlier contention of Scholte (1996), Adekanye (2004, p. iii) also states that globalization has become one of the most frequently used buzzwords in much of today's discourse, not just within the social sciences but across all academic disciplines and even among non-specialists. But, how do we ontologically conceptualize globalization? Such an ontological conceptualization would derive from an understanding of the phenomenon that is shorn of any disciplinary attachment,[1] an understanding that strikes at the essence of globalization.

According to Sklair, there is no single agreed definition of globalization (1999, p. 144). This admission, however, is not dismissive of making new attempts at understanding the ontology of the phenomenon of globalization, devoid of any disciplinary attachment, which tends to make our understanding of its ontology conceptually parochial. Towards this direction, Badru (2003, p. 17), quoting Martin Shaw (2002), summarizes three accounts of the meaning of *global.*

The first account has to do with the literal translation of the word, belong to the *globe.*[2] From this perspective, global means "connected with the natural habitat of human kind. . ." The second account explains the concept of global as "the quality involved in the world-wide stretching of social relations." The third explanation regards the concept as the development of "a common consciousness of human society on a world scale."

From the conceptions given, some inferences could be made. First, the two latter conceptions somewhat depend on the former conception. Without the existence of the natural habitat of man, there would be no man. If this is the case, then the issues of stretching social relations among men beyond national boundaries and developing a common consciousness of human society on a world scale seem unrealistic and impracticable if men had no natural habitat (Badru, 2003, p. 17).

Furthermore, the third account somehow accords with the second one. If there is a common consciousness of human society on a world scale, peoples of the world would see themselves as having a common destiny. This understood, then they would be more willing to stretch social relations among men beyond national boundaries (Badru, 2003, p. 18). In other words, the second account is reinforced by the third account.

In the words of Cohen and Kennedy, globalization means "the ways in which the world is being knitted together" (2000, p. 10). Scholte characterizes the phenomenon as "the process of the world becoming a single place" (1996, p. 43). He further makes a distinction between international and global relations:

> Whereas international circumstances involve crossing considerable distance over more or less extended time intervals, global conditions are situated in a space beyond geometry, where distance is covered in effective no time. (1996, p. 46)

The distinction made by Scholte (1996) contributes to our understanding of the phenomenon of globalization because it strikes at the spatio-temporal compression, which is taking place in the conduct of the present-day transcultural human relations. However, some critics have submitted that the stated spatio-temporal compression is largely a myth, that "there is no fundamental difference between the international submarine, telegraph cable method of financial transactions (of the early twentieth century) and contemporary electronic systems" (Hirst & Thompson, 1996, p. 197). The criticism can easily be dismissed by appealing to two commonplace facts in the contemporary world. First, the use of Internet facilities, for example, has made it possible for peoples to send and receive trans-border messages within seconds. Second, the use of ATM cards, a new phenomenon in Nigeria, makes it effortlessly easy to make financial transfers without traversing long distances.

The spatio-temporal compression in the conduct of contemporary trans-border human relations is also evident in Held's conception of globalization. For him, the phenomenon denotes:

> the stretching and deepening of social relations and institutions across space and time such that, on the one hand, day-to-day activities are increasingly influenced by events happening on the other side of the globe and, on the other, the practices and decisions of local groups or communities can have significant global reverberations. (Held, 1995, p. 20; see also, Held, et al., 1999, p. 15)

Furthermore, since the language of "stretching and deepening" implies an ongoing enterprise, then we can state that the phenomenon of globalization "describe(s) a process, not an end-state" (Habermas, 2001, p. 66). In other words, the phenomenon of globalization is in a state of becoming; it has not fully become.

Reasoning from the foregoing understandings of global and globalization, one could make some inferences about globalization on the ontological plane:

1. It is a spatio-temporal phenomenon; it is expressive of a commitment to the contraction or total annihilation of the spatio-temporal gap separating different nations and peoples of the world;
2. It is an unfurling process; it has not fully materialized; and
3. The end-state of the spatio-temporal process is the institution of a global sphere where common human values are promoted. All the global forces of economy, culture, politics, and communications that we are presently witnessing are manifestations, which point to, and also work towards, the given ideal end-state.

Morality, Compatriotism, and Cosmopolitanism

Morality

The concept of morality can be examined from two perspectives, descriptive and normative (see Gert, 2005). The first perspective can be conceived of in three senses:

Sense A: "Morality" is used simply to refer to a code of conduct put forward by a society (Gert, 2005, para. 3). One would call this morality in the social sense.

Sense B: "Morality" refers to a guide to behavior put forward by some group other than a society—for example, a religious group (Gert, 2005, para. 6). One would call this morality in the group sense.

Sense C: "Morality" refers to a guide that a person, perhaps himself, regards as overriding and wants adopted by everyone else (Gert, 2005, para. 11). One would call this morality in the individual sense. According to Gert (2005, para. 10),

> [T]his sense of "morality" is a descriptive sense, because a person can refer to an individual's morality without endorsing it. In this sense, like the original descriptive sense, morality has no limitations on content.

From the normative perspective, Gert (2005, para. 24) states that "morality is an informal public system applying to all rational persons, governing behavior that affects others, and has the lessening of evil or harm as its goal." Valequez (1999, p. 496) also accords with Gert's normative thinking of morality when he notes that "morality is a set of rules stating what you ought and ought not to do."

In his conceptual analysis of morality, Frankena (1995) distinguishes three kinds of moral thinking. First, there is descriptive-empirical inquiry, historical or scientific, such as is done by anthropologists, historians, psychologists, and sociologists. The focus here is to find out how people do behave in order to describe or explain their behavior coherently. Second, there is moral thinking which revolves around questions, such as What is good or what is obligatory? Essentially, this moral thinking is prescriptive and tries to prescribe what ought to be done or what ought not to be done. It differs from the earlier explanatory/descriptive moral thinking. Third, there is "meta-ethical" moral thinking, which focuses on critical analyses of the terms used in making evaluative statements. This thinking deals with logical, epistemological, or semantical questions, such as—What is the meaning of being morally right or being morally wrong? How can ethical and value judgments be established or justified? Can they be justified at all? What is the meaning of "free" or "responsible?"

Certain basic points must be noted from all the different understandings of the concept of morality espoused so far. First, the concept of morality is capable of different interpretations. It would be an inversion of conceptual clarity if this fact is not recognized.

Second, in the prescriptive/normative sense, morality is part of the subject matter of ethics, which is itself a subset of the discourse of philosophy. Therefore, morality is philosophical in the prescriptive/normative sense. Furthermore, morality and ethics are intimately related. We cannot ask about the right thing to do at any point in time without taking into account the sort of agents concerned in the decision-making process and the values to which they are attached (Solomon & Greene, 1999). In the same thinking, normative ethics is also called moral philosophy (Garner, 2003, p. 610). Thus, ethics and morality are interchangeable in the prescriptive/normative sense. The foregoing sense of morality is adopted in the study.

Compatriotism and Cosmopolitanism

Both the concepts of compatriotism and cosmopolitanism have rich philosophical backgrounds; the former derives chiefly from the Platonic and Aristotelian philosophical reflections on civic citizenship, and the latter from the stoic philosophy.

According to both Plato and Aristotle, the state exists to supply the necessities of life to man (see Coplestone, 1962a, p. 251; 1962b, p. 92). Therefore, to preserve the state, Aristotle stated that,

> [E]ach citizen will possess a plot of land near the city and another near the frontier (so that all may have an interest in the defence of the state). This land will be worked by the non-citizen labourers. (Coplestone, 1962b, p. 98)

From the foregoing, since Aristotle somewhat makes a distinction between citizens and non-citizens, we may rightly surmise that a citizen in the Aristotelian sense is one who holds a stake in the survival and flourishing of the state and who participates in "giving judgment and holding office" (Aristotle, 1981, p. 169). Hence, the emergence of the concept of civic citizenship with the cognate concept of patriotism.

But what is patriotism per se? Patriotism is a strand of what some scholars of morality have called partialism (see Cuttingham, 1986; Wolf, 1992); the thesis that "*it is* (not merely psychologically understandable but) *morally correct to favor one's own*" (Cuttingham, 1986, p. 357-358).[3] Nathanson, quoting Maclntyre, states that patriotism involves loyalty and a preference for the well-being of one's own country over others (1989, p. 536). Keller also strikes at the heart of the discussion when he notes that a patriot loves and is loyal to his own country (2005, p. 576).

Perhaps, the foregoing scholars have drawn on the philosophical resource of the classics. In the *Republic* (375e), *Platonic*[4] Socrates calls for a citizen army that resembles "the philosophic dogs" who are "as gentle as can be with their familiars and those they know and the opposite with those they don't know" (Pangle, 1998, p. 382). Aristotle also insists that the psychological core of citizenship is a tamed version of what Plato calls "spiritedness" (thumos)—that part of the soul that generates a passionate, often indignant, sense of honor, together with a fiercely proud and stubbornly loyal love for one's own people (Pangle, 1998, p. 382).

A reflection on the above reveals that the defining characteristic of the concept of patriotism reduces to loyalty to one's nation. Now, if we understand "compatriot" as including all long-term, law-abiding fellow-residents of a country (Miller, 1998, p. 205), then we can see it in the light that patriotism implies compatriotism. The logic is this:

1. The notion of a nation without people is unthinkable. Therefore, the concept of people is vital to any conception of a nation;
2. Patriotism means loyalty to one's nation;
3. Loyalty to one's nation implies development of the well-being of fellow nationals in preference to that of other nationals, since they commonly constitute the nation;
4. Development of the well-being of fellow nationals in preference to that of other nationals is compatriotism; and
5. Therefore, patriotism leads to compatriotism.

In simple terms, it is logical inconsistency to love one's nation without loving or giving moral preference to the service of one's fellow citizens in relation to the nationals of other nations. Thus, compatriotism is defined as a morality that expresses a normative commitment to giving priority treatment to compatriots living within a political community over moral agents living in a foreign political community. This understanding forms the basis of the concept of compatriotism in the study.

According to Cheah (2006, p. 487), quoting D'Alembert, "cosmopolitan" derives from the Greek words for "world" (cosmos) and "city" (polis). Specifically, the moral dimension to the concept of cosmopolitanism derives extensively from the reasoning of stoic philosophers. However, the first philosopher to have given explicit expression to cosmopolitanism was the Socratically inspired Cynic, Diogenes in the fourteenth century BCE. It is said that "when he was asked where he came from, he replied, 'I am a citizen of the world'" (Kleingeld & Brown, 2006, para. 5).

The above notwithstanding, the stoic philosophers provided a philosophical basis for the development of the concept of cosmopolitanism. Perhaps the classical philosophical high-ground for the whole idea of cosmopolitanism was provided by the stoic philosophers when they argued that all men are participants in the spark of divine reason; hence the idea of universal brotherhood (see Stumpf, 1994, p. 119). Cicero put it thus:

> . . . since reason exists both in man and God, the first common possession of men and God is reason. But those who have reason in common must also have right reason in common. And since right reason is law, we must believe that men have law also in common with the gods. Further, those who share law must also share justice, and those who share these are to be regarded as members of the same commonwealth. (Stumpf, 1994, p. 119)

Cicero's notion of cosmopolitanism is that moral duties and obligations ought not to be restricted only to those who have communal attachments. Rather, moral relations ought to be extended to those with whom we do not have obvious communal relationships. The reason being that we are all required to be benevolent to all persons. Seneca captured the thinking thus:

> Nature bids me to be of use to men whether they are slave or free, freedmen or free born. Wherever there is a human being there is room for benevolence. (Coplestone, 1962b, p. 175)

Another philosopher who contributed to the cosmopolitan thinking was the German philosopher, Immanuel Kant. Kant's contribution is both moral and political. Perhaps taking a cue from his Stoic predecessors, Kant defines the ontology of man as being constitutive of reason. Since all men possess this reason, then they are all persons who have equal moral worth. He states that,

> . . . rational beings are called persons in as much as their nature already marks them out as ends in themselves, i.e., as something which is not to be used merely as a means and hence there is imposed thereby a limit on all arbitrary use of such beings which are thus objects of respects. (Kant, 1981, p. 428)

From the political angle, Kant proposes an institutional structure at the transnational level. Using the contactarian approach, Kant contends that states should . . . relinquish, just as do individual human beings, their wild (lawless) freedom, and . . . accustom themselves to public, binding laws, and . . . thereby form a (continually expanding) *state of peoples* (civitas gentium), which would ultimately comprise all of the peoples on earth (Kleingeld, 2004, p. 306).

For the legal framework of the transnational institutional order, Kant also introduces the concept of "cosmopolitan law" in which both states and individuals have rights, and where individuals have these rights as "citizens of the earth" rather than as citizens of particular states (Kleingeld & Brown, 2006, para. 28). Kant notes that the cosmopolitan law is a "necessary complement" to the unwritten code of existing national and international law, and a means to transform the latter into a public law of humanity (Kant, 1970, p. 108). Kant goes on to emphasize the norm of action to the individual in his proposed transnational institutional order when he states that a world-citizen acts from the pluralistic standpoint of humanity as a collective actor as opposed to that of an egoistic individual (Kant, 1968, p. 411).

Read carefully and critically, the reflections of the above philosophers give us the understanding that moral cosmopolitanism is a normative thinking, which expresses a commitment to the view that all human beings ought to be regarded and treated as of equal moral value and respect. This position constitutes a clash with compatriotism.

Compatriotism vs. Cosmopolitanism

The central normative thesis of moral cosmopolitanism reduces to moral impartialism. However, some philosophers of compatriotism have argued that this thinking is defective, and that we are morally justified to be partial to those that are "near and dear."[5] The latter position is founded on some grounds.

Argument from fair play

This borders on the duty/logic of reciprocity. It states that we have obligations to give benefits in return for benefits received, and we receive benefits from our fellow citizens (Kleingeld & Brown, 2006, para. 57). Now, when the benefits we ought to give our fellow citizens by virtue of the duty/logic of reciprocity are being contended for by the distant needy, we know at once that the interests of our fellow citizens trump those of the others. The merit of the reasoning is obvious. One has a moral responsibility to reciprocate good gestures from his compatriots; failure to do this is ingratitude, and this is a vice. In as much as this vice is a moral wrong, then the virtue of gratitude ought to be promoted.

But, the argument is weak in at least two basic respects. First, the duty triggered by the principle of fairness is not a duty of a sort that could establish patriotic priority (Arneson, 2007, para. 26). This is simple:

> Even if the principle of fairness generates a duty to provide goods to one's fellow countrymen, this is a return for services rendered, not any sort of response to the neediness of badly off condition of those to whom the duty is owed. Those to whom I owe a duty of fair play arising from the principle of fairness might all be wealthy individuals who are among the very best off persons on earth. (Arneson, 2007, para. 26)

The second weakness is that the whole duty/logic of reciprocity borders on enlightened self-interest: you give me benefits now because you expect something of equal value from me in the future, though I may not be able to repay you immediately. Why operate on the basis of enlightened self-interest? Morality might require the well-off to help the badly-off forever with no actual behavioral reciprocity demanded of the recipients of help (Arneson, 2007, para. 29). This is moral altruism, which a sincere moral agent ought to adopt.

Argument from salience

Salience of need refers not only to the obviousness and inescapability of noticing need but also to the continuing imposition of this knowledge on us (Kamm, 2000, p. 664). The reasoning goes that we would be morally unfeeling not to assist those whose needs are salient to us by virtue of their proximity to us, rather than trouble ourselves over the problem of distant needy foreigners whose needs are not salient to us. Doubtless, it is morally reprehensible to refrain from helping those who we surely know, because of their proximity to us, are worse off. But this also applies to distant needy foreigners. In the present age of communication systems with transnational capacities to transmit and receive information within seconds, rarely can we say that we are unaware of the needs of distant foreigners.

Argument from "contract of consent"

From the Hobbesian and Lockean perspective, especially, the consent of the people in the pre-social life forms the basis for the justification of the modern society (see Wolff, 1996).[6] Thus, any duties and obligations of justice thereafter are equally a product of the "contract of consent," which only applies to those who have consented to it.[7] Obviously, the thinking provides, in the abstract, justification for political obligation and compatriotism. If the state truly exists to correct the evils of the pre-social life, which contractarian philosophers pointed out, then it would be contra-reason for the people in the modern state not to support its institutional structures. But, cooperative obedience is one thing; the state may still collapse due to lack of internal cohesion caused by the inability of the citizens to give priority treatment to the welfare of one another. Thus, if the end-point of cooperative obedience is stability of the state, then this cooperative obedience should also imply compatriotism.

However, Dzur (2002, pp. 203-204) argues that "we have already seen that consent is an insufficient theory of obligation for liberal states because in practice few actually *do* consent to political membership and, more fundamentally, because some *would* not consent to much liberal policy that benefits the less well-off."

As noted earlier, the cosmopolitan thinking is founded on a commitment to giving equal value of life to all the rational sentient beings in the world. Obviously, this is a virtue since it is morally opposed to various irrational forms of discrimination, such as racism, sexism, and clanism, which people perpetrate against one another, the discrimination all truly rational moral agents take to be morally wrong.

However, giving equal value to the lives of all rational sentient beings is one thing; giving them equal concern is quite another since the latter does not inevitably follow from the former (see R.W. Miller, 1998, p. 207). As a moral agent, I may hold the lives of all rational sentient beings as of equal value. However, I may be constrained by the finitude of my economic resources to show equal concern for their multifarious needs. And, those I may end up aiding may be on what D. Miller (1995) calls "relational facts," the thinking that my relationship with fellow citizens is constituted by reciprocal obligations.[8]

As the forgoing has shown, compatriotism and cosmopolitanism are in conflict on moral grounds.[9] Compatriotism encourages feelings that develop and sustain social cooperation that ultimately leads to social cohesion. However, strictly holding on to it weakens the common link of humanity across national boundaries as well as equality of all rational human beings, since compatriotism ontologically elevates the *being* of one people over that of another people. Conversely, cosmopolitanism makes a normative claim for equality of all rational human beings. Therefore, it strengthens the common link of humanity across borders. The weakness therein is that it attaches no serious importance to values, which strengthen internal cohesion of nations. Without those values of common appeal, there would be social implosion, leading eventually to state collapse. However, there is still a way of reconciling both compatriotism and cosmopolitanism.

A New Cosmo-Morality of Human Relations among the Yoruba in the Age of Globalization[10]

A new thinking that attempts a reconciliation of the contending moral claims of compatriotism and cosmopolitanism is deducible from the concept of *alajobi*, which is both cosmological and morally normative. Specifically, the study draws in part on an interesting exposition of the concept of *alajobi* from Yoruba cosmology, that is, the totality of the world views of the Yoruba, by Akiwowo (1983).

First, Akiwowo (1983, p.18) clarifies two concepts that are of cosmological significance, *ajobi* and *ajogbe*. According to his approximate translations, *ajobi* means consanguinity and *ajogbe* means co-residentship. He goes on to define consanguinity, as the facts of lineal and collateral relationships based upon blood and birth, while co-residentship is the fact of sharing the same or contiguous shelter whether or not the sharers are related by blood. From the two concepts, Akiwowo (1983, p.18) derives two further concepts of *alajobi* and *alajogbe*. He defines the former as that which sustains all kinds of lineal and collateral relationships, while the later is taken as that which sustains person or individualized groups who are living together under one roof or in contiguous shelters in a locale. To make the concepts clearer, one could define *alajobi* as that metaphysical familial bond holding together groups of people who subscribe to the spirit of common descent. However, *alajogbe* could be seen as that spatio-temporal bond holding together groups of people who might not subscribe to the same spirit of common descent; though, they are resident together. Seen in this light, it is obvious that the two concepts, socially speaking, generate two different norms of human association and interaction. *Alajobi* is committed to a norm of *necessary unity* in human interaction in society, whether or not the people in interaction are spatio-temporally contiguous. However, *alajogbe* is committed to a norm of *contingent unity* in human interaction in society—that is, the unity only obtains when the people involved in interaction are spatio-temporally contiguous. Thus, one could validly argue that the concept of *alajobi* embraces that of *alajogbe,* but the relationship does not hold in the converse. Furthermore, one could inferentially argue that the relationship bond of *alajobi* is longer and stronger than that of *alajogbe*.

Based on the above explication, it is clear why the concept of *alajobi* is significant in reconciling compatriotism and cosmopolitanism. The point is that the proponents of the divergent forms of ethical thinking usually see themselves "in opposition to," but not "in relation to"—that is, they interact on the basis of self-other dichotomy. However, as noted above, the basic norm of social association and interaction of *alajob*i contributes more to peaceful social existence and cooperative interaction than that of *alajogbe*. In other words, a strong commitment by the peoples of the world to the *alajobi* thinking makes them see one another as brothers and sisters, who ought to subscribe to the same spirit of common descent, no matter the degree of racial, religious, and ideological differences as well as spatio-temporal gap between them. This is the cosmological side to the thinking. The moral side derives from the foregoing. One must remember that the essence of the cosmological aspect is unity of all the peoples of the world in terms of their subscription to common descent. Thus, to practically demonstrate this spirit of common descent, they ought to see all aspects of their interaction as self-other complementarity as an ideal norm of human association and interaction.

An objection which could be raised against the position of the chapter is, How could the *alajobi* perspective solve the problems of obvious discrimination, domination, and suppression of the lowly by the mighty, the major problem in the present age? The answer is clear. Inasmuch as we could not consistently discriminate against, dominate, or suppress and still hold ourselves in brotherly terms, then the logical conclusion is that the foregoing problems are resolved in the cosmo-morality of *alajobi*.

It has, however, been pointed out that this proposal throws up the problem of implementation.[11] This problem is largely addressed if the policy makers of modern nation-states are committed to the following program of implementation. The constitution of each nation-state should be drawn up in such a way that sets aside a given portion of its wealth, depending on the economic buoyancy of the nation-state, to cater for the welfare of the clearly perceived unfortunate others in neighboring lands. The phrase "clearly perceived" means that the needs of the so-called unfortunate others in those lands must be firstly properly ascertained. This guards against any imprudent use of the wealth committed to their welfare. Thereafter, the reserved wealth is expended to provide for those identified needs. The moral justification for this transnational redistribution of wealth is founded on the *alajobi* thinking. Thus, observance of this scheme of redistribution is morally obligatory rather than supererogatory. Furthermore, this transnational redistribution of wealth is to be channeled through a specially established institution that equally has transnational capacities to operate across borders.

When all nation-states and peoples are morally committed to this proposal, then at least three fundamental things would be achieved: (1) people would be responsible in a morally obligatory way to the welfare of the unfortunate ones among them; (2) nation-states and peoples would have no excuse to exclude themselves from this morally binding scheme, since it is constitutionally backed at the domestic level; (3) no nation-state or people would be worse off in this scheme of redistribution, since what a nation-state or people might lack because of contribution to unfortunate ones in neighboring lands would be provided by another nation-state or people contributing to the welfare of the former.

Conclusion

The chapter has argued that the ontology of globalization is a commitment to the ultimate institution of a global village, where common human values are promoted. However, the opposed moral claims of compatriotism and cosmopolitanism constitute a problem to the realization of this ideal. In the final analysis, the chapter locates the solution to the problem in *alajobi* philosophy. It concludes that adopting this thinking as the new morality of human relations would contribute to the institution of a more just global village. Furthermore, the chapter also attempts to address the problem of implementation of the proposal made. Ultimately, one could state that in the ideal global village, founded on the *alajobi* philosophy, "self" is not conceptualized in isolation of "other." Rather, it is conceptualized on the basis of self-other complementarity. In the ideal global village, the concept of *otherness* is extensive rather than restrictive.

Notes

1. Conceptualizing globalization from a disciplinary matrix tends to be non-objective in the sense that it does not truly give us the essence of the phenomenon of globalization. What it offers us is just the interpretation of the concept from a given disciplinary angle.
2. The emphasis is in the original.
3. Other forms of partialism, according to Cuttingham, are familism, kinshipism, clanism, racism, sexism, and planetism (pp. 359–360).
4. Emphasis mine.
5. This is borrowed from Nathanson's work, p. 538.
6. This work presents illuminating summaries of the political philosophies of Thomas Hobbes and John Locke, the two philosophers that classically laid the metaphysical foundations of the modern state in contractarianism. See pp. 8–18; 18–26.
7. This is a logical derivative from the foregoing.
8. The distinction between "equal value" and "equal concern" to life as well as the specific example given is made in the Richard Miller's work cited earlier in the study, p. 207.
9. I thank the anonymous reviewers of the chapter for pointing out that there is a tension between compatriotism and cosmopolitanism on political, economic, and other grounds as well.
10. This thinking, although modified in what follows, is part of my present work on the cosmo-morality of *alajobi* as a norm for human interaction in the contemporary world
11. I also profusely thank the reviewers for making this valuable suggestion/contribution to the quality of the chapter.

References

Adekanye, J.B. (2004). Globalization: An introduction. *Ibadan Journal of the Social Sciences*, 2(1), pp. iii-vi.

Akiwowo, A. 1983 (1980). *Ajobi and Ajogbe: Variations on the theme sociation*. Inaugural Lecture Series 46. Ile-Ife: University of Ife Press.

Aristotle. (1981). *The politics*. Harmondsworth: Penguin.

Arneson, R.J. (2007). Do patriotic ties limit global justice? *The Journal of Ethics*, 9(1-2), pp. 127-150. Retrieved on January 11, 2007, from http://philosophy2.ucsd.edu/%7Erarneson/globalegalitarianjustice1.pdf.

Badru, R.O. (2003). *Globalization as an instrument of neo-colonialism in Africa: A critical exposition*. Unpublished MA thesis, Department of Philosophy, University of Ibadan, Nigeria.

Chase-Dunn, C. (1999). Globalization: A world-systems perspective. *Journal of World-Systems Research*, V(2), pp. 187-215.

Cheah, P. (2006). Cosmopolitanism. In M. Featherstone, C. Venn, R. Bishop, & J. Philips (Eds.), *Theory, Culture and Society: Special Issue on Problematizing Global Knowledge*, 23(2-3), pp. 486-496. London: Sage Publications.

Cohen, R., & Kennedy, P. (2000). *Global sociology*. New York: Palgrave.

Coplestone, F. (1962a). *A history of philosophy*. Vol. 1, Part 1. New York: Image Books.
Coplestone, F. (1962b). *A history of philosophy*. Vol. 1, Part II. New York: Image Books.
Cuttingham, J. (1986). Partiality, favoritism and morality. *The Philosophical Quarterly*, 36(144), pp. 357-373.
Dzur, A.W. (2002). Nationalism, liberalism and democracy. *Political Research Quarterly*, 55(1), pp. 191-211.
Frankena, W.K. (1995). *Ethics* (2nd ed.). (E. Beardsley & M. Beardsley, Eds.). New Jersey: Prentice Hall of India Private Ltd.
Garner, R.T. (Ed.). (2003). *The Encyclopedia Americana* (Vol. 10). Danbury, Connecticut, U.S.A.: Grolier Incorporated.
Gert, B. (2002, 2005). The definition of morality. Retrieved on January 19, 2007, from *Stanford encyclopedia of philosophy*, http://plato.stanford.edu/entries/morality-definition/.
Habermas, J. (2001). *The postnational constellation*. (M. Pensky, Ed. and Trans.). Cambridge, MA: MIT Press.
Halwani, R. (2003). Care ethics and virtue ethics. *Hypatia*, 18(3), pp. 161-192.
Held, D. (1995). *Democracy and the global order: From the modern state to cosmopolitan governance*. Cambridge: Polity Press.
Held, D., McGrew, A., Goldblatt, D., & Perrnton, J. (1999). *Global transformations: Politics, economics and culture*. Cambridge: Polity Press.
Hirst, P., & Thompson, G. (1996). *Globalization in question: The international economy and the possibilities*. Cambridge: Polity Press.
Kamm, F.M. (2000). Does distance matter morally to the duty to rescue? *Law and Philosophy*, 19(6), pp. 655-681.
Kant, I. (1968). Anthropologie in pragmatischer Hinsicht (Pragmatic anthropology and universal history). In W. Weischedel (Ed.), *Werkausgabe* XII. Frankfurt am Main: Suhrkamp.
Kant, I. (1970). *Kant's political writings*. (H. Reiss, Ed. and introduced by). Cambridge: Cambridge University Press.
Kant, I. (1981). *The grounding for the metaphysics of morals*. (J.W. Ellington, Trans.). Indianapolis and Cambridge: Hacket Publishing Company.
Keller, S. (2005). Patriotism as bad faith. *Ethics*, 115(3), pp. 563-592.
Kleingeld, P. (2004). Approaching perpetual peace: Kant's defence of a league of states and his ideal of world federation. *European Journal of Philosophy*, 12(3), pp. 304-325.
Kleingeld, P., & Brown, E. (2006). Cosmopolitan. Retrieved on May 2, 2007, from *Stanford encyclopedia of philosophy*, http://plato.stanford.edu/entries/cosmopolitanism/.
Miller, D. (1995). *On nationality*. Oxford: Oxford University Press.
Miller, R.W. (1998). Cosmopolitan respect and patriotic concern. *Philosophy and Public Affairs*, 27(3), pp. 202-224.
Nathanson, S. (1989). In defense of "moderate patriotism." *Ethics*, 99(3), pp. 535-552.
Pangle, T.L. (1998). Justice among nations in Platonic and Aristotelian political philosophy. *American Journal of Political Science*, 42(2), pp. 377-397.
Scholte, J.A. (1996). Beyond the buzz-word: Towards a critical theory of globalization. In E. Kofman & G. Youngs (Eds.), *Globalization: Theory and practice*. London and New York: Pinter.

Shaw, M. (2002). *Globalization, governance and integration*. Retrieved on June 11, 2002, from http://www.martinshaw.org/intro/36.htm.

Sklair, L. (1999). Competing conceptions of globalization. *Journal of World-Systems Research*, V(2), pp. 143-163.

Solomon, R.C., & Greene, J.K., (Eds). (1999). *Morality and the good life: An introduction to ethics through classical sources*. New York: McGraw-Hill Companies, Inc.

Stumpf, S.E. (1994). *Philosophy: History and problems* (5th ed.). New York: Mc-GrawHill Companies, Inc.

Valequez, M. (1999). *Philosophy*. London: Wadsworth Publishing Company.

Wolf, S. (1992). Morality and partiality. *Philosophical Perspectives*, 6, pp. 243-259.

Wolff, J. (1996). *An introduction to political philosophy*. Oxford/New York: Oxford University Press.

SECTION II

GLOBALIZATION AND CULTURE

CHAPTER FIVE

KISWAHILI LANGUAGE AND THE FUTURE OF EAST AFRICAN INTEGRATION IN THE AGE OF GLOBALIZATION

MWANAKOMBO MOHAMMED NOORDIN

The year 2007 represents a crucial turning point in the development of East Africa. It witnessed the expansion of the East African Community (EAC) to include Rwanda and Burundi, apart from Kenya, Uganda, and Tanzania. This expansion immediately raised the fundamental question of the role of Kiswahili in relation to other languages in the process of identity formation in the EAC. This study explores how Kiswahili competes with English and French (spoken largely in Rwanda and Burundi) to retain and expand its influence in the cultural and economic space of East Africa. Data for this study include government policy papers, reports, and legislation; media debates on the East African integration; in-depth interviews with policy makers and Kiswahili educators in Kenya; and focus-group discussion with the East African Integration Task Force in Kenya.

Introduction

This study is set within two simultaneous developments: the escalation in migration of people into and within East Africa; and the expansion of the East African Community to include Rwanda and Burundi. These processes represent important opportunities for East African society, but they also result in significant social and political tensions. The revival of the community, through the signing of the Treaty for the Establishment of the East African Community (EAC) in 1999, presents the partner states with the opportunity and framework for realizing the interest and the desire to co-operate in the cultural and linguistic fields. In recognition of the fundamental importance of this collaboration, there was a need to provide for Kiswahili to be developed as the *lingua franca* of the EAC.

Kiswahili has been recognized by the EAC as a language of unity for political, economic, social, cultural, educational, scientific, and technological development. This paper explores the role of Kiswahili in the integration of East Africa noting a fundamental challenge of the five East African states' different language policies and separate ideologies on education and cultural development and practices posed by the communities of people living within East Africa. Language plays a fundamental role in the process of identity formation. This study explores this concept in the promotion of national and ethnic identities in the region.

The original member states—Kenya, Uganda, and Tanzania—enjoy close regional, educational, scientific, technological, social, economic, cultural, and linguistic ties for their mutual benefit. This has existed since the colonial times. Between 1930 and 1964, there existed an inter-territorial language committee whose central aim was to promote the standardization and development of Kiswahili.

These three countries had been cooperating and sharing their resources, exemplified by the rotation of the headquarters of this language committee as follows: Dar-es-Salaam 1930-1942; Nairobi 1942-1952; Makerere 1952-1961; and Dar-es-Salaam again 1962-1964 (Kenya, 2007, pp. 2-8). In 1964 the committee was incorporated into the Institute of Kiswahili Research, University of Dar-es-Salaam.

In 1977, the East African Community broke up mainly due to selfish leadership and phobia. Despite this breakup, and despite the subsequent establishment of educational and language bodies in individual countries, the pan-regional language initiative continued to informally interact and formally seek mechanisms to establish a framework for formal cooperation.

The revival of the EAC in 1999 presented the partner states with another opportunity. Article 137 of the Treaty for the Establishment of the EAC provides that Kiswahili shall be developed as the lingua franca of the community (Kenya, 2007, pp. 2-8). Kiswahili plays a vital role in collaboration among the East African countries for political, economic, social, educational, cultural, and technological development. The admission of Rwanda and Burundi into the Community in 2007 opened up a whole new challenge due to the fact that Kiswahili had not been widely used there.

With this in mind, the East African Commission of Kiswahili was established in 2007 as a tool for advising the partner states on matters related to Kiswahili research, teaching, learning, and development through policy formulation, knowledge generation, curriculum review, standardization of terminology, and promotion of Kiswahili as a lingua franca. This meant that a mechanism had to be put in place and implemented in an effort to equalize the situation in the partner states (Kenya, 2007, pp. 2-8).

The main objective of having Kiswahili as a lingua franca in the EAC is to encourage regional unity and sustainable socio-economic development. There also developed the need to harmonize Kiswahili education programs, curricula, and certification in order to ensure that teaching and research achieve acceptable standards.

Statement of the Problem

This study raises several fundamental questions. The role of Kiswahili language in the future of the East African integration scheme has several problems due to differing language policies in all the five East African countries. The inclusion of Rwanda and Burundi also poses fundamental challenges. Rwanda has Kinyarwanda and French as the official languages; Kenya has Kiswahili and English; Uganda has English and several ethnic languages; and Tanzania has Kiswahili. This diversity of language policies in the EAC countries challenges the implementation of article 137 of the Treaty. Thus, making Kiswahili the lingua franca of East Africa needs a major overhaul of policies in the five countries and political will to do so. To achieve this, there is the need to find answers to the following:

- What is the role of Kiswahili in relation to other languages in the process of identity formation in the East African states?
- What is the role of Kiswahili in the promotion of national and ethnic identities?
- With globalization giving the push and ethnicity giving the pull, how do we enhance social inclusion and integration in the EAC?
- Could Kiswahili function as a unifying language for socio-economic growth within East Africa?

Kiswahili for Socio-Economic Development

With an estimated population of 125 million people, East Africa has a combined GDP of $44 billion, and it is ranked as one of the fastest reforming regions in terms of business regulation. A vibrant capital and securities market is being strengthened in the region with a high level of intra- and cross-border investments which range from the agricultural, manufacturing, tourism, mining, building, construction and housing, and capital markets, and the financial, education, and health sectors. The infrastructure is also calling for investors in road transport, railways, water and air transport, port facilities, information and communication technology, energy, and water and sanitation services.

By pooling their resources and promoting free trade within the region, the EAC aims to emerge as a leading trade entity in Africa. These are some of the reasons why major economic expansions of such magnitude require the services of a vibrant language like Kiswahili to facilitate communication within the region.

Further, it was noted that through the Inter-University Council for East Africa, a mechanism is being established for mutual recognition of higher educational qualifications in the region. This is an important prerequisite for the free movement of labor. Kiswahili can also function as a unifying language for trade, education, transport, agriculture, and finance.

Linguistically, Rwanda is oligolingual with Kinyarwanda used by practically the total population, while Uganda is multilingual with more than 30 languages. There are similarities in the use of both the English (official) and African languages. Kiswahili is the official national language of Tanzania and is used in higher education. Kenya has Kiswahili and English as official and practical languages, whereas the rural areas continue using mother-tongue language.

Historically, Kiswahili has been the lingua franca of the coastal region of East Africa since the fourteenth century. It is spoken by over 120 million people in the Eastern and Central African region. Kiswahili is used internationally in this region for economic, political, and social transactions, and in government as an official language. It has been a written language using the Arabic script since the fourteenth century and the Roman script since the nineteenth century (Massamba, 2002). Due to these functional attributes of Kiswahili, it was standardized in the 1930s and became a language of instruction in East African schools. As a consequence of its being one of the earliest standardized languages of Africa, it was made an official language of the African Union in 2004.

Socially, Kiswahili, as the language of the Swahili people of the East African coast, is a Bantu language. In his book, Massamba (2002) insists that it is through trade and religion that Kiswahili spread in the Eastern African region. The Arabs had used it to spread Islam into the hinterland of Congo and, later, it was utilized by the European missionaries in spreading Christianity. This made Kiswahili acceptable as the language of choice by the people of this region.

The same point can be made politically and educationally. Trade was the single most compelling vehicle that brought Kiswahili across the East African countries to Rwanda, Democratic Republic of Congo, and the Central African region. Kiswahili also facilitated the movement of Arab merchants into the interior of Africa.

It also became the language of politics. Political awareness and the clamor for independence in Kenya and Tanzania during the colonial era mainly used Kiswahili as the language to unify Africans and lock out the colonialists. The missionaries in Kenya and Tanzania also employed the use of Kiswahili to spread Christianity and open up schools in the hinterland. After the standardization of Kiswahili in 1930, however, the white colonial administrators employed the use of Kiswahili for education in the African schools.

Khatib (2004) looks at the unifying capacity of Kiswahili as a language for the liberation of the African people. He traced the use of Kiswahili since the Abushiri dynasty of seventeenth century East Africa where the Swahili united against Arab invasion. Subsequently, there was the Maji Maji rebellion against the Germans, the Mazrui rebellion against the British settlers, and the Mau Mau struggles for Kenya's independence—which all used Kiswahili as the language of communication and mobilization to end foreign occupation.

Kiswahili was used as a liberation language in Mozambique, Zimbabwe, South Africa (during the apartheid era), Uganda, Rwanda, Burundi, and the Congo. Kiswahili has also served as a language for research in various universities in Africa, Europe, Asia, and the United States. Due to the above functions, various international agencies support research in higher education on Kiswahili. These are some of the compelling advantages which enabled the African Union (AU) secretariat to choose Kiswahili as one of the official languages of the organization.

Globalization and Kiswahili as a Language of East African Integration

While the forces of regional integration focus on the promotion of Kiswahili, the forces of globalization seem to be pushing for the promotion of the English language. With the development in information technology in the region and the laying of fiber-optic cables, the goal of many East African countries recently has been to attract foreign investments, particularly call centers. The dream is to become like India where many major corporations have outsourced their phone operators in order to access a cheaper but well-qualified labor market. For East African nations to "be like India," it is argued, the use of the English language—rather than Kiswahili—needs to be promoted.

But East Africans, as a whole, stand to benefit immensely from Kiswahili as a unifying language. As an indigenous language of Africa, it would provide diversity in international fora and promote acceptance, unity, and homogeneity among the people of Africa.

Nevertheless, there is talk about the "imperialistic" nature of adopting Kiswahili by non-Swahili peoples of Eastern Africa and beyond. Here it has been found that, though being a language of the Waswahili, other ethnicities had historically embraced it without fear as the Swahili are cosmopolitan and accommodating of others by nature. With a literate history dating back to the seventh century, many non-Swahili people found that effective communication in Kiswahili was a useful skill.

Undoubtedly, trading blocs like the EAC can indeed help African countries evolve and pursue common and coordinated positions on various international trade issues and establish strong multilateral negotiating coalitions.

Having joined the EAC in 2007, the two francophone countries of Rwanda and Burundi have started promoting Kiswahili, and English, in order to harmonize their socio-cultural environments with those of Kenya, Uganda, and Tanzania. The use of mass media in this exercise cannot be overemphasized. Radio stations using Kiswahili as their broadcasting medium are indispensable instruments of integrating the people.

Consequently, the IPP media group of Tanzania has rolled out a regional Kiswahili newspaper to disseminate regional news. This has been a welcome development as the readership goes beyond East Africa to the world. With its accessibility in the web, this newspaper underscores the regional character of the media in East Africa.

One should also observe that many Rwandans and Burundis who have lived in Tanzania over an extended period as political refugees speak Kiswahili. They have adopted it and institutionalized it through the use of the Swahili culture (Kawoya & Makokha, 2007).

Significance of Kiswahili in Africa and Beyond

Kiswahili was initially used in Addis Ababa at the AU summit in 2004 and at the Pan African Parliament in the same year. There is a need to develop and expand the functions of Kiswahili in the Continent. This can be done by including Kiswahili in the ,various language policy documents of the countries affiliated to the AU. Major regional languages of Africa like Arabic in the North, Hausa/Yoruba in the West, and Zulu/Sotho/Tswana in the South can also be taught in East Africa. This will ensure that member states donate research funds for developing these regional languages in the continent.

The success of these policies would be definite with the inclusion of a social perspective on the attitudes and needs of the receptors. Both countries' policies had been defined in the colonial era and fully adopted at independence. Not much thought had been put on the opinions of the receptors. At independence more realistic options should have been sought. The language for the development of the people of Kenya and Uganda should be a language that has social ramifications, historical relevance, cultural integrity, and economic significance.

In this context, Kiswahili fits in very well as it has historical stature and economic relevance now that the expansion of the EAC to include Rwanda and Burundi has opened the East African market up to 150 million people. Rwandans and Burundis do speak Kiswahili especially after their migration into Tanzania during the 1994 genocide.

With English, the failure has been in the extra-linguistics phenomena whereby the lower primary pupils in urban areas had difficulties conceptualizing the cultural norms of the language. There have been recorded misinterpretations and misunderstandings of meanings in written works like compositions. At that level, English lacked the social significance of communications. Having been the language of colonialists, it conjured up negative feelings from users and needed to be tolerated for the sake of upward mobility.

The Protocol on the Establishment of the East African Kiswahili Commission declared: "The East African Kiswahili Commission formed in 2007 has the vision of being the leader in the promotion and coordination of the development and usage of Kiswahili for regional unity and sustainable socio-economic development in partner states." This is a very noble vision, but language has historical and contextual roots in the community. Recent reports allude to the suspicion of Kenya's neighbors as to the potential threat the human resource base of Kenya is to the partner states. More qualified to occupy most jobs in E.A. makes the neighbors weary of integration. Rigorous border scrutiny of passports and body searches make migration into another partner state an ordeal.

The role of Kiswahili would be to tap the human resource base of Kenya by supplying teachers, learning resource materials, and logistics to partner states so as to harmonize Kiswahili language education programs and curricula in East Africa.

Debates on Kiswahili: A Critique

Media debates have amplified the significance of Kiswahili in recent times. In an editorial article of one of the dailies, the editor decried the reluctance and lack of political will among the politicians in propelling the East African integration forward.

> Six months down the road, Kenya is reluctant to facilitate the constitution of the second assembly. Instead, flexing of muscles, insincerity, selfishness and lack of political will dominate. (Bundotich, 2007, p. 12)

All this was done to frustrate the formation of an East African Legislative Assembly by not electing the nine nominees from Kenya's parliament. This delayed and derailed the regional governance program.

For Kiswahili to function as a unifying language for socio-economic development within East Africa, according to Dellinger (2001), there has to be political will and intent to use it to facilitate integration. If the political sector of East Africa is in disarray, the social life is affected and Kiswahili will be used more as a language of disassociation than one of unity. We cannot deny the economic inequalities between the member states, with some being more industrialized than others, but this can be an advantage to all in that the EAC can negotiate better tariffs for sale of the goods to the world as a regional block. Language then can go beyond politics to promote, through relevant activities in the partner states, the meaning and value of community unity. One state's strengths can boost the capacity of all the other states.

The East African Integration Taskforce on the issue of language noted that the Kenyan populace was wary of adopting the Kiswahili as a lingua franca due to the fact that "we are better than the rest and we do not need them. Why waste our resources in stooping down to their level?" (Report of the EAIT, 2007, p. 9). These views were expressed by locals in one of the public hearings called by the Taskforce. In critically analyzing these statements, one gets the impression that the Kenyans who were speaking were suffering from a superiority complex and failed to grasp the bigger picture of the advantages of the integration. Much as the partner states share a history of colonialism, Swahili culture, and economic development, the people did not get a chance to internalize the meaning of integration. They conceived it as a step backwards. Several developments could have led to this, such as lack of a national referendum in Kenya for people to air their views, little time to discuss issues, past hurts after the breakup of the EAC in 1977—all these had not been resolved, and the people needed time to understand why the breakup happened and what measures had now been put in place to ensure that such a loss would not occur.

The historical injustices of closing borders, cutting off families and relatives, experienced in 1977 had not been resolved. Being socially situated, speakers needed to be informed of the new political, economic, social, and cultural language structures that had been put in place to avert such a crisis. Governments had used the top-down approach in total disregard for historical, cultural, and political contexts. For Kiswahili to succeed, therefore, all these have to be considered.

Conclusion

The foregoing discussions have shown that the partner states must put in efforts to implement the mission of the East African Commission on Kiswahili by providing resources to train teachers, exchange students, and develop uniform curricula in the five states. More research needs to be done in all the partner states on the language policies and the best practices of implementation.

The study is profoundly aware that contemporary East Africans confront a characteristic set of dilemmas in seeking to define themselves within a system that offers them few viable alternatives and subjects them to many unresolved conflicts. This is the reality, but Kiswahili as a lingua franca of East Africa can bridge the gaps and offer a moral ideal that can be related to the success of the integration process in East Africa, the African Union, and the world in general.

References

African Union. (2004). *Cultural charter for Africa*. Addis Ababa.

Bundotich, J. (2007). Fumbling undermining East African integration. *The Saturday Standard*, April, p. 12.

Dellinger, Brett (2001). *Views of CNN television news: A critical cross-cultural analysis of the American commercial discourse style*. Vaasa: Universitas Wasaensis.

EAIT. (2007). Unpublished report of the East African Integration Taskforce, sitting at the Town Hall in Eldoret, Kenya, June 2007.

Hall, Edward T. (1959). *The silent language*. New York: Doubleday.

Kaplan, Robert. (1990). Concluding essay: On applied linguistics and discourse analysis. In Robert Kaplan (Ed). *Annual Review of Applied Linguistics*. II.

Kawoya, V., & Makokha, J.S. (2009). The case of Kiswahili as a regional broadcasting language in East Africa. *Journal of Pan African Studies*, 2(8), pp. 11-35.

Kenya. (2007). Protocol on the establishment of the East African Kiswahili Commission. Nairobi, Kenya, pp. 2-8

Khatib, M.S. (2004). Kiswahili na Umoja wa Africa. Paper presented at the 3rd meeting of CHAKAMA, Arusha, Tanzania.

Kress, Gunter. (1990). Critical discourse analysis. In Robert Kaplan (Ed). *Annual Review of Applied Linguistics,* II.

Massamba, D.P.B. (2002). *Historia ya Kiswahili: 50 BK hadi 1500 BK*. Nairobi: The Jomo Kenyatta Foundation.

Muthwii, Margaret. (2001). Language policy and practices in education in Kenya and Uganda: Perceptions of parents, pupils and teachers on the use of mother tongue, Kiswahili and English in primary schools. Unpublished Report, Nairobi, 2001.

The Saturday Standard, Editorial. Fumbling undermining East African integration. April 2007.

Wodak, Ruth. (1989) (ed.) *Language power and ideology: Studies in political discourse*. London: Benjamins Publishing Company.

CHAPTER SIX

THE *KABBA* DRESS: IDENTITY AND MODERNITY IN CONTEMPORARY CAMEROON

FLAVIUS MAYOA MOKAKE[1]

This chapter examines the origin of *Kabba* and the growing importance of the gown among Cameroonian women. It discusses the multiple functions of *Kabba* over the years and shows how recent waves of modernization gave the dress a national character which justifies the need for its canonization as a national attire for women and a salable cultural artifact in a speedily globalizing world.

Introduction

The *Kabba* dress has been popular with most Sawa[2] women since the early periods of European visits to the coastal regions of Cameroon. Available evidence traces its origin to the early period of intimate contact with the outside world. Through this contact the coastal people have had a long and interesting history with European sailors, Anglo-West Indians, and West Africans (Wright, 1958, pp. 16-39). Within this period the principal mission of the pioneer Europeans was exploration, but later batches of Europeans included Christian missionaries, traders, and political adventurers.

Unlike the Christian missionaries who came to spread the Christian doctrine, the pull factor for traders was to exploit and benefit from the lucrative trade in slaves along the West African coast (Northrup, 1978, pp. 23-31). Events along the coastal regions were to change dramatically with the abolition of this trade in human chattel. Over the years, many more European and West Indian traders arrived on the scene following the suppression of the trans-Atlantic slave trade to benefit from the emerging trade in goods. The institutionalization of what was later described as legitimate trade preceded as much as it precipitated the annexation and colonization of African territories.

Indigenous Dressing Styles

Prior to the arrival of Europeans the indigenes had designed certain forms of dressing styles with the use of local material. These ranged from leaves, bark of trees, and animal skins and raffia-skirts. These were worn by the coastal peoples of Cameroon. Other forms of dress included *ngwashi*, a traditional dress worn exclusively by men. Similarly, among the Bakweri women a small skirt-like dress called *wanda* was very trendy. The history of these early dresses, though unclear, points to the fact that different modes of dressing had evolved over a long period.

Other dressing patterns were in vogue along the coast of Cameroon other than those mentioned above. By the nineteenth century, trading had become characterized by the exchange of European goods for African raw materials such as cotton, ivory, rubber, and palm produce. Generally, before such exchanges took place, it was not unusual for traders to induce the local rulers with gifts such as mirror and loin cloth. The offering of such gifts and their consumption by indigenous rulers perhaps influenced the dressing style of the coastal people of Cameroon. A sophisticated dress-code thus developed among the coastal people and those around trade centers who turned out in colorful Western fabrics to the envy of those in the hinterlands.

Before the *Kabba* dress was introduced in the nineteenth century, the indigenous women wore the fashionable loincloth. A piece of loincloth was tied below the breast and another from the waist right down to the upper knees. This was common among unmarried women. However it was considered reprehensive for married women to dress in this manner. The married women were expected to tie a loincloth over the breast with another piece falling from the waist well below the knees. Local customs warranted that once a woman was in matrimony, it was indecent to expose her body. Besides, men were obliged to be uninterested in another man's wife.

The popularity of the loincloth among the coastal people in the twentieth century was acknowledged by the District Officer of Victoria Division, A. R. Whitman.[3] In a 1922 preparatory report on the division for the League of Nations, Whitman reported the absence of any distinctive tribal articles of apparel or headdress in use, but loincloths were still the garment in fashion among the population (1922, p. 2).[4] The report further acknowledged the influence of foreign intrusion on the dressing style of the population in these words, "Loincloth is still the garment mostly worn by both sexes, though European clothing for the men and long-loose gowns for the women, known as liberty gowns . . . introduced by the Christians from Fernando Po, are becoming popular"[5] (Whitman, 1922, p. 6).

The practice of body adornment among indigenous women from pre-colonial times consisted of using tattoos to decorate the body. Tattoos were pricked around vital spots of the body like the breast, navels, and laps. The tattoos provided additional beauty to a woman and influenced the tradition of body exposure. In giving new tastes to women, the tattoos spoke a solemn language well understood by the indigenes. The marks and signs on the body in an extremely subtle way revealed the social status of the wearer among peers. Perhaps it was the practice of body exposure that made the women to move half-naked paving the way for the introduction of *Kabba* in late nineteenth century.

Kabba: Origin and Significance

Though literature on the origins of *Kabba* is sketchy, oral tradition dates it back to the nineteenth century when the pioneer Christian missionaries, particularly the English Baptist missionaries, established the first churches in Cameroon. According to oral tradition the dress was introduced to the local women by the wife of the Baptist missionary, Alfred Saker.[6] According to the oral account, Helen Saker[7] was uncomfortable each time she encountered indigenous women who were naked. To eradicate this practice, efforts were launched in the catering center she operated in Akwa, Douala, to correct the anomaly. At the center, indigenous women were taught basic services like cookery, laundry, and sewing as well as the Christian doctrine.

Accounts have it that Helen was constantly embarrassed and unable to withstand the presence of nude women who freely exposed their natural beauty and patterned contours. To her judgment this was a permanent source of temptation to the white missionaries. In an attempt to circumvent further embarrassments, Helen decided to introduce a gown designed like that of Her Majesty Queen Victoria I. The original idea behind this was to design a dress that covered the entire body of a woman. It was never expected that it would eventually become of ramifying significance. It is perhaps based on its growing significance that Poubum (2007) described the modern *Kabba* as a historical accident of the most "genuine common product in this era of cultural métissage" (p. 1). The unprecedented consequence has been that the gown became the first complete dress of the Douala and subsequently other Sawa women.

The original gown had unique features. It was voluminous, covering every part of the body from the lower neck to the ankle. The original gown also had long sleeves with part of the fingers covered. The gown looked more or less like the pastor's cassock. Perhaps the design was partly influenced by Helen's missionary background. A typical traditional *Kabba* worn by the *Sawa* women was voluminous and yoke-shaped. The sleeves of the gown were designed to be very long so as to expose only the tip of the fingers. It ran all over the entire body right down to the ankles hiding the toes. The gown was to be accompanied with a head-tie to match with the dress, a thing very unpopular today except with the older and rural *Sawa* women. In the past, the neck of the dress was made up of four pieces of trimmed cloth with the sleeves and body added to it. When the women wore *Kabba*, their breast and backs were not exposed in any way, especially as the Eurocentric idea had hyper-sexualized the breasts. The purpose was to conceal vital parts of the body (Matute, 1988, p. 22).

The material commonly used for the dress came from Europe and later from West African countries like Ghana (formerly Gold Coast) and Nigeria. In addition, the size of the gown—determined by the amount of material used—also revealed the economic power and social status of the wearer. For instance, in the first half of the twentieth century, prominent women preferred the expensive cloth locally called *modibo mo essova liwato* to stitch their *Kabba*. This material, locally referred to as the "material that does not fade," was high-priced and different from what commoners used. The cost of a fathom of *modibo* was estimated at about six pennies or one shilling, and very few persons could afford this amount especially as about three fathoms were needed to sew a typical traditional *Kabba*.

Not long after its introduction, the new gown symbolized authority and power. Initially only new converts, wives of chiefs and notables could wear the dress. This was so because only those indigenes who wielded economic power could afford the material used in sewing the dress. Those indigenes that had gained enormous influence and power as middle-men (Austen & Derrick, 1999, pp. 5-92) could afford the dress for their wives. Some acquired pieces of European cloth through the trade with whites, while others bought it with the proceeds from trade.

The association of the dress with Christianity created barriers as well as tensions. As soon as the first gowns were sown, Alfred Saker was urged by his wife to forbid nakedness in the "Holy House of God." The consequence of this law was far-reaching. As a result of its pronouncement, only local Christians were enthusiastic to wear the new dress. Those who did not appear clothed in *Kabba* were not allowed into church. This created an air of superiority among those who wore the dress. This group saw themselves as being close to the Europeans and thus more civilized than those who resisted wearing the gown. They also perceived themselves as being closer to the heavens as the gown was seen as not only a passport to sermons but as one into the Kingdom of God. This feeling of intolerance was also expressed against non-converts wearing the dress. Since the gown was perceived as a tool in the hands of the missionaries, those who rejected the doctrine also rejected it. The refusal to wear the dress could be interpreted as an extreme message of political, cultural, and religious contempt (Hopkins, 2006, p. 132). Tension did not only increase between indigenes and Europeans; non-initiates and other less privileged women were severely punished for wearing the dress.

Changing Patterns and Meaning of *Kabba* in Cameroon

With the advent of modern fashion designing, changes were introduced in the pattern of the traditional *Kabba*. Still, most women feel more comfortable in the original design of the gown. Embroidery and other products of the process of globalization have given it new taste and functions. Besides the multiple meaning discussed under the cultural, economic, social, and political spheres, this section examines the factors responsible for the change in designs. It enquires whether changes could be explained as a move to be trendy or practical.

Different patterns are sewn for different occasions and ceremonies, from wake-keepings to parades and from travel outfits to loose gowns for domestic uses. *Kabba* has evolved from something worn by Sawa women to a national attire. Climate change has influenced the change in design. It is not clear whether in the past the climate of the area contributed in the designing of the original traditional *Kabba*. It will be hard to determine this because the same design was worn in the warmer and cooler climatic zones. The fact that much the same pattern dominated across the geo-cultural region seems to suggest that the gown presented a deeper meaning to the people. The argument is made that because of the disturbing phenomenon of global warming, temperatures are unbearably high in most parts of the country especially during the dry season, making it extremely uncomfortable to wear the dress. Nonetheless, the women have been able to adapt the original idea to conform to present climatic situations by wearing mini-*Kabba* without sleeves or with perforated sleeves.

The only marked difference of the *Kabba* in the past was in terms of the measurement lengthwise. The size of the gown was also determined by the occasion. As such three relatively different types of *Kabba* were common among the women. For instance among the Douala women, the first type was the *Kabba Nisadie*, of a small size worn during house chores, fishing, or in fields during the planting season. It was more common among peasant women.

The second type was the *Kabba Mukuku*, a sexy and provocative style, usually worn by spinsters but also by married women who wanted to attract their husband's attention away from "local husband snatchers." Some unmarried women also wore it to win the admiration of married men. The third was the *Kabba Midene*, or the solemn *Kabba*, common among the city women and other great women in the society (Mokake, personal communication, 2007). It was also worn by queens and wives of chiefs. This was the very large, expensive *Kabba*, made of superior quality material. Only the "high-class" women could afford this type. Women from the lower class who wanted to acquire this type had to forgo other items on their market list so as to purchase it. Even within the upper class, there were differences in the style of the *midene*. The main difference was in the decoration. The decoration of the queen's *midene* was usually exceptional to depict class and status. There was yet another difference between the *Kabba* worn by the early Christians and the *mukanja* women. The *mukanja* were pagan women who had refused to infuse the Christian doctrines into their spiritual lives. The *Kabba* worn by the *mukanja* immediately communicated to the viewer her status, belief, and family history. Thus the dress item became a source of individual and family stigmatization. This somewhat separated a section of women considered as *mukanja* from the Christian women.

Different ceremonies also determined the pattern of *Kabba* in the past. The gown usually worn to funeral ceremonies was uniquely short. The purpose behind this short design was the need for flexibility and smartness, and communicated an image of communal solidarity in time of trouble. It also served as a medium for group and family identification. It was common for families to attend such solemn ceremonies in a *Kabba* sewn with a unique material known as *ashwabi*. Incidentally, this sounds similar to *aso ebi* (kinsgroup uniform) among the Yoruba of Nigeria, indicating a regional influence of great ramification.

Cameroonian women desire to be fashionable and to appear modern in the public eye. In executing its function as a mediator of space for individuals in a complex society, fashion heavily influence the types of clothing (Back, 1985, pp. 1-13; Hansen, 2004, pp. 371-373). Determined by social and cultural norms, fashion itself is a function of place and time, of society and period. It is also strongly influenced by an individual's self-expression. As such the present complexes of the global advances have gradually but steadily brought about many different types of *Kabba* in Cameroon within the reach of ever-larger groups of people. Fashion in this perspective should not necessarily be understood as long-term trends in clothing in the sense of fads, but as expressions of historical trends (Back, 1985, p. 1).

Evidence from oral tradition points to the role fashion plays in the evolution of *Kabba* patterns and explains why it has taken a national character. With the changes that have been ushered in by recent global processes and tastes, new styles and patterns have been created. Cameroonian women now design new forms of *Kabba* to suit particular body frames, individual taste, occasions, and socio-cultural groups (Mokake, personal communication, 2007).

Though culture and society attempt to dictate limits on modernity, especially in its emphasis on individual self-expression in this rapidly globalizing world, modernity interacts with fashion in a subtle way to fabricate new styles of *Kabba*. Modernity is understood in this context as innovations brought about by changes in advancements in technology and symbolic representation (Back, 1985, p. 10). Historical evidence of human behavior indicates that human beings have a culture of breaking with tradition. The world currently encounters a revolution in terms of industrial development. At present, there are better and sophisticated sewing machines, which are also widely distributed. The difference between old and new styles is partly a consequence of recent technological development and an economic system supported by a largely white-collar system. Individual achievement is revealed by the type of *Kabba* the person wears, thus easing the conventionalization of individual tastes. The proliferation of a wide variety of this gown could be understood as having been facilitated by new technologies.

But, while in general, technical advances precipitate varieties of *Kabba*, it also has in no small way decreased the difference in material and style according to wealth. Artificial fabrics and sophisticated methods of mass production make it possible to replicate high-quality textiles. These are strikingly so close to the original that it is often difficult to determine the origin of the apparel or to derive the socio-economic status of the wearer. New technology has rendered the variety of the *Kabba* to become so attractive that its value has been displayed by particularly seamstresses or designers.

With the influx of modern machines and imported textiles from sources like Benin, Ghana, and neighboring Nigeria, the gown has appropriated new roles and patrons. In a way, the easy access to colorful print fabrics dismantles the social walls erected around the *Kabba* by class and economic status. Also, it cuts across generations as more young girls are able to acquire foreign textiles to sew *Kabba* not necessarily for the sake of identifying with a particular cultural heritage (Boswell, 2006), but as a means to possess something African rather than a modern, Western, or global dress. Indeed, what we wear could be considered a site of convergence for transnational, global, and local forces, as Boswell discovered of *kanga* among women of the Island of Zanzibar (2006, p. 444).

The change in the patterns of the dress has invariably necessitated new roles for the *Kabba* and vice versa, other than the traditional functions it performed in the past. Culturally, it serves as an ambassador for the culture of the *Sawa* and Cameroon as a nation in international cultural interchange. *Kabba* remains the traditional attire during the *ngondo* festival[8] (Austen & Derrick, 1999, pp. 184-190). This annual cultural festival of the Doualas brings indigenes and tourists to the city. During the festival the custom was for women to wear the gown without underwear. The *ngondo* was also an occasion for a husband to offer the *Kabba Ngondo* gift to his deserving wife. This symbolic gift was an expression of love. Failure to offer this gift could have sexual repercussions, as a disgruntled wife may turn down the sexual advances of the husband.

In the political sphere, the *Kabba* has a history as a tool of manipulation of the rural women by the power elites. As early as the 1960s, the women's wing of the ruling Cameroon National Union (CNU) used the *Kabba* to win the sympathy of the Sawa women. Because of the use of the *Kabba* by the leaders of the sections in Douala and the effect that it solicited the sympathy of the local women during rallies and political confrontations, the party's national chairperson made it a national policy for all women wing of the party to wear the *Kabba* during political rallies. This move by the party's chairperson achieved its desired objectives with more *Sawa* women developing sympathy for the party.

Another political attribute of the *Kabba* which gives it a global dimension is its use during international celebrations. During international ceremonies like the International Women Day and African Rural Women Day, it is very common to see all women in Cameroon—including very little children—dressed in *Kabba* in a uniform material. The most interesting part of this treat of the *Kabba* of becoming a national costume during such national celebrations is the picture of the wives of political figures and women politicians in the midst of rural and low-class women. For instance, during the International Women Day commemoration in 2007, the First Lady, Madam Chantal Biya, appeared in a well-designed *Kabba* marching ahead of a multitude of women from diverse cultural, social, economic, and political backgrounds.

Also, some female politicians like the current Minister of Culture, Madam Ama Tutu Muna, mostly appear in beautiful designs of *Kabba* in public. It is important to note that neither of these women originated from any of the *Sawa* sub-groups. The action of these figures is evidently easily understood by the public. Their admiration for the gown has not necessarily been motivated by the beauty of the dress. It expresses the dialectics of *Kabba* and the integration of women into positions of power. Though during such occasions the dress bridges social gullies, the masses hardly gain any touch with political figures thereafter.

Conclusion

The chapter has attempted to examine the origin and the present multiple functions of *Kabba* in Cameroon. The dress originated from the era of missionary activities along the coast of Cameroon and has since become not only the first complete dress but also the traditional dress of the *Sawas*. Assorted designs represent different things to different people. It serves to develop and manifest individual, religious, socio-cultural, class, group and gender identity. It developed and strengthened cultural, religious, and national solidarity. The new patterns not only represent a window into social change and cultural adaptation, but also the mutuality of tradition and modernity, and the determinant role of fashion in this mutual relationship. In addition, it emphasized class differences while at the same time it erased distinction, announced new shared goals and aspirations, contributed to public discourse in a subtle way, and contributed to the development of a national identity. These multiple attributes of the *Kabba* in contemporary Cameroon justify the need for the canonization of the dress as a national attire.

Notes

1. The author acknowledges with profound thanks the assistance given by Kate Nanyongo Vevanje in the collection of data for this paper.

2. The term *Sawa* in the phonology of the *Douala* and *Bakweri* peoples means the coast. It represents the people that inhabit the coastal region. Therefore the noun form of the word describes the place, while the adjectival form represents the people. Not all the people that the term represents at the micro level are strictly coastal people. Neither *Bakossi* nor *Bafour* are coastal people but forest people. Their connection to the coast is only through the cultural ties with the coastal peoples like the *Douala* and *Bakweri*. The enveloping *Sawa* identity is, however, a recent creation of the political confrontations of the 1990s in Cameroon.

3. Victoria was founded by Alfred Saker in 1858 after he was evicted from Fernando Po. After the annexation of Cameroon by the Germans it was among the first administrative districts during German annexation. When the British took over British Cameroons following World War I, Victoria was elevated to an administrative division. It was a

cosmopolitan area harboring most of the ports, colonial plantations, and administrative services.

4. File No. Ba (1922) 2, "Report on the Victoria Division, Cameroons Province, Written for the League of Nations by A. R. Whitman, District Officer," *Preparation of Report for League of Nations, 1922*, p. 6, National Archive Buea).

5. Ibid.

6. Alfred Saker, after his eviction from Fernando Po, bought a piece of land between Bota and Man-of-War Bay from King William in Bimbia, which he named Victoria in honor of the Queen. Together with a team of missionaries, he moved from Victoria to Douala to continue missionary activity, and his wife opened a center to train indigenous women on basic catering skills.

7. Oral accounts link the origin of the *Kabba* dress to the Sakers' daughter, Emily. This is largely a result of a confusion of names or that she probably helped the mother at the center. By the time the Sakers left Cameroon in 1876, Emily was still a tot and could not have been the one to introduce the dress to the indigenous women. While the origin may be debated, the influence has been regional. In Lagos and among the Yoruba, a dress of similar size bears the same name till today. See reference to *Kabba* wearers in Yorubaland in chapter 7 of this book.

8. The *ngondo* festival day is a cultural festival of the coastal people, particularly the Douala, which assembles locals along the shore of the rivers during which certain ancestral rituals are performed. During this festival some young girls are selected for marriage after a parade. This festival that started in the colonial period is still being witnessed annually and pulls *Sawa* indigenes and individuals of other ethnic groups within the national territory and abroad. In fact, the *ngondo* festival is an epitome of a national touristic jamboree. One of the recent innovations during the festival is the award of an honorary prize to a "Miss *Ngondo*." The festival is one of the marked media to market the *Kabba* as it is expected of all the ladies to the festival to appear in *Kabba*. Women from other ethnic groups than *Sawa*, in a bid to identify with this ethnic group as well as with the nation, also wear *Kabba* on occasion. See Austen and Derrick (1999, pp. 184-190) for a discussion on the evolution of the *ngondo* festival.

References

Allman, J. (Ed.). (2004). *Fashioning Africa: Power and the politics of dress*. Bloomington: Indiana University Press.

Ardener, S. (2002). (Ed.). *Swedish ventures in Cameroon 1883-1923: Trade and travel, people and politics. The memoirs of Knut Knutson, with supporting material.* New York & Oxford: Berghahn Books.

Austen, R., & Derrick, J. (1999). *Middlemen of the Cameroon rivers. The Duala and their hinterland c. 1600-1960.* Cambridge: Cambridge University Press.

Back, K.W. (1985). Modernism and fashion: A social psychological interpretation. In M. R. Solomon (Ed.), *The Psychology of Fashion*, pp. 3-14. Lexington: D.C. Heath and Company.

Barnes, R., & Eicher, J.B. (1992). Introduction. In R. Barnes & J. B. Eicher (Eds.), *Dress and gender: Making and meaning*, pp. 1-7. Oxford: BERG.

Boswell, R. (2006). Say what you like: Dress, identity and heritage in Zanzibar. *International Journal of Heritage Studies,* 12(5), pp. 449-457.

Eicher, J.B., & Roach-Higgins, M. E. (1992). Definition and classification of dress: Implications for analysis of gender roles. In R. Barnes & J.B. Eicher (Eds.), *Dress and gender: Making and meaning*, pp. 8-28. Oxford: BERG.

Hansen, K.T. (2004). The world in dress: Anthropological perspectives on clothing, fashion, and culture. *Annual Review of Anthropology,* 33, pp. 369-392.

Hopkins, M.C. (2006). Review of *Fashioning Africa: Power and the politics of dress. Africa Today*, 52(4), pp. 130-135.

Matute, D.L. (1988). *The socio-cultural legacies of the Bakweris of Cameroon.* Yaounde: CEPER.

Northrup, D. (1978). *Trade without rulers: Precolonial economic development in South-eastern Nigeria.* Oxford: Clarendon.

Poubum, L. (2007). *Kaba days are here.* Retrieved September 23, 2007, from http://www.postnewsline.com/2007/05/kaba_days_are_h.html.

Whitman, A.R. (1922). *Report on the Victoria division.* (British Colonial Report to the League of Nations, File No. Ba (1922) 2, National Archive Buea, Cameroon).

Wright, A.K. (1958). *Victoria, southern Cameroons 1858-1958.* Victoria, Southern Cameroons: Basel Mission Book Depot.

CHAPTER SEVEN

BEYOND MEMOIR: ECHOES OF GLOBALIZATION, IDENTITY, AND GENDER STRUGGLE IN SOYINKA'S *AKE: THE YEARS OF CHILDHOOD*

AYO OGUNSIJI

Apart from being a childhood story of Wole Soyinka, *Ake* is also a story of the people, events, and places associated with Soyinka's early life and experiences. Anchored on the insights of Critical Discourse Analysis (CDA), this chapter reveals that the text is more than an autobiography, more than a memoir. It radiates echoes of globalization, identity, and gender struggle. Issues relating to Christian religion, Western education, and colonial administration occupy a considerable space in the text. Certain events crystallize identity construction and ideological polarity, especially from cultural, racial, and gender perspectives. In this way, the text is seen as a site for the interrogation of the contests of women's protest against socio-economic and political exploitation and marginalization. Considered in this light, Soyinka's *Ake*, becomes a multivocal (re)construction of realities whose interpretations cannot be divorced from its socio-cultural and historical contexts.

Introduction

The working definition of a memoir adopted by this study is as "a book or other piece of writing based on the writer's personal knowledge of famous people, places or events" (*Cambridge*, 1985, p. 885). From this definition, it becomes clear that there is a link between a memoir and an/a (auto)biography. In fact, Birbalsingh (2004, p. 29) corroborates this by asserting that "autobiography overlaps with memoir." Therefore, Soyinka's *Ake*, an autobiography, also qualifies as a memoir, especially because of its considerable emphasis on some personalities, events, and places that impact Soyinka's life.

Ake is a narration of the childhood experience of the young Soyinka, especially the first eleven years of his life, terminating at a time he is about to leave Ake for the Government College, Ibadan. Done from a child's point of view, the narration recounts the experiences of the author as he moves from innocence to experience, focusing on common or popular scenes/sights, sounds, events, places, and people. The story dramatizes the Christian family background of Soyinka as metaphorized by the parsonage at Ake and the traditional background symbolized by Soyinka's grandfather (called "Father") and Isara as a community. Soyinka's father nicknamed "Essay" is a strict, meticulous head-teacher; he is a Christian and a disciplinarian. Soyinka's mother, nicknamed "Wild Christian" (probably because of her religious zeal) is a devoted Christian who will pray seriously to remove "emi esu" (the devil's spirit) when observed in any of her children or wards.

Ake is a good background to the life and personality of Wole Soyinka as well as his subsequent writings. The narration demonstrates Soyinka's precociousness and inquisitiveness as well as the doggedness and determination which later blossomed in his adult life. As a memoir, the text relives the personalities and influences of Soyinka's grandfather, and those of Rev. and Mrs. Ransome Kuti (Daodu and Beere) as well as the memory of Ake community.

Thematically, *Ake* is preoccupied with the innocent childhood experiences of a young boy whose daily activities make him predisposed to and conscious of his identity. He is exposed very early in life to two different traditions—the modern, Western culture represented by mainly Christianity, Western (formal) education, and colonial administration, and the traditional, African culture which Father and the Isara Community, among others, stand for. This situation predisposes Soyinka to cultural hybridity. According to Larsen (1983, p. 181), the world depicted in *Ake* is greatly influenced by both Christianity and ancient, native traditions. The text may be seen as a metaphor of drama of individual and collective existence as the author journeys from innocence to experience, sensing and feeling (although from a child's perspective) religious devotion, traditional customs and beliefs, parental protection and care (or control), women protest against economic and political exploitation, and so on.

It thus becomes obvious that although Soyinka's *Ake* is a record of a child's personal experiences in life, the story touches on broader global issues such as identity (re)construction, political and economic emancipation, women's empowerment and gender struggle. It moves from a memoir (autobiography) to a site for the interrogation of certain aspects of globalization, especially when approached and deconstructed or, more appropriately, reconstructed via CDA which, among others, ". . . views the systematic analysis and interpretation of texts as potentially revelatory of ways in which discourses consolidate power." (Locke, 2004, p. 2).

Echoes of Globalization, Identity, and Gender Struggle in *Ake*

Globalization has been defined in many ways by many people. Iwara (2004, p. 20) cited Mazrui (2001) as defining globalization "as a process by which different regions of the world are pulled together through an expanding network of exchanges of people . . . ideas and cultures." Also, Awonusi (2004, p. 87) takes globalization to refer to "the universalization of concepts, movements, technology, markets, etc. in the context of a compressed world." *Wikipedia* (2009, p.1) considers it as "the process by which the people of the world are unified into a single society and function together." Globalization, therefore, carries such connotations as "hybridised/diffused culture" (Ashcroft, Griffiths & Tiffin, 1995, pp. 183-184), "the death of distance" (Cairncross, 2001), the collapse of cultural boundaries, deterritorialization, "trade liberalization" (Awonusi 2004 p. 86).

Although globalization and modernity are not exactly the same thing, they are closely related. Taking globalization as the transnational diffusion of ideas, beliefs, languages, etc., culminating in the growth of popular culture, we certainly see it as both a product and an agent of modernity. Modernity itself refers to the present and suggests a stage in human development. It implies advancements in such areas of human endeavors as science and technology, economy, politics, education, communication, etc. In other words, globalization is a feature of modernization, and it is applicable in many contexts. The context in which we apply it in this chapter is essentially cultural. Within the context of Soyinka's *Ake,* some form of cultural diffusion becomes discernible. This cross-cultural influence leads to the construction of new identities and stimulates female gender struggle.

A postmodern reading of Soyinka's *Ake* reveals that the text contains echoes of globalization. Some indicators of the new world order in the text include the references to a transistor radio and a gramophone (Soyinka, 1981, pp. 108-110), the soldiers and Hitler (pp. 110-114) to produce echoes of the world wars, photography, and fashion designing (pp. 38-40), magicians "train in India" (p. 151), confectionaries and provisions (p. 78), cosmetics, snacks, and European food such as hamburgers and sausage rolls (pp. 156-160). As shown in the text, all these modify the life of the Ake community. For instance, some friends of Soyinka's father (Essay) would come to his house to listen to radio news. To show the importance that these people attach to the news, Soyinka foregrounds the expression THE NEWS in capital prints and says that it becomes "an object of worship to Essay and a number of his friends" (Soyinka, 1981, p. 108). Elsewhere in town there are sign posts bearing "AKINS PHOTO STUDIO: LONDON-TRAINED PORTRAITIST" (p. 38) and "MRS T. BANJOKO. LONDON-TRAINED SEWING MISTRESS" (p. 40). The expression

"LONDON-TRAINED" depicts the people's love for exotic style. But ironically, the apprentice-girls of Mrs. Banjoko wear ". . . uniforms of blue, shapeless dresses" (p. 40). More importantly, the text employs the medium of English—the language which is now almost synonymous with globalization. *Ake* is a product of a second language situation and consequently it reflects the criss-cross influences between the English language and the Yoruba language as well as between the Western and the African (Yoruba) cultures as shown in such expressions as "chewing stick" (Soyinka, 1981, p. 77), "native doctor" (Soyinka, 1981, p. 70), and "junior wives" (Soyinka, 1981, p. 182). Such formations are features of Nigerian English; they are a product of the attempt to nativize the English language in Nigeria. In addition, we also see these features as being conditioned by the necessity of diffused/hybridized culture. Other coinages which help to define the identity of *Ake* as a product of a second language situation include "elevenses" (p. 117), "akaralogics" (p. 55), "atarodimensis" (p. 55), etc. "Elevenses" is used to refer to light refreshment taken between meals, while "akaralogics," and "atarodimensis" make reference to "akara" (bean cakes) prepared with "atarodo" (ground fresh pepper). "Akaralogics" and "atarodimensis" are a blend of Yoruba and English. At a macro level, the linguistic ingenuity demonstrated by Soyinka with these formations may be seen as an attempt at both "glocalization" and globalization. At a micro level, the linguistic game helps to encapsulate the hybridized identity of Wole Soyinka as a writer. This becomes clearer as we witness instances of code-mixing and code-switching in the text.

Examples of code-mixing in the text include:

1. *Omo*, let's go (Soyinka, 1981, p. 56).
2. Three years old *wo* (Soyinka, 1981, p. 24).
3. He cannot *la* anything (Soyinka, 1981, p. 102).
4. Now, the matter has reached *gongo* (Soyinka, 1981, p. 208).

The following examples also illustrate code-switching:

1. "What is this?" "*Omo tani*?" (Soyinka, 1981, p. 127).
2. "We've heard enough. *O ya, e nso l'Ake*" (Soyinka, 1981, p. 202).
3. "A man cannot argue with his soul. *Ibanuje ko m'omode, ko m'agba*" (Soyinka, 1981, p. 146).

These expressions help to define the identity of the text as well as that of the author as products of biculturalism/bilingualism. The code-mixing and code-switching involve English and Yoruba languages and by extension English and Yoruba cultures. The two sociolinguistic phenomena produce the yoking of two languages and cultures to forge new realities—just as it has become evident in the age of globalization.

Apart from language, Western education and Christian religion are demonstrated as symbols of globalization in *Ake*. The presence of the school and the church (the Anglican communion) in the text is of a thematic effect. Very early in life, the boy, Soyinka, shows his interest in Western education as he follows

Tinu (his sister) to school. His presence in the school causes laughter among the teachers, and when asked whether he had come to school to keep his sister's company, Soyinka replies: "No, I have come to school" (p. 24). With further probing, he affirms his determination and readiness to come to school always, saying, "I shall come everyday" (p. 25). Epistemically, this statement expresses Soyinka's commitment to what he believes in and, deontically, the statement commits him to a course of future action. At another level of delicacy, the statement can be said to amount to primary performative which can be made explicit thus: "I hereby promise to come always" (Lyons, 1995, pp. 238-239).

The effect of Western education on the people of Ake as a whole is immense. Even at an informal level, the Women Group under the leadership of Mrs. Ransome Kuti makes effort to teach some illiterate young women how to read and write in order to improve the quality of their lives (Soyinka, 1981, pp. 180-181). The women see the need for education as a means of empowerment, and they vigorously pursue its spread (although informally) among their members. In this connection, education is also portrayed as a tool for identity (re)construction; it makes a difference between the "*onikaba*" (gown wearers)—wives of professionals such as teachers, pastors, pharmacists, etc. (Soyinka, 1981, p. 177); and the "*aroso*" (wrapper wearers)—the illiterate women.

The religion of Christianity is no doubt a close ally of Western education. In *Ake* the two variables work hand-in-hand to modify the lives of the inhabitants of Ake community as well as the region as a whole. This crystallizes as we witness the influence of Rev. and Mrs. Ransome Kuti, particularly on the Women Group. Mrs. Ransome Kuti, an educated Christian woman, is shown as a galvanizing force behind the women's ideological stance. With collective resolve, they protest against taxation when they say, "special o, ordinary o, levy o . . . our Beere says . . . no more. The women of Egba say, NO MORE TAX, of any kind . . . We reject all forms of taxation" (Soyinka, 1981, p. 298). As shown above, the women's demand is foregrounded in capital letters, and the pronoun "we" suggests collective resolve.

In the heat of their protest, the women dare the Alake of Egbaland and stun the District Officer, the agent of colonial administration. Mrs. Kuti charges at the District Officer: "You may have been born, you were not bred" (Soyinka, 1981, p. 211). Even the dreaded *Ogboni* cult is not spared. As a form of "faction," a sub-genre of literature which blends fact with fiction, *Ake* uses this real historical event to encapsulate female gender struggle in the pre-independence Egba community to re-define social, economic, and political structures. Ordinarily, no Yoruba woman would have dared a paramount ruler like the Alake of Egba, to talk of confronting the *Ogboni* cult, but with the influence of Christianity and Western education, Mrs. Ransome Kuti infuses her women group with new consciousness that equips them to assert themselves.

Again, identity is shaped on religious-cum-cultural basis. For example, at Soyinka's residence at Ake, there are some inscriptions on the embroidered, framed, glazed homilies hung on the wall which read thus: "REMEMBER NOW THY CREATOR IN THE DAYS OF THY YOUTH;" "EBENEZER

HITHERTO HATH THE LORD HELPED US," "HONOUR THY FATHER AND THY MOTHER," etc. (Soyinka, 1981, p. 94). These homilies are not mere decorations—the inscriptions are biblical echoes which serve as religious injunctions; they help to define the religious mood in Soyinka's family. In order to underlie the importance of the messages they bear, the inscriptions are foregrounded in capital letters. We can compare this Christian religious mood with the aura of fear that surrounds the *Ogboni* cult:

> The *Ogboni* slid through Ake like ancient wraiths, silent, dark and wise, a tanned pouch of Egba history. . . . *We* were afraid of *them* . . . *we* heard of them that *they* sent out child kidnappers whose hand was essential to some of their rites and ceremonies. (Soyinka, 1981, p. 203) [emphasis added]

There is a form of polarity that is set up between Soyinka's Christian household at Ake and the clandestine *Ogboni* group. The pronoun "we" refers to the members of Soyinka's household while "they" and "them" refer to the *Ogboni* members. Here, the pronouns "we" on the one hand, and "they" and "them" stand in antithetical relationship.

Towards the end of the novel, a note of racism is introduced to reinforce the issue of identity. In reference to the bombing of Japan during World War II, Mrs. Ransome Kuti shows her bitterness against the whites saying:

> The white man is a racist . . . to him the black man is only a beast of burden, a work-donkey. As for Asians—and that includes the Indians, Japanese, Chinese and so on—they are only a small grade above us. So, dropping that terrible weapon, experimenting with such a horrifying thing on human beings—as long as they are not white—is for them the same as experimenting on cattle. (Soyinka, 1981, p. 227)

Mrs. Kuti's revelation of the racist tendency in the whites as shown above throws up for interrogation the issue of racial identity and inequality, and questions the basis of the whites' inhuman treatment of the non-whites. It still needs to be said that even now in the present age of globalization with its good sides is not without the charge of inequality as it is largely one-sided, especially on economic and technological planes.

Conclusion

Soyinka's *Ake* is an interesting autobiography, a memoir that is rich in content, language, and style. The text describes Soyinka's family background, his love and desire for education at a very tender age, his inquisitive nature, and the effect of Christianity and Western education on Ake and its inhabitants. In addition to doing this, *Ake* radiates echoes of globalization, identity (re)construction and female gender struggle against certain repressive forces. Seen through the lens of CDA, *Ake* becomes a multi-semiotic (Fairclough, 1995, p. 4) text that can be properly understood by going beyond its grammar (phono-graphology, structure, lexico-semantics) to relate it to its social, cultural, and historical contexts. The text is multilayered, and perhaps this is why some post-*Ake* writings of Soyinka still allude to it as a demonstration of intertextuality. To confirm this, Ogunba (1994, p. 18) submits that Soyinka's *Ake* is "a very useful glossary to some of his writings." The philosophical and critical tone set in the text blossoms in the subsequent literary and even non-literary, political writings of Soyinka.

References

Ashcroft, B., Griffiths, G., & Tiffin, H. (Eds.). (1995). *The post-colonial studies reader*. London: Routledge.

Awonusi, S. (2004). Globalization and hegemonic English in Nigeria: Identity conflicts and linguistic pluralism. In D. Oni et al. (Eds.), *Nigeria and globalization* (pp. 85-102). Lagos: Centre for Black and African Arts and Civilization (CBAAC).

Birbalsingh, F. (2004). The autobiographical writings. In B. Lindfors & B. Kothandaraman (Eds.), *The writer as mythmaker: South Asian perspectives on Wole Soyinka* (pp. 27-40). Eritrea: African World Press.

Cairncross, F. (2001). *The death of distance*. Boston: Harvard Business School Press.

Cambridge International Dictionary of English. Cambridge: Cambridge UP, 1985.

Fairclough, N. (1995). *Critical discourse analysis: The critical study of language*. London: Longman.

Iwara, A. (2004). Identity, politics, globalization and socio-political engineering in Nigeria. In D. Oni et al. (Eds.), *Nigeria and globalization* (pp. 19-36). Lagos: CBAAC.

Larsen, S. (1983). *A writer and his God: A study of the importance of Yoruba myths and religious ideas to the writing of Wole Soyinka*. Stockholm: University of Stockholm.

Locke, T. (2004). *Critical discourse analysis*. London: Continuum.

Lyons, J. (1995). *Linguistic semantics: An introduction*. Cambridge: Cambridge University Press.

Mazrui, A. (2001). Unpublished public lecture given at the Center for African Studies, Livingston Campus, Rutgers University, New Jersey.

Ogunba, O. (1994). *Ake* as a background to Soyinka's creative writings. In O. Ogunba (Ed.), *Soyinka: A collection of critical essays* (pp. 1-18). Ibadan: Syndicated Communications Ltd.

Soyinka, W. (1981). *Ake: The years of childhood*. London: Rex Collings.

Wikipedia. (n.d.). Globalization. Retrieved July 23, 2009, from en.wikipedia.org/wiki/Globalization.

CHAPTER EIGHT

FROM THE GLOBAL TO THE LOCAL: THE MEDIA AND ISLAM IN NIGERIA, 1979-2007[1]

H. O. DANMOLE

This chapter examines the global nature of media forces on Nigerian Muslims. The study alludes to the ways through which new media technologies have been impacting on the lives of Nigerian Muslims from the last quarter of the twentieth century. In particular, it explores the reactions of many Muslims in Nigeria to appropriated messages from new media technologies especially the Internet on developments in other parts of the world.

Introduction

The term "globalization" encapsulates various things; it has included the swift flow of information, exchange of ideas and knowledge, appropriation of cultures, closer economic ties, and the movement of people across national boundaries (Stiglitz, 2007, p. 4; Giddens, 1990, p. 64; Ferguson, 1992, p. 63; Robertson, 1987, pp. 20-30). Most of these developments are made possible through mediated interactions, which were themselves the result of great strides in satellite technologies of the post-World War II era (Thomas, 2005, p. 17; Gurevitch, 1997, pp. 204-224). Lawrence Babb (1995, p. 3) has noted that media products such as printed words, photographs, audio recordings, and videotapes can be transported over long distances, and these can be mass reproduced and sold cheaply to the public. Equally, the media has reduced physical distance, which in effect has been impacting religion in South Asia (Babb, 1995, p. 3). Babb's observation is also true of Africa in general and Nigeria in particular. Indeed, the general public, according to Meyrowtiz (1985), consumes media products and often creates harmony among religious communities, although at the same time, it fosters discontent.

Reinforcement of Islamic Values

The media has in recent years helped to reinforce Islamic values (Sreberny-Mohammadi & Mohammadi, 1994; Morley, 1994). Media materials such as audio- and videotapes, compact discs, and the computer have been in widespread use amongst Nigerians including Muslims. These materials collectively referred to as "small media" have been improving the knowledge of Muslims and non-Muslims alike on the tenets of Islam. The Qur'an for instance is now available on all these aforementioned media products. Anecdotal evidence suggests that many Muslims learn and re-learn the Qur'an and all other Islamic duties through repeated playing of cassettes or discs. Thus, the memorization of some chapters or verses of the Qur'an amongst Muslims has improved because of the application of media technologies by many Nigerian Muslims.

Before the present age of globalization, Islam, like Christianity, has been a global religion. However, the religion has been experiencing its own share of the gains of globalization as well as its discontents. Through direct satellite communication, Nigerian Muslims have continued to maintain close contacts with other Muslims, most especially in the Arab world. These contacts have led to some level of enforcement of Islamic values.

By the last quarter of the twentieth century, Muslim organizations were involved in using television for the propagation of the tenets of Islam. In addition, audio- and videotapes were used by Muslim clerics to disseminate their ideas to the larger public. An important organization in Northern Nigeria that used the media to shape the lives of its members was the *Jamaatul Izalat al-Bid'ah wa Iqama as Sunnah* (The Movement for the Eradication of Innovation and the Establishment of *Sunnah*). Sheikh Abubakar Gumi founded the organization in 1978 (Sanusi, 2004; Kukah, 1993, pp. 216-242). The group popularly called *Izala* had considerable access to the media for several years. Not only were the preaching of Shaikh Gumi aired on television, they were also recorded on audio- and videotapes, and were sold at very cheap prices. If such media gadgets were means of spreading information in the last years of the twentieth century, the new media technologies particularly the Internet, have been very important media outlets through which Nigerian Muslims have been involved in global issues.

Media, Islam, and Religious Crisis in Nigeria

Radical Islam that grew in leaps and bounds in the 1970s could be traced to the role played by the media. Between 1978 and 1980, there was hardly any day the media would not report events in Iran and the Middle East. These reports carried images of the rise of Islamism in Iran and conflicts in the Middle East. Many Muslim youths were impressed with the developments especially in Iran and borrowed the garb of Islamism that pervaded the Islamic revolution in Iran. One of such groups in Nigeria was the Muslim Brothers who displayed a lack of understanding of Nigerian history by seeking to turn Nigeria to a Muslim state (Sanusi, 2004).

The unity of the Muslim Brothers, however, was not to endure for a long time. Two important reasons can help explain this development. First, the attention, which the media turned to Iran, was receding after years of the successful revolution. Second, the Muslim Brothers received considerable assistance from the Iranian government through the award of scholarships to study in Iran (Sanusi, 2004). The resultant effect of this was the penetration of Shiite doctrine into Northern Nigeria and this inevitably led to doctrinal conflicts in Sunni dominated areas. A third but less important reason is that the charismatic El-Zakzaky left the group because of the Shitte tendencies to form his own group. Yet, in spite of the fact that the group broke into different parts, radical Islam that had been borrowed during the Iranian revolution continued to be their pattern and approach to Islamic issues. It is perhaps not an exaggeration to imply that the global media's coverage of the Iranian revolution of 1979 did pave the way for young Muslims in several parts of the world to emulate Ayatollah Khomeini. This emulation gave a lift to the Shitte which, in turn, led to conflicts with Sunni Muslims in many areas of the northern states of Nigeria.

However, another development that was irksome to Muslims old and young was the Rushdie Affair (Piscatori, 1990, pp. 767-789; Esposito, 1999, pp. 249-252). The Rushdie Affair stemmed from the publication of a book entitled *The Satanic Verses* (1988) by a former Muslim, the British writer Salman Rushdie. This book was, and still is, regarded by Muslims as an attack on Islam, which as Kohn Voll suggests, was seen by Muslims as a continuation of the Western World's Crusade against basic Islamic values of community responsibility and obedience to God. Kohn Voll (1989, p. 2) is probably correct because many Nigerian Muslims perceived Rushdie's book as an affront on Islam and its values. This was perhaps why many notable publishing companies in the United States did not accept the manuscript, as they were apprehensive of the anger and protests that the publication of Rushdie's book would attract from Muslims across the world (Mazrui, 2006, pp. 246-247). The companies possibly realized that such protests would be dangerous to their companies and business interests. Both the electronic and the print media in the Western world gave attention to reactions that followed the publication of Rushdie's book. Reports in the international media were aired on television stations in Nigeria. Newspapers in the country also reported reactions to Rushdie's book. The reactions of Nigerian Muslim youths followed the pattern in other parts of the world with a large population of Muslims.

In March 1989, over 300 Muslim youths protested against the publication of Rushdie's book in Kaduna because the book was seen as blasphemous against Islam. These protesters handed a letter of protest to the British Consul in Kaduna

(Noble, 1989). The protests by many Nigerian Muslims did not stop at the condemnation of the book alone, some Nigerian Muslims were so angry that they endorsed Ayatollah Khomeini's *fatwa* of death sentence on Rushdie (Noble, 1989). Apart from that, the protesters threatened to kill the Nigerian Nobel Laureate, Wole Soyinka, because of his criticism of Ayatollah Khomeini over the *fatwa* on Rushdie. Some of the placards carried by protesters read "Handover Rushdie for justice" and "Soyinka Must Die" (Noble, 1989). Be that as it may, many Muslims in Nigeria did condemn Rushdie and his *Satanic Verses*; nevertheless, the views of the protesters on Wole Soyinka did not receive wide support. The controversy which the book generated in Nigeria made the Nigerian Supreme Council for Islamic Affairs to recommend that,

> Salman Rushdie having blasphemed God, the Holy Prophet Mohammed (May the Peace of Allah be Upon Him) and Islam, deserves the maximum punishment for his grievous offence as laid down in the *Sharia*, and that the Federal Government should prohibit the importation of the infamous publication and its serialization in any print or electronic medium in Nigeria. (*The Guardian*, March 1, 1989)

The position of this powerful umbrella organization for Muslims in Nigeria was meant to reduce the growing religious tension which the publication was generating in Nigeria. However, the Sultan of Sokoto, Ibahim Dasuki, believed that the Ayatollah's *fatwa* was Allah's directive (Noble, 1989). On its part, the Federal Military Government (FMG) declined any official position. In other words, the government, while maintaining dignified neutrality because of the secular nature of the Nigerian state, believed that there should be respect for the "sensitivities of people of different cultures and backgrounds" (Noble, 1989).

Vivid images are much more likely to bring about serious emotional reactions than verbal messages or written words (Sparks, 2006, p. 182). Indeed, television images and works of art that Muslims consider as violating Islamic culture and beliefs have always attracted reactions from Muslims. The Danish newspaper cartoons of 2005 clearly illustrate this point. These cartoons evoked angry emotions among Muslims in Europe and other parts of the world, including Nigeria. The controversy that followed the publication of these cartoons received some attention from the media in Nigeria especially because there were protests and riots which were directly connected with the controversy that the publication of the cartoon generated.

It is perhaps instructive to provide a brief background of the controversy before analyzing the response of Nigerian Muslim youths and some members of the political elite in the country. On September 30, 2005, a Danish newspaper, *Jyllands Posten*, published cartoons caricaturing Prophet Mohammad.[2] These cartoons were reprinted in many European newspapers.

The cartoons were meant for a Danish audience where they were not construed as offensive. However, from the Muslim point of view, the cartoons were offensive as Islam forbids any representation of Prophet Mohammad in any form because of fear of idolatry. Subsequently, Muslims in Europe and other parts of the world reacted swiftly. Between September 2005 and the first quarter of 2006, there were protests and violent riots in many parts of the Muslim world. The controversy that the cartoon evoked created tension in inter-governmental relations and re-opened the debate on the extent of free speech and the lives of Muslims in Europe and the Western world. The cartoon controversy represented in this era of globalization a classical example of a clash of cultures.

The publishers of the newspapers in which the cartoons originally appeared held the view that it was normal in Denmark to disseminate satirical information to their readers. According to them, they satirize Jesus Christ and write funny stories of the Danish royal family. The publishers did not possibly take into consideration the religious and cultural feelings of Muslims in their country or any other place that may likely have access to the paper in the present-day flow of information. As Hilal Khashan (Bransten, 2006) rightly observed when he opined that:

> Political socialization is extremely deep and religious inculcation is essential in raising Muslim kids since we live in a highly interactive world, characterized by rapid communication and access to information, it becomes extremely difficult to talk about targeting a specific audience.

Violence against Danish and European interests spread across Europe. While the Danish government insisted that it was not going to apologize, the paper that first published the cartoons tendered an apology because of the violence that the cartoons provoked while still standing by the cartoons. It was therefore not surprising that the controversy spread to Nigeria just as it was still raging in Europe and other parts of the world.

Before the violence linked with the publications of the cartoons began in Nigeria, the media in the country carried reports of violent reactions to the cartoon publications in other parts of the world. These included the killing of a Catholic priest in Turkey and other deaths in other countries of the Muslim world. There were also reports of protesters losing their lives in encounters with security agencies in Lebanon, Pakistan, Afghanistan, and several other countries. The violence that accompanied the controversy was so widespread that Muslim leaders in Europe, the Organization of Islamic Conference (OIC), and other world leaders including the United Nations Secretary General, Kofi Anan, appealed for peace. The reactions from these Muslim countries would appear to have influenced Muslim youths in Nigeria in their reactions to the publication.

Nigerian Muslims, like other Nigerians, were aware of the developments as they were unfolding on the Internet. Many Muslim organizations in Nigeria such as the Muslim Students Society of Nigeria, Ansar-Ud-Deen Society, and Nasrullahi-Fathi Society of Nigeria (NASFAT) maintained their own websites, and their members across the country employed e-mails and text messages to contact each other on many global issues. Apart from websites belonging to Muslim organizations, a large number of Muslims patronized cyber cafes in major cities of the country. These cyber cafes, which sourced power from standby generators for constant supply of electricity, were major centers of dissemination of information by Muslims during the controversy. Through the information superhighway provided by the Internet, Nigerian Muslims joined the global furor by Muslims around the world on the cartoon controversy.

Traditionally, the Nigerian media—radio, television, and newspapers—were, and still are, cautious in the reportage of controversial religious issues because of the sensitive nature of religion amongst Nigerians. Indeed, a perusal of the media during the cartoon controversy and those before it, indicated that the Nigerian media had been a careful distiller of news about religion. However, the information highway as represented by the Internet in Nigeria has continued to change the face of flow of religious news in the country as the employment of this media technology is increased geometrically.

In this connection, the Muslim youths from different Islamic organizations in Lagos joined the crusade against the publication of the cartoons by carrying placards, condemning the publication of the cartoons to the governor's office. They did so, not so much from the information on the controversy from the Nigerian media *per se*, but from what some of them read on the Internet in their various institutions and cyber cafes. Indeed, their swift assemblage at the governor's office was reportedly facilitated by electronic mails and text messages through their cell phones. These youths were addressed by the governor of the state, Bola Ahmed Tinubu (Thomas, 2007). The governor admonished the protesters to continue to be law abiding because their protest was not only peaceful, it was also a legitimate way of expressing their feelings (Thomas, 2007).

Unlike the peaceful protest in Lagos, however, attacks were directed at churches and Christians in the northern cities of Bauchi, Maidugiri, and Katsina (Democratic Underground, 2006). Media reports also indicated that hoodlums who perhaps were not interested in the cartoon controversy joined the violent protests to vent a deep-rooted anger over other social and economic issues in the country. Thus, the protests provided opportunity for many Muslims and non-Muslims alike to show their resentment against the government because of increasing unemployment in the country.

In the history of religious disturbances in Nigeria, the crises evoked by the cartoon controversy had some peculiar features. The first was the fact that, in southeastern Nigeria, there were retaliatory attacks on mosques because of the churches that were burnt in northern Nigeria. Two mosques in Onitsha were reportedly burned down, and many Muslims lost their lives. Muslims, most of whom were from northern Nigeria, also took refuge in army barracks in the town before the situation was brought under control (VOA News, 2006). The burning of mosques in Onitsha and the loss of lives by Muslims there can be explained in terms of the fact that Christians and their places of worship in northern Nigeria were always at the receiving end in most religious-driven crises there. However, the retaliation increased religious tensions and could have destroyed the nascent democratic dispensation in Nigeria if actions had not been quickly taken by the government.

Secondly, protests associated with religion in the country before 2005 were always avoided by the political elite because of the sensitive nature of religion in the Nigerian polity. In the case of the cartoon controversy and the subsequent religious riots, members of the Kano State House of Assembly supported the protests albeit in a non-violent manner. These legislators burned the flags of both Denmark and Norway in the presence of a very large crowd. Just like many Muslim countries, particularly Saudi Arabia and Kuwait, the Kano State House of Assembly called for a boycott of Danish goods and did pass a resolution for the cancellation of a €23 million order for buses. Sale of Danish and Norwegian products were also to be affected by the resolution (Wikipedia.org).

The cartoon controversy was not the only incident that fueled religious riots in Nigeria. Many religious riots in the past had their origins in ethnicity and other social problems within the Nigerian state. Some religious crises especially in northern Nigeria began on perceived lack of respect for the Quran by non-Muslims or displeasure with publications in Nigerian newspapers judged by Muslims as insulting to their religion. A good example which was similar to the circumstance that produced the cartoon controversy was the Miss World religious crisis in Kaduna where many lives were lost. The crisis was sequel to an opinion by Daniel Isioma of *This Day* newspaper that Prophet Muhammad would have approved the Miss World contest and even married a beautiful queen. There is no doubt that the journalist carried her satire of the Prophet too far. She also demonstrated a poor understanding of Islam and consequently failed to think about the sensitivities of Muslims in the country. Nevertheless, the violent eruptions that followed the comment of the journalist in northern Nigeria created religious tension. The report spread very fast in Nigeria and the north in particular, not because a large number of the protesters read the issue of *This Day* but the news was greatly circulated by those who had access to the Internet as the newspaper posted its daily issue on its website, like most leading newspapers in the country. The protesters were reportedly mobilized by Muslim students in tertiary institutions in the area (Yahya, 2006; Adewuyi, 2006).

By 1989, the wearing of the *hijab* had become a controversial issue in France. By the 1990s, most especially with the introduction of the Shari'a in 1999, some states in northern Nigeria introduced the *hijab* as a compulsory part of girls' uniforms in state schools. However, this soon assumed political dimensions. The *hijab* controversy and the dilemma this posed to the secular Nigerian state followed rapidly on the heels of anti-*hijab* controversies in the Western media. In France, President Jacques Chirac had called for a law banning Muslim headscarves, Jewish skullcaps, and large Christian crosses from French state schools. France banned the use of *hijab* and other religious items in its state schools in 2004. The *hijab* debate soon spread across countries of the West and subsequently found resonance in Nigeria.

The *hijab* controversy became distinctly located in Oyo State, Nigeria, as a symbol of the new contest. On February 24, 2003, irate Islamic activists invaded some secondary schools in Ibadan, the state capital, beating and injuring students and teachers. They claimed to be protesting against alleged discrimination against female Muslims in the practice of their faith. The incident led to the closure of the entire primary and post-primary institutions in the state for several days. On March 13, 2003, this incident was repeated at another secondary school in Ibadan, the Queen of Apostles, Oluyoro, where the principal was man-handled for disallowing students from putting on the *hijab* as part of their school uniforms. The Islamic militants later got the principal arrested and detained until her students mobilized, marched on the police station, and forced the police to release her (Socialist Democracy, 2003).

Towards the end of the first decade of the twenty-first century, the role of the media in the *hijab* controversy had become clearer. According to Mahdi (n.d.):

> . . . With a barrage of indoctrination through the media, induction in schools and Islamic state laws and other instruments of control, women's dressing is being steered towards monotypic codes.

Media and Religious Harmony

Veritable opportunities for religious understanding between Muslims and people of other faiths, especially Christianity had been provided through news and images from new media technology. Two examples will be sufficient to illustrate this point. The completion and opening of a large mosque in Rome in 1993 was given wide coverage by the traditional media as well as comments and chats on the Internet by individuals across the world. This was because the mosque was not only large, it was to many Muslims the most important in Europe as it was the only one "located in the heart of Christianity, in the Mecca of Catholicism" (Haberman, 1989). Apart from that, the mosque was an eye opener for inter-religious dialogue between Muslims and Christians. Oral evidence in Nigeria suggests that many Muslims were happy with the opening of the mosque, and Islamic preachers in Nigeria who watched the reportage on local television made reference to the event as a sign of the spread of Islam to areas where hitherto Islam was not accepted in their preaching effort (Kasim, 2007; Ibrahim, 2007; Olowodola, 2007). These preachings prompted many Muslims in Nigeria to patronize cyber cafes for more information on the mosque at a time when Internet facilities were not too common in the country (Yusuf, 2007; Hassan, 2007). However, many Christians also felt, and still feel, that the same hand of friendship should be extended to the Christians in Saudi Arabia (Bamidele, 2007; Akinsola, 2007).

Also in February and March 2000, Pope John Paul II undertook a tour of some Middle Eastern countries, notably, Egypt and Israel. The visit was widely reported in both the electronic and the print media all over the world. The publicity given to the visit was probably borne out of the fact that Pope John Paul II was the first Pope to visit Egypt—a mainly Muslim country. There is no doubt that many Muslims in Nigeria knew that the Pope is the head of the Catholic

Church; indeed, the visit to the Middle East encouraged many others to resort to the Internet to find more information about the visit and reactions to it across the world. In addition the Internet served as a veritable source of reference on the Vatican for those Muslims who had a passing knowledge of what it represents (Adisa, 2007; Olarewaju, 2007; Yahaya, 2007).

Significant as the visit was, the crucial point of the tour, as evidenced by the reportage, was the call by the Pope for harmony between different religions. Indeed, Nigerians across the religious divide, who watched the visit on both terrestrial and satellite television stations, believed that the visit marked a new era of religious understanding amongst people of different faiths in the country (Awoyemi, 2007; Njoku, 2007). It is perhaps not surprising, that the King of Saudi Arabia, Abdullah bin Abd-al-Aziz al Saud, visited Italy in November 2007 (AdnKronos International, 2007). He also made reference to the need for religious dialogue with a view to promoting peace between Islam and Christianity. Clearly, the flow of information from global media networks aided by the Internet and other gadgets to different parts of the world no doubt created an enduring atmosphere for the building of bridges between Muslims and non-Muslims.

Conclusion

Great strides in the development of technology have facilitated the process of globalization; this in turn has brought some degree of transformation in the practice of Islam amongst Muslims in Nigeria. Through the media, Nigerian Muslims have been able to achieve a greater participation on global issues particularly when such issues are a matter of concern to their religion. Constant contacts with Muslims in other parts of the world through new media technologies—Internet, cell phones, e-mails—Islamic cultural values have continued to be transmitted and transformed. However, the same process of media-aided transformation in religious activities of Nigerian Muslims has contributed to religious protests and clashes particularly amongst Muslim youths and organizations who were reacting to news, images, and information on the Internet which to them were against Islamic beliefs and were meant to undermine the status of Muslims and Islam. Nevertheless, the same media technologies through images and news have created opportunities that have pointed directions to harmony amongst different religions.

Notes

1. This study has benefited from the research on the Media and Religious Publics in Southwestern Nigeria sponsored by the British Academy between 1996 and 1999.

2. Between January and the beginning of February 2006, newspapers in Norway, Germany, Italy, and Spain reprinted the cartoons. See Reynolds, P. (2006). Cartoons and the globalization of protests [Electronic version]. *B.B.C. News.*

References

Adisa, S. Personal interview. May 1, 2007.

Adewuyi, R. Personal interview. May 10, 2006.

AdnKronos International. (2007, November 6). Saudi king in Rome for historic visit. Retrieved August 6, 2009, from http://www.adnkronos.com/AKI/English/Politics/?id=1.0.1519197270.

Ahmed, A.S., & Donaan, H. (Eds.). (1994). *Islam, globalization and post modernity.* London and New York: Routledge.

Akinsola, S. Personal interview. August 13, 2007.

Arjomand, S.A. (1987). *The turban for the crown: The Islamic revolution in Iran.* New York: Oxford University Press.

Awoyemi, Pastor Oladele. Personal interview. August 20, 2007.

Babb, L. A. (1995). Introduction. In L. A. Babb & S. S. Wadley (Eds.), *Media and the transformation of religion in South Asia* (p. 3). Philadelphia: University of Pennsylvania Press.

Bamidele, J. Personal interview. August 10, 2007.

Bransten, J. (2006). World: Muslim protests highlight free speech issues. Radio Free Europe. Retrieved August 6, 2009, from http://www.rferl.org/content/Article/1065282.html.

Democratic Underground. (2006). Death toll rises in Nigerian violence. Retrieved August 6, 2009, from http://www.democraticunderground.com/discuss/duboard.php?az=view_all&address=102x2125568.

Esposito, J. L. (Ed.). (1983). *Voices of Islamic resurgence.* New York: Oxford University Press.

Esposito, J. L. (Ed.). (1990). *The Iranian revolution: Its global impact.* Miami: Florida International University Press.

Esposito, J. L. (1999). *The Islamic threat: Myth or reality.* New York: Oxford University Press.

Ferguson, A. (1992). The mythology about globalization. *European Journal of Communication*, 1(7), pp. 63-93.

Giddens, A. (1990). *The consequences of modernity.* Cambridge: Polity Press.

Gurevitch, M. (1997). The globalization of electronic journalism. In J. Curran & M. Gurevitch (Eds.), *Mass media and society* (pp. 204-224). London: Edward Arnold.

Haberman, C. (1989). Rome journal; A mosque is built, finally, in the city of St. Peter [Electronic version]. *New York Times*. Retrieved August 6, 2009, from http://www.nytimes.com/1989/07/31/world/rome-journal-a-mosque-is-built-finally-in-the-city-of-st-peter.html.

Hassan, I. Personal interview. August 13, 2007.

Ibrahim, M. A. Personal interview. September 8, 2007.

Jyllands-Posten. Muhammad cartoons controversy. (2009, August 6). In *Wikipedia, The Free Encyclopedia*. Retrieved August 6, 2009, from http://en.wikipedia.org/w/index.php?title=Jyllands-Posten_Muhammad_cartoons_controversy&oldid=306037964.

Kasim, A.U.O. Personal interview. August 3, 2007.

Kukah, M.H. (1993). Politicization of fundamentalism in Nigeria. In P. Gifford (Ed.), *New dimension in African Christianity* (pp. 216-242). Ibadan: Sefer.

Mahdi, Hauwa. (n.d.). The *hijab* in Nigeria, the women's body, and the feminist private/public discourse. Center for Global Gender Studies, Gothenburg University (mimeo).
Mazrui, A. (2006). *Islam between globalization and counter terrorism.* Oxford: James Currey.
Meyrowitz, J. (1985). *No sense of place: The impact of electronic media on social behaviour.* New York: Oxford University Press.
Morley, D. (1994). Between the public and the private: The domestic uses of information and communication technologies. In J. Cruz & J. Lewis (Eds.), *Viewing, reading listening: Audiences and cultural reception.* San Francisco: Westview Press.
Njoku, C. Personal interview. August 24, 2007.
Noble, K. B. Special Report to *The New York Times.* Retrieved August 20, 2009, from http://query.nytimes.com/gst/fullpage.html.
Olarewaju, H. Personal interview. June 16, 2007.
Olowodola, A. Personal interview. October 15, 2007.
Piscatori, J. (1990). The Rushdie affair and the politics of ambiguity. *International Affairs,* 66(4), pp. 767-789.
Reynolds, P. (2006). Cartoons and the globalization of protests [Electronic version]. *BBC.*
Robertson, R. (1987). Globalization theory and civilization analysis. *Comparative Civilization Review*, No.17, pp. 20-30.
Sanusi, S.L. (2004). Fundamentalist groups and the Nigerian legal system: Some reflections. Retrieved August 6, 2009, from http://www.wluml.org/english/pubs/pdf/wsf/09.pdf.
Socialist Democracy. (2003). Sharia crisis in Oyo schools: Religion should be a private affair. April-May. Retrieved 24 October, 2009, from http://www.socialistnigeria.org/paper/2003/april-may/6.html.
Sparks, C.G. (2006). *Media, effects research: A basic overview.* Florence, KY: Wadsworth.
Sreberny-Mohammadi, A., & Mohammadi, A. (1994). *Small media, big revolution: Communication, culture and the Iranian revolution.* Minneapolis: University of Minneapolis Press.
Stiglitz, J.E. (2007). *Making globalization work.* New York: Norton W. W. & Company.
Thomas, A. O. (2005). *Imagi-nation and borderless television: Media, culture and politics across Asia.* London: Sage.
Thomas, D. Personal interview. October 2, 2007.
Voice of America News. (2006). Death toll rises in Nigerian sectarian violence. Retrieved August 6, 2009, from http://www.voanews.com/english/archive/2006-02/Death-Toll-Rises-in-Nigerian-Sectarian-Violence.cfm.
Voll, K. O. (1989). For scholars of Islam, interpretation need not be advocacy. *Chronicle of Higher Education*, p. 2.
Yahaya, W. Personal interview. June 24, 2007.
Yahya, I. Personal interview. May 10, 2006.
Yusuf, B. Personal interview. August 9, 2007.

Section III

Marginality: Africa and the Political Economy of Globalization

CHAPTER NINE

GLOBALIZATION AND THE PRIVATIZATION OF STATE-OWNED ENTERPRISES: AN EMPIRICAL ANALYSIS OF THE IMPACT OF PRIVATIZATION ON THE NIGERIAN ECONOMY

DAVID OMEIZA MOVEH

Spawned largely by the ascendancy of global forces, Nigeria's privatization program generated a lot of controversies, especially with regards to its underlying motives and the likely implications. This chapter is a critical evaluation of the outcome of the privatization program in the Nigerian economy within the context of a globalized economic system. It determines that privatization has not resulted in any significant improvement in the Nigerian economy. Instead, privatization is exposed for what it really was: one of the features of a new phase in the export of capital from the advanced capitalist countries.

Introduction

The inherent inability of states to independently satisfy their socio-economic needs has always been a fundamental impetus for international economic interaction. It is against this background that the international economic system has witnessed increased interdependence and changes, so much so that the contemporary world has become a global village.

Globalization, which has become the most defining feature of the contemporary international system entails a process and pattern of interaction—through which nation-states, societies, international institutions, non-governmental organizations, and multinational corporations are linked and networked together towards achieving their objectives (Balarabe, 2002). While its proponents and supporters argue that the globalization process encourages the sharing of basic knowledge, technology, investments, resources, and ethical values, there has been increasing disillusionment among many policy makers, analysts and academics concerning the benefits of globalization.

As noted in Khor (2003, p. 1), the reasons for the negative attitude towards globalization include: first, the lack of tangible benefits to most developing countries from opening their economies—despite the well-publicized claims of export and income gains; secondly, the economic losses and social dislocation caused to many developing countries by rapid financial and trade liberalization; thirdly, the growing inequalities of wealth and opportunities arising from globalization; and finally, the perception that environmental, social, and cultural problems have been made worse by the workings of the global free-market economy.

Against this backdrop, it has been argued that the asymmetry of power and interests of member states in the global village, as well as the lopsidedness in the rules of the game therein, cannot benefit Africa and her people (Akindele & Gidado, 2002). Yet, virtually all African countries including Nigeria have continued to adopt—hook, line, and sinker—policies engendered by contemporary economic globalization. This chapter examines the outcome of the privatization program in the Nigerian economy within the context of a globalized economic system.

The chapter is divided into six parts. Following this introduction is an examination of the nexus between globalization and privatization. This is followed by an examination of Nigeria's economic crisis and the emergence of privatization, followed by an examination of globalization and the ascendancy of neoliberalism as a key factor in the emergence of privatization in Nigeria. The fifth part of the work is an examination of some macro-economic indicators before and after the introduction of the privatization program. The final part of the work is the summary, conclusions, and recommendations.

Globalization and Privatization Nexus

Globalization refers to the process of the intensification of economic, political, social, and cultural relations across international boundaries. It is principally aimed at the transcendental homogenization of political and socio-economic theory across the globe (Akindele & Gidado, 2002, p. 3). Globalization is equally aimed at "making global," that is, being present world-wide—as in the primacy and emphasis on the activities of its agents—the World Bank, the International Monetary Fund (IMF), and the World Trade Organization (WTO)—in contemporary interstate economic interactions. Globalization therefore deals with the increasing breakdown of trade barriers and increasing integration of world markets. This is evident in its push of free market economics, liberal democracy, good governance, gender equality, and environmental sustainability among other holistic values for the people of member states.

Although globalization is multidimensional, and can be understood in different perspectives—social, economic, cultural, and political—it is essentially an economic phenomenon aimed at the increasing integration of national economies through its emphasis on neo-liberal economic ideas.

Table 9.1: U.S. Assistance to Nigeria ($ millions, fiscal years)

PROGRAM	2002 Actual	2003 Actual	2004 Actual	2005 Actual	2006 Est.	2007 Req.
DA	15.8	23.2	13.6	14.8	14.00	21.2
CSH	36.6	47.9	42.5	28.2	21.5	19.6
ESF	8.5	3.8	4.9	4.9	4.9	5.0
FMF Grants					.990	.800
GHAI				85.9	138.1	272.0
INCLE				2.2	.990	.400
NADR-ATF					.435	
IMET					.792	.590
TOTAL	66.5	75.1	61.1	136.2	181.9	320.1

Table Abbreviations:
DA = Development Assistance
CSH = Child Survival and Health Programs Fund
ESF = Economic Support Fund
FMF = Foreign Military Financing
GHAI = Global HIV/AIDS Initiative
IMET = International Military Education and Training (Notification required)
INCLE = International Narcotics Control & Law Enforcement
NADR-ATF = Nonproliferation, Anti-terrorism, Demining, and Related Programs

Source: Congressional Research Service (2006): United States Library of Congress

The resurgence of neo-liberalism in contemporary economic theorizing, which had been relegated by the dominance of Keynesian economics, was due mainly to the rise to power of groups espousing neo-liberal economic ideas during the political tenure of the Reagan and Thatcher governments in the United States and Great Britain respectively. These regimes not only strengthened the role of international financial institutions, but foreign aid and assistance to the crisis-ridden states in Africa and other developing states became increasingly tied to economic and political liberalization in the developing states hitherto characterized by the primacy of the state in all aspects of life including the economy. Table 9.1 above is a concrete example of the sustained assistance Nigeria enjoyed from the United States with the enthronement of a civilian regime and the general privatization of the Nigerian economy.

Thus, while the size of governments in the economies of Africa (and by implication Nigeria) was on the increase at the dawn of political independence, the 1980s saw the rise of a trend in the opposite direction—privatizations. It is, however, pertinent to note—as Petras and Veltmeyer (2001, p. 93) observe—that,

> The privatization strategy of the imperial centre is in the first instance to homogenize every region of the world economy subject to its penetration. The process of privatization is thus not principally a means of taking over enterprises and penetrating markets so much as it is a means of eliminating alternative structures of production which could compete or challenge an imperially dominated world.

Nigeria's Economic Crisis and the Emergence of Privatization

Privatization may narrowly be defined as the divestiture or transfer of state-owned enterprises to private initiatives. Broadly, however, privatization can also be seen as an umbrella term used to describe varieties of policies which encourage competition and emphasize the role of market forces in place of statutory restrictions and monopoly power. For the purpose of this chapter, privatization is seen from this perspective.

Nigeria's privatization programme was part of a trajectory of the general crisis in the Nigerian state and economy, which culminated in the adoption of an externally induced structural adjustment program in the mid-1980s. Indeed, the dependent capitalist orientation of the Nigerian state and economy, and its resultant degeneration, beginning from the late 1970s to the 1980s made the Nigerian state vulnerable to the increasing tendency towards globalization.

In the 1960s the Nigerian economy was based on the export of primary agricultural products. Consequently, the government was able to sustain its direct influence in the economy from the proceeds of such exports. The oil boom of the 1970s, however, brought with it fundamental changes that ultimately resulted in a traumatic economic crisis.

In addition to the prevalence of corruption in the nature and practice of politics and governance, the Nigerian economic crisis of the late 1970s and early 1980s was the result of two major interrelated factors. These are, firstly, the shift from a diverse agricultural economy to a mono-cultural economy dependent solely on oil exports and secondly, the glut in the oil market in the 1970s and 1980s. The glut in the world oil market and the resultant fall in oil export and its prices were reflected in the corresponding fall in revenue. Crude oil prices which rose rapidly from $20.94 U.S.D. per barrel in 1979 to $36.94 U.S.D. in 1980 and $40 U.S.D. in 1981, fell to $29 U.S.D. in 1983, and to a low level of $5.2 U.S.D. in 1986 (Musa, 1998, p.23). Consequently, the country's external reserves fell sharply, and its foreign debts mounted. In addition to this, the prevailing structure of policy incentives and control encouraged an import-oriented consumption pattern.

In the face of rising imports, government deficits widened and efforts at containing the adverse developments created some other serious problems such as economic depression, rising prices, inflation (from 21 percent in 1981 to 40 percent in 1984), unemployment which in 1986 was 5.3 percent, and persistent balance-of-payment deficits (Musa, 1998, p. 24).

The first response of the Nigerian government to the deteriorating economic conditions in the country was to introduce some stabilization austerity and countertrade measures between 1982 and 1984. The Economic Stabilization Act (1982) imposed more stringent exchange control measures and import restrictions supported by appropriate monetary and fiscal policies.

In order to secure foreign assistance to solve its balance of payment problems, the government approached the International Monetary Fund for a three-year extended loan facility in 1983. In line with its neo-liberal policies, however, and the logic of the process of globalization, the IMF introduced some conditions that must be met for the loan to be given. These were a 60 percent devaluation of the national currency, rationalization of the size of the public service, trade liberalization, and removal of petroleum subsidy. By December 1983, however, the Shagari administration was ousted in a coup, and the Buhari administration came to power.

The articulation and implementation of the Buhari adjustment program included among others, increasing the rate and volume of internal revenue raised through the payment of taxes, fees, and levies, and privatization of public enterprises (Usman, 1985, p. 15).

According to Usman (1985, p. 15) the Buhari program of adjustment did not start with any genuine recovery process. Oil still dominated the economy, and the weak and dependent structure persisted as indicated by the high debt profile.

The economy was almost the reason for the overthrow of the Buhari regime; it was described as showing no signs of recovery, and that contrary to expectations, the nation was subjected to further decline thereby pushing ordinary Nigerians into conditions of scarcity, low living standards, and suffering. In this situation, it was not surprising that the State-Owned Enterprises (SOEs) in Nigeria became characterized by apparent low-capacity utilization. This situation preceded the introduction of the first comprehensive privatization program by the Babangida administration in 1988 with the promulgation of the Privatization and Commercialization Decree No. 25. Under this phase of privatization the objectives of the program, according to the government, included:

1. To send a clear message to the local and international community that a new Nigeria is open for business.
2. To restructure, rationalize, and improve the efficiency of public enterprises.
3. To raise funds for financing socially oriented program.
4. To reduce the burden on the treasury.
5. To expose Nigeria to international competition and performance by attracting foreign resources. (Bureau for Public Enterprises-BPE, 2005: 12)

The privatization and commercialization program ran till 1999, with modifications from time to time. By 1999, the Obasanjo administration ushered in the second phase of the privatization program with the enactment of the Privatization and Commercialization Act. At the fourth Pan-African privatization summit, which was held at Abuja in November 2002, President Obasanjo declared:

> From the Adebo panel (1969), Udoji panel (1973), Onosode panel (1981) through Al-Hakim (1984) the performance of public enterprises has been the subject of extensive studies in Nigeria. Without exception these studies agree that our public enterprises have not added value to our economy rather they have consistently reduced value through wastage, mismanagement and overdependence on the treasury. (Bureau for Public Enterprises (BPE) 2005: 15)

In spite of a plethora of works on the negative impact of SAP in Nigeria, its element of privatization and commercialization of SOEs continued unabated amid controversies. SOEs, which were once seen as imperative for the development of Nigeria, were described as "inefficient and unproductive." Without prejudice to internal factors like corruption, one other important factor that accounted for this paradigm shift lies within developments in the global economic system.

Globalization and the Ascendancy of Neo-Liberalism: A Key Factor of Privatization in Nigeria

Contradictions inherent in the emerging capitalist economies of Europe necessitated the export of capital to foreign lands at the earliest period of globalization. The export of capital from these societies which began from the era of monopoly capitalism has not receded; rather it has taken new forms. The latest form being characterized by the push for structural adjustments and privatization. Kozlov notes:

> One of the most important forms of capitalist export that have developed since the Second World War is the activities of international state monopoly credit organizations of which the most prominent are the International Bank for Reconstruction and Development (IBRD), the International Finance Corporation

> (IFC) and the International Development Association (IDA). Since the United States makes the biggest contributions to these organizations in practice, it controls their activities and directs them primarily towards the external economic expansion of American monopolies. (Kozlov, 1977, p. 224)

Kozlov further notes that the structure and activities of these banks and other credit institutions reveal the distinctive features of present-day capitalist export. These activities include:

> (a) Every possible assistance is rendered to expand private capitalist enterprise in the developing countries against the growing state sectors of the economy.
> (b) Foreign monopoly capital is intensively merged with local national capital so that the latter can be involved as a junior partner in the exploiting and robbing of the people of developing countries.
> (c) These organizations themselves, the economic basis of which is the export of capital are typical of the new collective colonialism that is the union of imperialist powers, with the United States at the head for the financial enslavement's of new states. (Kozlov, 1977, p. 244)

The capitalistic nature of the global economic system as captured in the foregoing suggests that the emphasis on neo-liberal economic theories must take precedence if the system is to be sustained. Thus, the developed capitalist economies of the West have continued to seek new ways of ensuring the ascendancy of neo-liberal economic theories in a world characterized by increasing interdependence.

In order to sustain this asymmetric global economic system, an international capitalist financial system was established. This financial system comprises the IMF, IBRD, IDA, WTO, and IFC who, incidentally, became the champions of the privatization program. At a time when infrastructural decay was at its peak, the debt crisis on the increase, as well as a mounting pressure on government to deliver, the package of structural adjustment inclusive of privatization seemed to have been adopted in Nigeria and other developing countries on the basis of its political expedience. This was particularly the case in Nigeria. As Jega has noted:

> By the time the Babangida regime came to power, the economic crises had become acute in all its manifestations. International pressure had been mounted by all the Bretton Woods institutions and domestic demand for a resolution of the crisis had also heightened. (Jega, 2000, p. 18)

Table 9.2: Nigeria's Gross Domestic Product and Growth Rate before and after Privatization (1970-2004)

YEAR	GDP IN MILLIONS OF NAIRA	PERCENTAGE GROWTH RATE OF GDP
1970	54148.9	-
1971	65707.0	21.0
1972	69310.6	5.0
1973	73763.1	6.0
1974	82424.8	11.0
1975	79988.5	-3.0
1976	88854.3	10.0
1977	96098.5	8.0
1978	89020.9	-8.0
1979	91190.7	2.0
1980	96186.6	4.1
1981	70395.7	2.8
1982	70157.0	-0.3
1983	66389.5	-5.4
1984	63006.2	-1.5
1985	68916.1	9.4
1986	71075.9	3.2
1987	70740.6	-0.6
1988	77752.0	10.0
1989	83495.0	7.3
1990	90342.0	8.3
1991	94614.1	4.7
1992	97431.4	3.0
1993	100010.0	2.3
1994	101350.0	1.3
1995	103530.0	2.2
1996	107020.0	3.4
1997	110400.0	3.2
1998	113,000.0	2.4
1999	116,000	2.7
2000	4,547.1 bill	5.4
2001	5, 187.9 bill	4.6
2002	5,465.3 bill	3.5
2003	7191.1 bill	10.2
2004	8,553.3 bill	6.1

Source: Central Bank of Nigeria, *Statistical Bulletin* (various issues)

Macro Economic Indicators before and after Privatization

Among the supposed benefits of privatization is that more revenue shall be available for the financing of socially oriented programs, thereby reducing the hardship majority of Nigerians have had to contend with. In the light of this, what was the general economic condition in Nigeria before and after privatization?

Table 9.3: GDP Per Capita Growth Rate in Nigeria before and after Privatization

YEAR	GDP PER CAPITA GROWTH RATE IN PERCENTAGE
1980	1.0
1981	-0.15
1982	-3.3
1983	-8.2
1984	-7.7
1985	6.4
1986	-0.5
1987	-3.5
1988	6.7
1989	4.1
1990	5.1
1991	1.8
1992	-0.1
1993	-0.7
1994	-2.7
1995	-0.5
1996	1.3
1997	0.8
1998	0.8
1999	-1.4
2000	1.3

Source: Central Bank of Nigeria, *Statistical Bulletin* (various issues)

The Gross Domestic Product and Its Growth Rate before and after Privatization in Nigeria

Table 9.2 (above) shows the GDP and the GDP growth rate before and after the introduction of the privatization program. It also indicates that the Nigerian economy experienced the highest GDP growth rate of 21.0 percent in 1971. This was prior to the introduction of the privatization program, when there was a dominance of state-owned enterprises in the economy. However, the pre-privatization period also witnessed the highest decline in the GDP growth rate as the GDP growth rate fell from 8.0 percent in 1977 to -8.0 percent in 1978.

In the post-privatization period, the average GDP growth rate from 1988 to 2004 was 4.7 percent. This represented a slight increase in comparison with the pre-privatization period where the average GDP growth rate from 1970 to 1988 was 3.5 percent. The situation however is different with the GDP per capita growth rate as shown in Table 9.3 above. Indeed, Table 9.3 indicates that the pre-privatization period recorded an average per capita growth rate of 1.9 percent from 1980 to 1987. In the post-privatization period, however, the average per capita growth rate from 1988 to 2000 was 1.7 percent. This implies that the introduction of the privatization program has not been accompanied by an increase in the GDP per capita growth rate.

Table 9.4: Inflation Rate in Nigeria before and after Privatization

YEARS	INFLATION RATE IN PERCENTAGE
1980	9.9
1981	20.9
1982	7.7
1983	23.2
1984	39.6
1985	5.5
1986	5.4
1987	10.2
1988	38.3
1989	40.9
1990	7.5
1991	13.0
1992	44.5
1993	-
1994	-
1995	72.8
1996	29.3
1997	8.5
1998	10.0
1999	6.6
2000	6.9
2001	18.9
2002	19.6
2003	18.3
2004	15.0

Source: Central Bank of Nigeria, *Statistical Bulletin* (various issues)

From Table 9.4 above, it is also evident that the inflation rate in the pre-privatization period was lower in comparison with the post-privatization period. This is so because from 1980 to 1988 the average inflation rate was 17.8 percent, while from 1988 to 2004 the economy recorded an average of 22.2 percent inflation rate.

Table 9.5: Incidence of Poverty in Nigeria before and after Privatization

YEAR	POVERTY LEVEL	ESTIMATED POPULATION IN MILLIONS	ESTIMATED POPULATION LIVING IN POVERTY
1980	27.2%	65	17.7% millions
1985	46.3%	75	34.7% millions
1992	42.7%	92	39.7% millions
1996	65.6%	120	67.1% millions

Source: Federal Office of Statistics, *Digest of Statistics* (various issues)

Table 9.5 above reveals that there was a steady increase in the incidence of poverty in Nigeria even after the introduction of the privatization program. While in 1985 less than half of the population was living in poverty, more than half of Nigeria's population (65.6 percent) was living in poverty by 1996. Furthermore, the incidence of poverty in Nigeria was projected to increase from 65.6 percent in 1996 to 70.7 percent in 2000. However, the result of a Nigerian living standard survey 2003/2004 from the Federal Office of Statistics (FOS) showed that the incidence of poverty declined to 54.4 percent in 2003/2004 (CBN, 2004).

The increasing incidence of poverty in Nigeria is also evident in the country's ranking among the comity of nations. The United Nations Development Programme (UNDP), Human Development Index (HDI) ranked Nigeria as 137th among the 174 countries listed with HDI of 0.384 in 1996. By 1997, the country slipped to 142nd position and ranked among the 44 poorest countries (CBN, 1999)

Unemployment and Privatization

Despite the absence of concrete data on the trend of unemployment in pre- and post-privatization Nigeria, there are suggestions that the level of unemployment too has been on the increase even after the introduction of the privatization program. According to the Central Bank of Nigeria,

> . . . The level of unemployment in Nigeria has increased at an alarming rate. This is evident in the high incidence of criminal activities and violence the country has witnessed since 1999. (CBN, 2000, p. 45)

Discussion of Findings

The foregoing macro-economic indicators suggest that while the Nigerian economy continued to record growth, other socio-economic indicators like the GDP per capita growth rate, inflation rate, poverty, and unemployment levels did not record any positive improvement with the introduction of the privatization program. This is in spite of the fact that within four years of the privatization and commercialization exercise in Nigeria, the Technical Committee on Privatization and Commercialization (TCPC) realized over 3.7 billion naira as gross privatization proceeds from the affected enterprises whose original investment was 652 million naira. In all, the TCPC during its tenure privatized 88 out of a total of 111 enterprises slated for privatization (Anyawu, 1997). Similarly, from 1999 to 2004, the Obasanjo administration continued the privatization of public enterprises with a total of 13 privatization transactions completed. These transactions also brought in a total of over 30 billion naira (Akpotor, 2005, p. 224) with no evidence as to how the proceeds were utilized. Thus, the argument suggesting that more revenue will be available for the financing of socially oriented programs due to privatizations is false, as the alleged benefits were yet to materialize almost 20 years after it was first introduced.

It should suffice at this point to assert that the fears expressed in the opposition to globalization, particularly its element of privatization, was not misplaced. Evidence from this study suggests that, just like the assumption that SOEs have not added value to the Nigerian economy, privatization too has not resulted in any significant improvement in the Nigerian economy. In fact, the above findings confirm the argument by Smith and Niam (2000, p. 43) that "globalization and its element of privatization have carried with it a remarkably uneven distribution of cost and benefits. The results for the most part have been to exacerbate inequalities of wealth, consumption and power within and between countries."

Summary and Conclusions

This chapter has attempted to show the connection between globalization and privatization in Nigeria as well as the outcome of this connection. It establishes that privatization in Nigeria was part of the trajectory of the globalization process. However, when weighed against the supposed benefits of the privatization program, evidence indicates that the general developmental trends of the Nigerian economy did not record any significant improvement with privatization. This is particularly the case when seen in the light of the lopsided nature of the implementation of privatization and the failure to channel the proceeds therefrom into efforts at poverty reduction. It is on this basis that the following recommendations are made.

Recommendations

First, a conscious and genuine effort must be in place to combat poverty and inequality. This therefore, means that the role of the state must be proactive. Privatization in Nigeria, it has become obvious, is premature because the initial motives underlying the establishment of SOEs are yet to materialize. Thus, reforms should be cautious and for the benefit of all and not a few. Pro-poor policies like massive investments in agriculture and the provision of subsidy in the rural areas should be a priority in order to achieve a balanced development program.

Second, rather than the outright sale and transfer of ownership of state-owned enterprises to private entrepreneurs, the emphasis should be on commercialization. In this regard, there must be efforts geared towards the following:

i. Making the enterprises receptive to changes in the environment
ii. Resolving the problems of under-management
iii. Encouraging employee identification with the enterprises.

Finally, in industries with a relative degree of development, the government may systematically withdraw and lease or sell the enterprise to a company formed by workers. In this case, steps may be taken to limit the shareholding of any one worker so that the company does not get dominated by a few persons.

References

Akpotor, A.S. (2005). *Deregulation and globalization in Nigeria: Issues and perspectives*. Ekpoma: Ambrose Ali University Publishing House.

Akindele, S., & Gidado, T. (2002). *Globalization, its implications and consequences for Africa*. Ile Ife: Obafemi Awolowo University Press.

Anyanwu, J.C. (1997). *The structure of the Nigerian economy (1960-1997)*. Onitsha: Joane Educational Publishers, Ltd.

Balarabe. K. (2005). *Democratization and globalization: A dialectical framework for understanding democratization in Nigeria*. Birmingham, AL: University of Birmingham Press.

Bureau for Public Enterprises BPE. (2005). Proceedings of the fourth Pan-African privatization summit, 6-8 November, 2002, International Conference Centre, Abuja.

Campbell, A. (2006). United States grants to developing countries. Washington, D.C.: Congressional Research Service, United States Library of Congress.

Central Bank of Nigeria. (1999). *Annual report and statement of account for the year ended 31 December, 1999*. Abuja: Central Bank of Nigeria.

Central Bank of Nigeria. (2000). *Statistical bulletin*. Abuja: Central Bank of Nigeria.

Central Bank of Nigeria. (2004). *Annual report and statement of account for the year ended 31 December, 2004*. Abuja: Central Bank of Nigeria.

Federal Office of Statistics. (2000). *Statistical bulletin*. Abuja: Federal Office of Statistics.

Jega, A. (2000). *Identity transformation and identity politics under structural adjustment in Nigeria*. Stockholm: Elanders Gotab.

Khor, M. (2003). *Globalization and the south: Some critical issues*. Lagos: Spectrum Books Limited.

Kozlov, G.A. (1977). *Political economy of capitalism*. Moscow: Progress Publishers.

Musa Y.S. (1998). *Privatization and commercialization in Nigeria: Analysis of causes and implementation*. Unpublished master's thesis, Ahmadu Bello University, Zaria, Nigeria.

Petras, J., & Veltmeyer, H. (2001). *Globalization unmasked: Imperialism in the 21st century*. Halifax, NS: Fernwood Publishing Limited.

Smith, G., & Niam, M. (2000). *Altered states: Globalization, sovereignty and governance*. Ottawa: International Development Research Centre.

Usman, Y.B. (1985). The Structure of the Nigerian economy and the real meaning of adjustment. A paper presented at a conference on the Nigerian Economy and Society since the Berlin Conference, Organized by Faculty of Arts and Social Sciences, Ahmadu Bello University, Zaria, Nigeria, from November 11-15, 1985.

CHAPTER TEN

CONTEMPORARY TRADE, INVESTMENT PRACTICES, AND THE CHALLENGES OF REGIONALISM AND POVERTY ALLEVIATION IN AFRICA

ALOYSIUS-MICHAELS OKOLIE

The chapter interrogates the processes underlying the production and distribution of global wealth and how these determine development initiatives in Africa. Specifically, the chapter focuses on poverty and the possibilities of either eradicating or reducing it. The chapter argues that concrete solutions to the high rate of poverty lie outside the current attempt to enthrone and consolidate regional economic blocs anchored on the New Partnership for African Development (NEPAD). Indeed, Africa should look beyond economic regionalism to re-emphasizing identity politics and consolidating domestic economic structure within the ambit of nationalistic resurgence.

Introduction

The global political economy is driven by capitalist ideals, principles, and preferment. Indeed, the period 1977 to 1990/91 was generally regarded as "a World of two Worlds" when socialist and capitalist values engaged in bitter and consuming competition for control and dominance of global production space. Since then, the global political order has continued to thrive on capitalist values and innuendos. Therefore, any discussion on globalization (as an idea or process) must come to terms with the fact that it is an inevitable outcome of capitalist expansion. It is intimately engrained in capitalist values and propensities. Global capitalism "fundamentally thrives and promotes expansion and externalization of investment finance and international finance and has continued to change in content and substance in line with changing pattern and character of the existing predominant mode of production" (Okolie, 2007, p. 1).

Basically, contemporary globalization seeks to free economies by dismantling all barriers to free movement of goods, services, labor, and investment capital. In this case, capital becomes international capital with seemingly patent and unrestricted investment potentials. Simply put, it implies that the world is facing "the end of geography" (O'Brien, 1992). Arising from the above discussions is the fact that trade and investments remain the key pillars of globalization in our world. This chapter will interrogate the challenges posed by contemporary trade and investment practices to poverty alleviation in Africa. It will explore the linkage between attempts at regionalism and the seeming resurgence of nationalistic fervor in Africa. The implications of these developments for poverty alleviation and/or reduction shall constitute the central focus of the chapter. The chapter is divided into four sub-themes, viz, globalization; trade and investment practices; Africa's response to contemporary trade and investment practices; evaluation, prognosis, and conclusion.

Globalization: Trade and Investment Practices

Most definitions of globalization do not take into cognizance the differing dimensions of the term. However, Rodrik (2000) noted that some scholars in their attempt to define the subject often see it as encompassing many different phenomena, some of which have little or nothing to do with globalization as economists define it. He noted that economists generally define globalization as encompassing declining barriers to trade, migration, capital flows, technology transfers, and foreign direct investment.

Globalization is largely a process. It is associated with movement of history itself and has political, economic, and socio-cultural ramifications. Seteolu (2004, p. 6) identified the following as some of the key elements of globalization: time-space compression, bi-polar to uni-polar system, international division of labor and polarized system, global economy through the integration of local economies using the instrument of structural adjustment program, flow of persons, culture, ideas, and finance. He stated further:

> Meanwhile, globalization, as a process, is informed by a set of ideas: free market capitalism or neo-liberalism. According to the ideology of the free market, the role of the state is to promote increased profit for business. In fact, globalization has created some challenges to the sovereignty and power of state and even regional blocs.

Eliagwu (2005, p. 315) remarked that "while these contradictions are glaring and provide new challenges for regional groups, they raise the issue of conflict management and coordination." He also stated that one of the first problems among members of a regional organization is that of striking a balance between two types of nationalism: supra national and nation-state.

After a critical review of several definitions of globalization in the literature, and taking into cognizance the manifestations and character of the phenomenon, this chapter conceives globalization as the process of evolving a global community that is anchored on shared developmental values, principles, and norms. As a process, it moves in a spectrum-like dimension and basically revolves around the dominant values of the prevailing global order. Such an order evokes conformity with acceptable developmental precepts; rules that govern such interrelationship naturally emerge from the dominant economic order and aim primarily at legitimizing the prevailing global order and sustaining the checklists associated with the globalization ideals.

The above naturally explains why globalization remains fundamentally an ongoing process, reflecting the gigantic movement of history and global trade and investment potentials. The central plank of contemporary globalization is essentially liberalization of trade and international finance. Indeed, liberalization "is a complex of measures aimed at reducing government involvement through policies of privatization, and deregulation, and implied the elimination of laws and rules that were assumed to hinder the market" (Hout, 2006, p. 10). Meanwhile, trade liberalization falls within the orbit of economic globalization. As noted by Khor (2001, p. 1):

> Economic globalization is not a new process, for over the past centuries firms in the economically advanced countries have increasingly extended their outreach through trade and portion activities to territories all over the world. However, in the past two to three decades, economic globalization has accelerated as a result of various factors, such as technological development, but especially the policies of liberalization that have swept across the world.

The principal aspects of this liberalization process are finance, trade, and investment. Trade liberalization suggests unfettered movement of goods across global boundaries. It involves dismantling territorial boundaries and removal of tariffs for free movement of goods and for trade to take place under the regulatory framework of the World Trade Organization (WTO).

The WTO is an international organization designed to supervise and liberalize international trade. It was established on January 1, 1995, to replace the General Agreement on Tariffs and Trade (GATT), which was created in 1947. Among other functions, the WTO deals with the rules of trade between nations at a near-global level. It is also responsible for negotiating and implementing new trade agreements and for ensuring compliance to trade rules by signatories to the charter.

Another important aspect of economic globalization is financial liberalization. According to Patnaik (1999, p. 1-2):

> The essence of financial liberalization consists in three sets of measures: first, to open up a country to the free flow of international finance; secondly, to remove controls and restrictions on the functioning of domestic banks and other financial institutions so that they properly integrate as participants in the world financial markets; and thirdly, to provide autonomy from the government to the Central Bank so that its supervisory and regulatory role vis-à-vis the banking sector is dissociated from the political process of the country, and hence from any accountability to the people.

Basically, financial liberalization is undertaken in the guise of attracting capital inflow. Thus Foreign Direct Investment (FDI) is a major component of international capital flows (investments). This investment involves not only a transfer of funds (including the investment of profits) but also a whole package of physical capital, techniques of production, managerial and marketing expertise, products advertising, and basic practice for the maximization of global profits (CBN, 2003, p. 8).

In sum, foreign direct investment can be conceived as embracing the following:

- New equity from the foreign company in the host country
- Long- and short-term net loans from foreign to host country
- Reinvested profits from foreign business concerns.

Subsequent discussions in this chapter will examine how the existing trade and investment practices impact on poverty alleviation and threw up new vistas of enquiry on regionalism and the resurgence of nationalism in Africa.

Incidence of Poverty in Africa

The intention here is to demonstrate empirically the incidence of poverty within Africa. Poverty can simply be conceived as a situation of want; a situation in which the people living within particular localities are placed, where they are naturally and/or artificially condemned to a hapless and helpless low level of social reproduction of their state of existence. They therefore wallow in abject want, misery, malnourishment, and malnutrition. Besides, such people have fundamentally very little opportunity to change their condition of social existence.

Basically, poverty is not specifically synonymous with inequality. As noted by Offiong (2001, p. 97), "Whereas poverty is concerned with the absolute standard of living of a part of society, that is, the poor, inequality is the relative living standards across the whole of society." Fundamentally, poverty affects both the physical and psychological dimensions of man's existential conditions.

Primarily, it disparages the mental apparatus and psychic motor and reverberates on the levels of attitudinal and behavioral patterns. It demeans innate values of man and dehumanizes him to a level of near irrelevance. Indeed poverty remains the worst experience a man could face. Indeed it is better seen as the worst depreciating currency of human ideals, propensities, and idiosyncratic qualities.

Meanwhile, two models of poverty exist in the literature; they include absolute and relative poverty. The former concerns economic deprivation in terms of an objective, fixed standard. As stated by Offiong (2001, p. 96), "This implies a level of income that imposes real physical suffering on people in hunger, disease and the massacre of innocent children." Moreover, absolute poverty refers to the inability of people to maintain psychical survival on a long-term basis, while relative poverty means the suffering that stems from inequality; it is thus the situation of being economically deprived compared to some other particular groups (Bryjak & Soroka, 1992, p. 185).

Arising from the above is that poverty can be measured in various ways. Ogboi (2003, p. 19) identified four criteria, viz:

a. Economic criteria measured in terms of income, expenditure, and welfare;
b. Sociological criteria measured in terms of ethnicity, minority group, religion, and social status;
c. Characteristics of household head measured in terms of occupation or employment status; or in terms of the sex of the household head; and
d. Locational criteria divide an area or region to capture the spatial pattern of inequality and poverty and the effect of public anti-poverty policies.

Nonetheless, the above criteria are not collectively exhaustive and mutually exclusive. Indeed there exists a double standard in the "scientific" measurement of poverty. For instance, the World Bank's one dollar a day criterion applies only to developing states; and indeed both the Bank and the UNDP fail to acknowledge the existence of poverty in Western Europe and North America. In fact, they base their measurement of poverty in the West on minimum levels of household spending required to meet essential expenditure on food, clothing, shelter, health, and education (see Chossudovsky, 2002, p. 7, for extension of the argument).

However, the preceding argument does not vitiate the fact that Africa is not thoroughly a poor continent. Available indices, however, validly demonstrate that Africa is not only the poorest region in the world, but it is also the only major developing region with negative growth in income per capita during 1980-2000 (Sachs et al., 2004, p. 117). The tragedy remains that "while other countries in Asia and Latin America are slowly but surely pulling themselves out of the poverty club, African countries are regressing into lower levels of deprivation, with the result that the number of poor people in this region is expected to rise from 315 million in 1999 to about 404 million in 2015" (Stephen, 2006, p. 2). Hence, Madavo (2005, p. 2) observed that Africa is the only region of the World where poverty is increasing in stark contrast to the dramatic gains in the fight against poverty that are seen elsewhere, most notably in Asia . . . at a time when globalization is integrating the World economy and contributing to growth in many least developed countries, Africans are being marginalized. The continent's share of world trade has declined from 3.5% in the 1970s to 1.5% today.

The above reinforced the argument that Africa is consistently lagging behind in such areas as access to piped water and sanitation, primary education completion rates, and gender equality. This pattern, as noted by Madavo (2005, p. 2), is compounded by the HIV/AIDS pandemic and by a series of destructive conflicts. Thus, presently, over 25 million Africans live with HIV/AIDS, and the disease has orphaned another 12 million children. He also remarked that an estimated 20 million people have been displaced by conflicts, with large numbers dying in such places as the Great Lakes region, and in Sierra Leone, Sudan, and Somalia.

The situation is even more critical in sub-Saharan African states where poverty has reached an intolerable level. Table 10.1 below shows that apart from sub-Saharan Africa, other regions in the developing world have reduced the incidence of poverty to a large extent over the period under review:

Table 10.1: Poverty in the Developing World, 1950-2000 (in percentages)

Region	1950	1960	1970	1980	1990	2000
East Asia	86.6	77.5	71.1	67.2	31.3	6.0
South Asia	44.3	37.2	32.1	34.4	18.5	7.8
Sub-Saharan Africa	59.3	53.2	52.2	49.9	55.3	54.8
Middle East & North Africa	26.3	24.3	13.4	4.3	5.2	7.8
Latin America	22.0	16.0	9.4	3.6	5.3	5.2
Eastern Europe	17.8	9.2	3.3	1.7	0	0

Source: Culled from Osakwe (2006, p. 7)

As noted from the table above, the poverty level in sub-Saharan Africa dropped sluggishly from 59.3 percent in 1950 to 49.9 percent in 1980 and rose again to 55.3 percent in 1999 before dropping a little again to 54.8 percent a decade later.

In addition, Table 10.2, which presents a share of population living on less than one dollar a day between 1987 and 1998 is even more instructive. In addition, Table 10.2 which presents selected development indicators for major developing regions is even more revealing. The thirty-three sub-Saharan African countries studied had a combined population of 617 million in 2001, with a population-weighted average annual income of $271 per person, or a mere 74 cents a day. All the countries had a life expectancy at birth below 60 years, and in all but Ghana, Madagascar, and Sudan, life expectancy at birth is below 55 years. Child mortality rates (deaths before the age of five per 1,000 live births) are above 100 in every country.

The above analysis vividly points to the fact that poverty is endemic in Africa. It therefore remains to be seen how contemporary trade and investment practices have addressed this hydra-headed cankerworm.

Table 10.2: Selected Development Indicators for Major Developing Regions

Region	GNI per capita 2001 (dollars)	Average growth rate in GDP per capita 1980-2000 (per-cent)	Life expec-tancy at birth, 2001 (years)	Under-five mortality rates, 2001 (deaths per 1000 live births)	Average annual growth in population, 2001 (per-cent)
Topical Sub-Saharan Africa	271	−1.1	46.0	172.5	2.3
South Asia	449	3.3	62.6	95.3	1.7
Latin America	3,669	0.5	70.6	32.7	1.4
East Asia and the Pacif-ic	3,710	6.4	70.2	38.3	0.8
Middle East and North Africa	2,207	0.9	68.4	49.8	2.0

a. Population-weighted averages of countries in the region.
b. GNI, gross national income.
c. Thirty-three-country sample listed in Table 10.2; other regions are as defined by the World Bank.

Source: World Bank (2003).

Africa's Response to Trade and Investment Practices

Most states in Africa have no doubt embraced the policy of trade liberalization and demands of foreign direct investment. For instance Table 10.3 below demonstrates, among others, that tariff walls in selected African countries for the period following the establishment of WTO have continued to be dismantled by most states in Africa.

Table 10.3: Tariff Walls in Selected African Countries, 1986-2000 (in percentages)

Country	1986-1990	1996-2000	% Change
Mozambique	15.6	15.5	-0.1
Ethiopia	29.6	25.5	-4.1
Cameroon	32.0	18.5	-13.5
Sierra Leone	30.9	18.3	-12.6
Burkina Faso	60.8	25.4	-35.4
Nigeria	29.7	24.1	-5.6
Cote d'Ivoire	26.1	18.5	-7.6
Tunisia	26.0	30.9	4.9
Congo, DR	32.0	16.2	-15.8
Rwanda	33.0	21.4	-11.6
Zambia	29.9	14.0	-15.9
Mauritania	22.3	15.9	-6.4
Uganda	25.0	10.9	-14.1
Senegal	13.5	19.3	5.8
Malawi	18.0	18.9	0.9
Algeria	24.6	24.9	0.3
South Africa	15.2	7.9	-7.3
Egypt	39.7	26.2	-13.5
Mauritius	36.3	25.6	-10.7
Madagascar	6.0	6.6	0.6
Kenya	40.3	17.1	-23.2
Ghana	18.8	14.6	-4.2

Source: Adapted from Osakwe (2006, p. 4).

The above table indicates that relative to the establishment of the WTO, a number of countries had a reduction of trade barriers in the 1996-2000 period—a period after the establishment of the WTO. Indeed apart from Tunisia, Senegal, Malawi, Nigeria, and Madagascar that raised their respective tariff walls above what it used to be before the WTO, the rest of the countries reduced their respective walls in positive response to demands of liberalization of trade. In fact, Table 10.4 below shows that since the 1960s, and especially in the 1990s, almost all African countries liberalized their trade regimes, at least in quantitative terms. Although there has been a progressive reduction of tariffs, the period after 1995 was remarkable.

Meanwhile, a review of development strategies adopted by most states in Africa in the years following the dismantling of the socialist bloc reveals a recurring developmental decimal, the refocusing of development strategies within the precept of devaluation, deregulation, privatization, commercialization, monetization, and other neo-liberal reforms. These reform agenda are largely predicated on liberalization of trade, finance, and foreign investment. Indeed several states had recorded remarkable investments into their economies. However, Table 10.4 shows, among others, that Africa's share of global inward FDI flows fell from 1.8 percent in the period 1986-1990 to 0.87 over the period 1999-2000. Indeed, these figures are well below the developing countries' average of 17.5 percent and 17.9 percent over the same period.

Table 10.4: Pattern of Tariff Changes in Africa, 1980-2002 (Average Scheduled Tariffs)

	1980-1985	1990-1995	2000-2002
All Africa (29)	32.8	23.2	16.1
Regions			
North Africa (4)	35.2	27.2	24.3
West Africa (10)	38.5	23.4	14.4
Central Africa (6)	33.1	20.4	16.4
East Africa (5)	32.5	26.1	16.0
Southern Africa (4)	19.5	17.7	12.9
Export Orientation			
Manufacturing	28.1	20.4	16.5
Agriculture	40.2	22.5	14.5
Mining/ Resources	50.5	18.4	13.2
Oil	30.7	25.2	20.2

Source: Ackah and Morrissey (2005, p. 14)

Evaluation

Available indices indicate, among others, that trade liberalization persistently decreased Africa's share of world trade. Indeed, the direct impact of trade liberalization should be to increase the exposure of economies to international trade and practices, which would be reflected in an increase in the volume and value of trade. In other words, one would have expected that the openness of Africa's economy would have resulted equally in an increase in the share of its world trade. But the share of Africa in world trade, especially that of sub-Saharan Africa, has been declining. The decline is as a result of some factors which include the fact that its exports have grown much more slowly than world exports. Secondly, its exports are dependent on primary products; and thirdly, its imports have grown much faster than its exports. In 1990, exports from sub-Saharan Africa were 1.2 percent of total world exports. In 1995, when the WTO was established, it declined to 0.9 percent. In 1999, it was still 0.9 percent (UNCTAD, 2001, p. 27).

The manipulation of agricultural subsidies by developed states went further to undermine development efforts in Africa. An evaluation of the European Union's (EU) Common Agricultural Policy (CAP) shows that agricultural products were heavily subsidized with $51 billion U.S.D., and this is a sector that accounts for less than 2 percent of employment in Europe (UNDP, 2005, p. 130). Sugar, the most important item in this policy, receives subsidies that enable the farmers to produce so many surpluses which are then dumped on world markets. The resultant effect is that Europe becomes the world's second largest exporter of sugar, a product in which it has no comparative advantage.

It is indeed the developing states that bear the brunt of these subsidies. This is because the subsidized EU sugar exporters lower the world prices. A country like South Africa loses $151 million U.S.D., while Mozambique, a country that is building a competitive sugar industry that employs a large number of agricultural laborers, is kept out of EU markets by an import quota allowing it to supply an amount equivalent to less than four hours' worth of EU consumption (UNDP, 2005, p. 131).

The above scenario further underscores the need for fair trade. Fair trade refers to trading partnerships which, inter alia, aim at sustainable development for excluded and disadvantaged producers. Primarily, it aims at providing better trading conditions that would be rooted in justice, fairness, and sound international morality. In fact, fair trade movement aims at achieving the following:

a. To improve the livelihoods and well-being of producers by improving market access, strengthening producer organizations, paying a better price and providing continuity in the trading relationship;
b. To promote development opportunities for disadvantaged producers, especially women and indigenous people, and to protect children from exploitation in the production process;
c. To raise awareness among consumers of the negative effects on producers of international trade so that they exercise their purchasing power positively;
d. To set an example of partnership in trade through dialogue, transparency, and respect;
e. To campaign for changes in the rules and practice of conventional international trade; and
f. To protect human rights by promoting social justice, sound environmental practices and economic security. (WTO)

Meanwhile the protagonists of the above are convinced that it will enhance trade justice. Hence the developing country governments would be able to freely choose best polices unimpeded by WTO restrictions. However, Sharman (2005, p. 2) noted that "fair-trade primarily helps those who sell their goods abroad. The very poorest farmers produce for local markets; not foreign ones. They are being priced out of those markets by subsidized goods 'dumped' by corporations based in rich countries." This therefore results in the persistence of "forced liberalization" that inherently re-creates trade deficits against African economies.

It must also be noted that most economies in Africa are primary community producers and thus are subjected to adverse and volatile world prices. The flooding of domestic economies in Africa with imported products brings adverse competition and undermines expansion of local manufacturing concerns. It can be observed that industrialized capitalist economies which propagate free trade still use discriminatory tariff and nontariff barriers to protect their respective economies. In other words, they build their economic policies largely on neo-mercantilism. For instance, the United States of America extends heavy subsidies to its cotton farmers. Again, the EU, in direct contradiction to free market and liberalization policy, has discriminatory common agricultural policy.

In line with the view stated by Cooper (2003, p. 119), the type of investment that enters developing economies adds little to the host country capital stock. Generally, most FDI have not been in process manufacturing or in general manufacturing or a productive sector of the economy. Rather, such investments are concentrated in exploitation of the natural resources of the host country.

Again, in real terms, investment in developing economies were, strictly speaking, not FDI but mopping up of speculative capital which adds little to domestic capital stock.

In sum, rather than bring improved management, new production techniques, quality control, and access to foreign markets, as well as exerting competitive pressures on local producers, foreign investments rather de-capitalize the economy and intensify capital flight (the actions of investors in Africa's communication sector is very instructive). Thus, even with remarkable liberalization of African economies, the continent's share of world trade has declined from 3.5 percent in the 1970s to 1.5 percent by 2005. Madavo (2005, p. 2) remarked that "the decline is equivalent to an annual loss of approximately $70 billion. When compared with the $25 billion that come to Africa each year in the form of overseas development assistance, the significance of Africa's declining participation in international trade becomes clear." Therefore, at a time when globalization is integrating the world economy and contributing to growth in many least developed countries, Africa remains marginalized; hence the persistence of the vicious circle of poverty.

Developmental Option

Most states in Africa had groped in the dark for decades after independence. The challenges of development and poverty alleviation had driven post-colonial political leaderships to wallow from one development strategy to another. Thus from import-substitution industrialization in the 1960s, most of these states experimented with various strands of export promotions, indigenization policy, structural adjustment programs, and presently with modified strands of IMF/World Bank-foisted economic reform agenda. However, these policies yielded meager returns as poverty becomes rather entrenched. The preceding discussions further strengthen our argument that poverty is more than ever more endemic. Presently, Africa's contribution to global GDP is less than 2 percent and her contribution to world trade has declined from 4 percent to less than 2 percent, and Africa attracts less than 1 percent of global capital flows.

Therefore, in an attempt to reverse the above trend and reposition the continent for robust global competitiveness associated with globalization, African leaders initiated the New Partnership for African Development (NEPAD) (for a comprehensive analysis of the origin, goals, principles and structure of NEPAD, see Okolie, 2004, pp. 287-299). Therefore, both NEPAD and the formation of regional and sub-regional organizations constituted direct responses by African leaders to turn around the economic fortunes of the continent. However, the formation of regional and sub-regional bodies such as Economic Community of West African States (ECOWAS); EU; African Union; East Asian Commission, etc., are concrete countervailing blocs against liberalization of trade and investment potentials. This is primarily because, by encouraging exclusive trading blocs and enhancing discriminatory tariff practices, these regional and sub-regional groups wittingly and unwittingly undermine unfettered movement of global goods and services. Hence rather than promoting universalization of globalization ideals, these groups engender segmented liberalization of trade and investment practices.

However, these regional and sub-regional organizations, together with the NEPAD initiative had failed to stem the tide because of the following reasons:

a. The economic foundations of most states in Africa are weak, inchoate, and dependent; and hence remain rather compliant to external dictates, shocks, and manipulations;
b. The factors of colonialism, neo-colonialism, and imperialism implanted divisive tendencies and mutual distrust among African states. This makes internal cohesion and development difficult;
c. The circulation of political leaderships masquerading as lackeys to global capital rather complicates development difficulties. In addition, the low autonomization of most states in Africa, arising from persistence of rudimentary productive forces, reduces State apparatus to mere personalized tools used for self-aggrandizement and expropriation;
d. Most of the development strategies were imposed by external machinations and hence do not accommodate internal development ingredients. Like NEPAD, these policies did not accommodate the civil society in the planning and execution of development strategies;
e. The existing structure of global political economy consistently sustains the existing domination and undermines all efforts to reverse the trend. Indeed, all existing international institutions including the UN, WTO, G8, NATO, etc., serve the aforementioned purpose;
f. The dominance of political leaderships in Africa with visionless, outlandish, and prostrate ideas on the way out of the woods; immersed in ideological *tabula rasa* further consolidates the asymmetrical relationship between the developed and developing states; and

g. By relying on NEPAD initiatives which was foisted with little or no consultation with the local population, the implementation of the strategies contained therein will at best produce development strategies that will continuously reproduce "a wholesale repudiation of the State of being of the African man."

Prognosis

Anchoring development planning and implementation on the above also suggests that constituent States should go back to their respective cultural-specific developmental conditions, rediscover and re-emphasize their unique material conditions, and re-build their national economies along the lines of a re-defined and re-tooled mercantilist orientation.

Primarily, this is not to make a case for protectionism, or for a policy of delinking or autarky. There is enough to support a belief in complex interdependent principle anchored by materialist understanding of global interaction. However, building and consolidating national economies with the intent of pursuing integration at a later date remains the way forward. Contemporary globalization moves under the fulcrum of competitiveness and liberalization; and with the present structure of the disoriented national economies in Africa, the task of alleviating poverty and meeting the demands and challenges of the Millennium Development Goals (MDG) by 2015 shall remain a mirage.

Conclusion

An attempt has been made to demonstrate that most states in Africa are very poor. This chapter has explored the persisting and escalating incidence of poverty and the challenges posed by contemporary trade and investment practices in alleviating or eradicating poverty in Africa. It noted, among others that, the prevailing checklists of contemporary globalization rather deepen the incidence of poverty and complicate development initiatives aimed at redressing the ugly situation. Thus, it observed that the poverty level in Africa, especially in sub-Saharan Africa has been critical and seemingly intractable.

However, this chapter considered development options and the primary ideas behind the establishment of regional and sub-regional organizations, including the NEPAD. Among others, it remarked that NEPAD, like preceding development initiatives, is bound to fail in its task of stimulating sustainable human development for reasons enunciated above.

To redress the situation, this chapter advocated for a resurgence of nationalistic fervor. While not advocating for delinking, it argued that constituent states should go back to their roots and re-strategize their development initiatives in line with their local conditions. African states should see development from their peculiar circumstances; and think more of how productive sectors of their respective economies are empowered, expanded, and made more competitive and positioned for collective competition against external domination and manipulation. The task is arduous but surmountable—it requires reviving their patriotic fervor, developing pride and commitment to a collective course, and re-orientating the political leaderships away from fixated and value-laden Western development scholarships to original inward-looking and genuine internally motivated development ideals.

References

Ackah, C., & Morrissey, O. (2005). Trade policy and performance in sub-Saharan Africa since the 1980s. (CREDIT Research Paper No.05/13). Nottingham: Centre for Research in Economic Development and International Trade, University of Nottingham.

Ake, C. (1981). *A Political economy of Africa*. Nigeria: Longman Group.

Amin, S. (1973). *Accumulation on a world scale*. New York: Monthly Review Press.

Baran, P. (1967). *Economic development and growth*, 2nd ed. New York: Monthly Review Press.

Bryjak, G., & Soroka, M.P. (1992). *Sociology: Cultural diversity in a changing world*. Boston: Allyn and Bacon.

Central Bank of Nigeria. (2003). Foreign direct investment in Nigeria. Proceedings of the twelfth annual conference of regional research units. Abuja: CBN.

Chossudovsky, M. (2002). Global poverty in the late 20th century: Economic depression and the new world order. *Global Research*, January 26. Retrieved on May 15, 2009, from http://www.globalresearch.ca/index.php?context=va&aid=365.

Cooper, R.N. (2003). The role of foreign trade and investment. In B. Pleskovic & N. Stern (Eds.), *Annual World Bank conference of development economics 2001/2002*. New York: Oxford University Press.

Dobb, M., (Ed.). (1970). *A contribution to the critique of political economy*. Moscow: Progress Publishers.

Elaigwu, J.I. (2005). Globalization and Nigeria's foreign policy: The challenges of adaptation to the twenty-first century. In D.A. Briggs (Ed.), *Nigeria in world politics: Trends and challenges. Essays in honour of Maj Gen Nanven Garba*. Kuru: National Institute for Policy and Strategic Studies.

Emmanuel, A. (1992). *Unequal exchange: A study of the imperialism of trade (With additional comments by Bethleheim*). New York: Monthly Review Press.

Frank, A.G. (1967). *Capitalism and underdevelopment in Latin America*. New York: Monthly Review Press.

Frank, A.G. (1969). *Latin America: Underdevelopment or revolution*? New York: Monthly Review Press.

Hout, W. (2006). The only game in town? European social democracy and neo-liberal globalization. *International Politics and Society*, 2, pp. 9-26.

Iyoha, M.A. (2005). Enhancing Africa's trade: From marginalization to an export-led approach to development (Policy Research Working Paper 3775). Washington, D.C.: The World Bank.

Keohane, R., & Nye, J. (1977). *Power and interdependence: World politics in transition*, 2nd ed. Boston: Little Brown.

Khor, M. (1998). Globalization and Africa's options. *AAPS Newsletter*, 3(2), pp. 1-5.

Khor, M. (2001). *Globalization and the south. Some critical issues*. Ibadan: Spectrum Books Limited.

Lenin, V.I. (1976). *The state and revolution*, 2nd ed. Perking: Foreign Languages Press.

Levi, L. (1997). Globalization and international diplomacy. The Federalist Debate, XN 1 cited in J.I. Elaigwu, (2005), Globalization and Nigeria's foreign policy: The challenges of adaptation to the twenty-first century, In D.A. Briggs (Ed.), *Nigeria in world politics: Trends and challenges. Essays in honour of Maj. Gen. Joseph Narven Garba*. Kuru: National Institute for Policy and Strategic Studies.

Madavo, C. (2005). Africa: The development challenge of the 21st century. *Africa Program Occasional Paper Series*. Washington, D.C.: Woodrow Wilson International Center for Scholars

O'Brien, R. (1992). *Global financial integration: The end of geography*. London: Printer/RIIA.

Offiong, D. (1980). *Imperialism and dependency: Obstacles to African development*. Enugu: Fourth Dimension Publishers.

Offiong, D. (2001). *Globalization: Post-neodependency and poverty in Africa*. Enugu: Fourth Dimension Publishers.

Ogboi, K.C. (2003). Poverty, environment and sustainable development: The spatial dimension. In P.C. Onokala et al. (Eds.), *Environment and poverty in Nigeria*. Enugu: Jamoe Enterprises.

Okolie A.M.N. (2004). NEPAD strategy: A study in dependency. *African Journal of Political and Administrative Studies*, 2(1), pp. 32-48.

Okolie, A.M.N. (2007). Trade liberalization and Nigeria's development imperative: A study in complex interdependence. *African Journal of Political and Administrative Studies*, 3(1), May, pp. 118-139.

Osakwe, P.N. (2006). Emerging issues and concerns of African countries in the WTO negotiations on agriculture and the Doha Round. Paper presented at the FAO Workshop, Addis Ababa, Ethiopia, organized by the UN Economic Commission for Africa February 16. Retrieved February 27, 2009, at http://mpra.ub.unide/view/language/en.html.

Patnaik, P. (1999). The real face of financial liberalization. *Frontline*, 16(4), pp. 1-22.

Prebisch, R. (1950). *The economic development of Latin America and its principal problems*. New York: UN Economic Commission for Latin America.

Rodrick, D. (2000). How far will international economic integration go? *Journal of Economic Perspectives*, 14(1), pp. 117-186.

Sachs, J.D., et al. (2004). Ending Africa's poverty trap. *Brookings Papers on Economic Activity*, 1, pp. 117-240.

Santos, D. (1970). The structure of dependence. *American Economic Review*, 60, pp. 231-236.

Scholte, J.A. (2002). The sources of neoliberal globalization. Paper for the UNRISD project improving research and knowledge on social development in international organization. Geneva: UNRISD. Retrieved August 4, 2004, from http://www.unrisd.org.

Seteolu, J.A. (2004). Globalization: Challenges for the state in Africa. *Nigerian Forum*, 25(1-2), pp. 2-18.

Sharman, T. (2005). Trade and the WTO: An introduction. Retrieved August 22, 2009, from http:www.actionaid.org.uk/_content/documents/trade_wto.pdf.

Stephen, R. (2006). The complexity of African poverty. *New Times*, July 23.

Todaro, M.P., & Smith, S.C. (2003). *Economic development*. India: Pearson Educational Press.

UNCTAD. (2001). *Economic development in Africa: Performance, prospects and policy issues*. New York: UNCTAD.

UNDP. (2005). *Human development report, 2005*. New York: UNDP.

United Nations Conference on Trade and Development. (2002). *World investment report: Transnational corporations and export competitiveness*. Geneva: United Nations.

United Nations Development Programme. (1997). *Human development report*. New York: Oxford University Press.

World Bank. (2000 and 2001). *World development indicators*. Washington D.C.: The World Bank.

World Bank. (2003). *World development indicators*. Washington, D.C.: The World Bank.

WTO. (1995). *Trading into the future*. Geneva: WTO.

CHAPTER ELEVEN

COMMUNITY-BASED ORGANIZATIONS: HOUSEHOLD FOOD AND LIVELIHOOD SECURITY IN SOUTHERN NIGERIA

STEPHEN ONAKUSE AND EAMON LENIHAN

This study explores the relationship between household food security and community-based organizations (CBOs) in rural villages in southern states of Nigeria. The research is underpinned by the established observation that rural CBOs are a significant factor in the process of livelihood security, particularly in rural villages. The relationship which is cultural in context indicates that the processes and involvement of indigenous CBOs empower rural poor people in demand time, in resource access and utilization, and in local support. The associations also explore the knowledge, culture which suggests that food insecurity might be a thing of the past if the ethos of CBOs is proactively employed to livelihood and food security programs among rural poor.

Introduction

Over the past 40 years, Nigeria has had about 44 poverty and livelihood insecurity eradication programs, which were either derailed or disrupted without achieving their objectives. Livelihood insecurity has become the norm; it has become so commonplace and almost taken for granted as a natural feature by the citizenry. Forty-nine years after independence, food insecurity remains one of the most pressing issues in Nigeria's development despite the global nature in which poverty and development issues are based and discussed in the twenty-first century. It has not only become entrenched and multifaceted over decades, but has also continued to elude efforts made towards eradicating it.

Nigeria is supposed to be a rich country given the enormous human and mineral resources available in the country. In particular, one issue that keeps recurring is the increasing poverty level in the country. Nigeria is a poor country judging from its $260 per capita in 1996 and during the 1990s the nation showed no appreciable growth in per capita GDP. In fact it declined for most part of the decade except in 1996 and 1997 when per capita growth is 0.54 and 0.32 respectively. This is however, in line with the average growth of real GDP which averaged about 2.5 percent in 1995, although the performance was marked by variations from 1.01 in 1994 to 3.38 in 1996 (CBN, 1998, WB, 1996).

The relative conceptualization of poverty is largely income based. Accordingly, poverty and food insecurity depicts a situation in which a given material means of sustenance, within a given society, is hardly enough for subsistence. Food insecurity in southern Nigeria is both widespread and deep. Southern Nigeria and the entire country in general has progressively slipped from being one of the middle-income oil-producing countries in the late 1970s and early 1980s to one of the lowest income countries in the early 1990s. Moreover, the 2004 edition of the UNDP's Human Development Report placed Nigeria in the 151st position, based on the Human Development Index. Casual evidence of the growing intensity of poverty and livelihood insecurity in the country can be glimpsed from the rising incidence of mass unemployment, urban poverty and homelessness among the poorest groups; diminished access to quality foods and nutrition, health care, and educational facilities; and the rising incidence of street begging; among others.

The basic causes of poverty in Nigeria have been identified to include inadequate access to employment opportunities for the poor; lack or inadequate access to assets such as land and capital by the poor; inadequate access to the means of fostering rural development in poor rural villages; inadequate access to markets for the goods and services that the poor produce; inadequate access to education, health, sanitation, and water services; the destruction of the natural resource endowments which has led to reduced productivity of agriculture, forestry, and fisheries; the inadequate access to assistance by those who are the victims of transitory poverty due to factors such as erosion, floods, pests, and civil disturbances; and inadequate involvement of the poor in the design of development programs. These multidimensional causes of material and non-material deprivation make livelihood insecurity endemic in Nigeria (FOS, 1999).

In rural Nigeria, seasonal and inter-annual income fluctuations pose a severe problem of livelihood security to a larger percentage of the population (70 percent) (UNAIDS, 2004). Household survival and welfare depend on the ability to anticipate and cope with income shocks. Over the past decade, the World Bank, Development Agencies, Research Institutes, and NGOs have made important theoretical and empirical contributions in the area of food security, poverty alleviation, nutrition, and HIV/AIDS control and prevention. These contributions have yielded new thoughts and insights on the roles of the poor (themselves) in achieving food security, sustainable livelihoods, gender empowerment, health services, education, etc. through indigenous systems that are specific in history, indigenous knowledge, and local traditions.

Important topical areas, however, such as the dynamics of livelihood security framework built around the mechanisms of human development and the issues of food security have attracted different approaches, and still raise many questions. Difficulties stem, on the one hand, mostly from controversies around theories of livelihood approaches (top-down approach) and conceptual models of individual, household, and community interactions and, on the other hand, from the non-use of traditional strategies to simulate livelihood security.

There is thus a clear gap between the standards of livelihood security approaches and the real facts; however, rural poor people have continually modified local traditions for or as survival strategies. There is a growing interest centered on the modelling of socially-articulated network arrangements across households, extended family, and the community (informal lending, sharecropping, and other risk-pooling strategies) as a major approach to livelihood security (Agarwal, 1991, Udry, 1990; Thi-Dieu-Phuong, 1998). Meanwhile the widespread use of CBOs has been observed throughout traditional livelihood settings in rural villages (Platteau, 1991: Olowu, et al, 1991). The partition of community in terms of tradition, religion, region, and ethnic groupings has made it difficult to demonstrate their framework of operation in a formal model (Nweze, 1991).

The informal, rural, and socially-articulated CBOs arrangements erase the doubt that networks, individual values, and moral behaviors to coping strategies could be viably harnessed into food security policy development. Carter (1997) found that rural households in the Sahel, if socially and economically isolated, would annually face a 21 percent probability of falling below food subsistence level. This probability decreases to 16 percent when reciprocal social sharing is involved. Rosenzweig (1988) also confirmed the critical role an extended household plays in insuring consumption against adverse income shocks. Therefore, households seek and rely on CBOs' livelihood strategy mechanisms that can provide a relative flow of livelihood resources organized around norms of conduct and moral principles of reciprocity.

The main objective of this study is to explore the relationship between CBOs' orientation and the livelihood experiences of rural poor people who are food insecure through lack of access to and exclusion from obtaining meaningful livelihoods. The study aims to explore the relationship and networks used by the rural poor through CBOs' activities in coping for short- and long-term periods of scarcity. The hypothesis therefore is that harnessing and exploiting community-based organizations' knowledge contribute to long-term household food and livelihood security. Furthermore, in order to explore the effects of CBOs' choices, indigenous beliefs and members' risk-sharing on food security, the study seeks to evaluate the diversity of rural households' strategies for adapting short- and long-term livelihood security responses. In addition, it is important to go beyond and explore the collective approach mechanism of CBOs, and to determine if the impact of these strategies on resource allocation could be responsible for the ties and dynamics of CBO formation in rural communities. Finally, the study set out to explore how government policies or programs impact on CBOs' activities (if any), and on food and livelihood security in the current global economy.

The Structure of Community-Based Organizations

CBOs are local and indigenous to the poor which are created, owned, and sustained by poor members themselves and are present in all parts of southern Nigeria in a wide variety of forms. This excludes the other CBOs that are urban with international business networks. Perhaps the most common form are the small, relatively informal, common-interest, trust-based groups, including savings groups and rotating savings associations, self-help groups, funeral associations, village banks, water user groups, and mutual aid societies (Van Duuren, 2004; IFAD, 2005; Marsh, 2003; FAO, 2002; Crowley, 1993). These are usually limited in size to between about 5 and 25 individuals, in which all or most members are of a similar social or economic status or physical ability and know each other personally. Members often reside near one another and enjoy bonds of friendship, kinship, or alliance.

Depending upon the objectives of the organization, the optimal size and structure vary. The structure of CBOs is determined by the felt need which is the endogenous process of group formation, and also by traditional regulations based on norms, values, and beliefs. The purpose of such organization does not warrant written rules because the conditions are based on mutual trust and understanding of felt needs. Also gender and size of the group determine its initial formation. Usually, the principal agents of CBOs formation are branded in age grade, occupation, size of extensive family, gender, and those with access to information. Importantly, the formation of these groups overwhelmingly is based on livelihood felt needs and harsh economic conditions. However, the resources available create for a substantial variation in organizational character and structure which are important elements in determining the kinds and types of membership.

The relationship between members of the same group (a particular group who live in the same hamlet or village) implies that local information exchange between members is facilitated while building a strong tie and mutual trust. This makes it possible for nearly, if not, all members to be related to each other; this is a reason for greater knowledge of each other's assets, liabilities, and livelihood status (Zeller et al., 2001). Devereux and Fishe (1993) conclude that individuals facing similar magnitude of risks have an incentive to form a group that is the heterogeneity of livelihood among households or community which facilitates mutual help.

Zeller et al. (2001) argued that a group beyond a certain size may experience increased difficulty in exchanging information and in coordination. But the binding norms, values, and belief coupled with equal livelihood economic situation negates the above assumption. On the one hand, Zeller's et al., (2001) argument could be valid in an urban condition where networks are severed due to formalized models of relation (erosion of "extensive family" with preferred nuclear family), but between rural village contexts where extensive family values, neighborliness, and familiarity are unique, the size of such extension becomes strength based on the density of their networks.

The ability of individuals to manipulate his or her network within CBOs resides on their social ties. Louch (2000), therefore, defines these networks of integration in terms of connection between pairs of individuals (dyads) within a network. He used transition to refer to the empirical situation where mutual connections exist between individuals in a network. These types of mutual connections are sometimes relatively small, contained in groups where everyone is likely to associate in some way with everyone else.

The aggregated explanation of social capital explores the actual or potential resources which are linked to membership in a group or in association working together to provide each of its members with the backing of the collectively owned capital against livelihood insecurity (Bourdieu, 1993). The emphasis is upon social networks that provide access to members of a connected group. The outcome of such association is ultimately economic reward reaped through ongoing participation in the network as mutual benefits accrue. Therefore, social capital is a means expressed through the activities of CBOs in a social connection to collectively gain access to resources which are keenly sought in poor rural communities. Bourdieu's (1993) particular application of the concept of social capital relates to understanding how individuals draw upon social capital networks to improve their livelihood conditions where access to assets remains a major problem to livelihood security amongst rural poor people.

Rural poor people in southern Nigeria belong to relatively expansive personal networks, many of whom are connected by virtue of common religion, ethnic group, family, occupation, economic situation, language, region, and geographical location; where all individuals in the network have a potential basis to associate with one another (livelihood insecurity) with common interest (needs and access to assets of production) and to communally manipulate their social networks within the constraints that affect their everyday life.

Majority of the CBOs examined show a multiple possible connection kind of relationship within the framework which is relied on—that is, the greater the number of members organized within the common area of interest, the more likely a better cohesion to achieving livelihood results through combined mutual assistance. Thus mutual sharing associates are more connected than those who are non-members of such groups or indifferent. Feld (1981), also argues that most ties develop around specific focus (livelihood security), including persons, places, social positions, activities, and groups. This understanding can be extended to deal with multiple overlapping roles among members of CBOs in terms of member's participation in multiple foci—work, family, etc.—with connections cutting across dense networks with heterogeneous character.

The most stated objectives of the informal mutual savings and loan organizations obtained through the survey exercise group discussion across the three regions are summarized as follows:

(a) To improve the socio-economic conditions of members, especially those in the rural areas through the provision of loan assistance, skills acquisition, reproductive health care service, adult literacy, and child education;
(b) To build community capacities for wealth creation among enterprising poor people and to promote sustainable livelihood by strengthening co-operation; and
(c) To attain livelihood security through the provision of microfinance support and skill acquisition development for income generation.

The southern states of Nigeria are a polyvalent cultural and ethnic estate with historical contiguities and linkages between the ethnic groups and region. Based on this polyvalence, it will be difficult to determine the genuine requirements and priorities of rural poor people in terms of household food and livelihood security. So, an understanding of inherent traditional means of survival presupposes that the common cultural values be carefully evaluated. This process provides a difficult task to actually perform a concise and specific research that spread across the colossal units of tribes and ethnic groups that spread across all the regions and villages in southern Nigeria.

The daily activities of rural poor villages in southern Nigeria are based on the actions of CBO networks which control livelihood security activities of the poor with a distinguished history traced to indigenous economic and moral realms in determining well-being, which has overly provided a diagnosis of rural household livelihood within individuals, households, and communities.

An understanding of the cultural dynamism of groups/communities in a way recognizes potential sources of livelihood security, which provides a cushion against food insecurity in the social support mechanisms of "extensive family" and local institutional maintenance. Rao et al. (2004) summarized these dynamics to mean the relationships among individuals within groups, among groups, and between ideas and perspectives, which is symbolic with identity, aspiration, exchange, co-ordination, structures, and practices that serve relational ends, such as ethnicity, ritual, heritage, norms, meanings, and beliefs.

The apparent complexity with the key dimension of social relation in households circulates within age and gender, which affect access to, control over, and use of resources (land, tools, and labor), output, and income (Ellis, 2000). Even though they may pursue the same strategies as men (e.g. migration, diversification of income source, borrowing), they do so under different institutional rules thus making intra-household resource allocation to vary significantly between cultures.

One key to understanding popular adaptive strategies and their underlying ideologies may be found in the terminologies, idioms, and phrases used in everyday life in an informal economy. There is no question, however, that the informal economy is large and that it forms an important piece of what keeps families alive and thriving and capable of participating in food security generating activities as the need and opportunity arise (Ratner, 2000). Therefore, CBOs are an enhancing strategy that focuses on the potentials and opportunities based in indigenous knowledge that rural poor people maximize in order to pull themselves. Because rural poor people have their own definition of desired livelihood outcome, indigenous organizations, or groups therefore undertake a variety of strategies (swapping, trading, sharing labor, barter system, and borrowing from one household to another) based on established networks which are primarily kinship and communal in nature.

Data and Method

The study was based upon primary data, collected through fieldwork and secondary data obtained from the critical assessment of relevant documents and published literature with a view to understanding the topic and the context of issues that evolve around household food and livelihood security. The study draws on a comprehensive field survey of 1620 households conducted in 2003 in 18 states of Nigeria. The three regions surveyed—the Southwest, Midwest, and Southeast—are based on the initial division soon after independence. The three regions chosen for this research have tropical environments with characteristic tropical rainfall patterns of two distinct seasons—the dry and the wet seasons.

The sampling procedure employed in this study is a multi-stage stratified random sampling, involving four stages. At the first stage, all the 18 states were identified and selected out of the 36 states, taking into consideration the regional division in operation in the country. At the second stage, 54 local government areas were randomly selected out of the 18 states in the southern part of Nigeria. Proportionality factor of three was introduced to derive the number of study villages in each state and also the numbers of existing local government areas. The study is strictly rural; therefore areas with cosmopolitan nature were purposively excluded from the study. Lists of 162 villages were randomly selected from the list of total villages in the eighteen states obtained from the Federal Office of Statistics (FOS) and the National Population Commission (NPC). From the list of villages, the first village was automatically selected, while three villages each were selected from the 54 local government areas.

At the third stage, a household list in the selected villages was obtained from community members based on household head representation. The number of respondent households from each village was selected using another proportionality factor such that the number of respondent households from each village was proportional and equal to the number of households obtained in other villages despite size and population difference.

At the fourth and the last stage, a household numbering was done. This was followed by random selection of households from the list of households by writing the number of the household on small pieces of paper and picking a number of papers, which correspond with the number of respondents, expected from the village.

The approach employed here will make it possible to compare whether any difference exists between households that rely on CBOs' activities and those that are not members of CBOs, in terms of benefits of CBO membership. Qualitative studies have reported the coexistence of traditional knowledge and CBOs on issues of biodiversity and environment conservation practices (UNEP/CBD, 2003).

The questionnaire was divided into different sections, which are interrelated, and together they explore individual household's characteristics. The questionnaire was designed to facilitate a concise and in-depth evaluation to access household strategies and also to exploit CBOs'/groups' interaction with livelihood security. The questionnaire not only gathers qualitative data, it also enables insight into household's livelihoods activities with additional questions about issues with wider context in which households struggle with, to produce livelihood needs.

Results and Discussion

The analysis is based on the survey of 1620 households in 18 states in the southern part of Nigeria. The study advances that CBOs' ethos exerts a significantly positive impact on individuals, households, and community livelihood security in rural areas where such CBOs are operational. Membership and levels of involvement in CBOs' activities makes it possible to investigate the benefits derived from such an association and its ability to smoothen food insecurity at the individual, household, and community levels. The research findings presented in this chapter show the wide range of CBOs found in rural villages across the three regions of southern Nigeria. Informal CBOs at the village-level often substitute for missing formal institutions and formal safety nets, but CBOs tend to persist even during very hard times. This type of understanding will avoid the pitfall of undermining (inadvertently, perhaps) existing formal institutions—by introducing competing institutions that may be attractive in the short run, especially from the point of view of the World Bank and UNDP.

The results of the research illustrate that there is a relationship between a flourishing associational life and livelihood security which portrays that households and villages with higher social capital, as measured by membership in functioning groups, have higher incomes (Narayan & Ebbe, 1997; Narayan & Pritchett, 1999).

The characteristics and socio-economic indices of household heads shows that 97.2 percent are men, while a marginal 2.8 percent are female head of households with the southwest having a higher percentage of 3.5 percent when compared to the other two regions. This disparity is probably due to the cultural context in which females rarely become heads of households unless they are separated/widowed or their spouse has migrated away for economic reasons and the women are left behind to keep the household together.

Between the 18 states in the three regions, the percentages of male were all above 90 percent, except for three states: Osun, Cross River, and Ekiti which recorded a significant percentage of female headed households of 7.8 percent, 6.7 percent, and 6.7 percent respectively. This distribution has two implications on livelihood security when disaggregated by age. While the distributions still rank all the respondents on the average at their economically active age, it is an indication that they are still at the active age for economic activities and child bearing. In the first reason cited, the ability of family to go about their daily activities in order to earn income with which they cater for their family basic needs is enhanced. Thus, these daily activities can result in reduction in livelihood insecurity as women and children are in most cases left behind while the active male or the head of the household migrates. Therefore, the larger the family size, the more thinly spread is the family's income on basic needs, leading to a further aggravation of livelihood insecurity. The above postulations are, however, subject to the respondent's level of education, family relation, income, access to assets of production, as well as affiliation to CBOs.

Literacy was not a mandatory condition in the determination of CBO membership, but it is an advantage. Analyzed data from the field survey shows that 47.3 percent of the entire population surveyed had no formal education while the age range of between 51-60 had the highest (54.4 percent) of those who had never been to school; 27.2 percent represent those who have finished primary education, and 19.3 percent with secondary levels. However, 6 percent obtained a diploma (these comprise pensioners and retirees, while 0.2% represents those with university degrees). There was a significant variation in educational attainment by head of household by state and region. This shows that most of the female heads had little or no education (13.3 percent), while men had 86.7 percent.

There is a strong correlation between the size of the household and livelihood security of the household. From the survey result, the 18 states from southern Nigeria had an average household's mean size of 5.6, while a typical household in rural southern Nigeria villages consist of between 1-18 persons. The survey result indicates that the relatively large household size is peculiar throughout the 18 states surveyed and there is no particular ethnic group or region which demonstrates a higher degree of preference for large family size. Livelihood insecurity has the propensity to be dominant in areas with low-level education while the gap between food security, knowledge, and ignorance are further expanding. One of the characteristics of the poor, which remains consistent over time, is their lack of basic education.

Current understandings of livelihood security place considerable emphasis on ownership or access to assets that can be put to productive use as the building blocks by which the poor can construct their own routes out of poverty (World Bank, 2000). Naturally, each of the regions and their villages has particular asset characteristics. The largest single contributing source of livelihood to the poor (income) was agriculture 81.48 percent, fishing 3.15 percent, business/hotel 9.75 percent, construction 5.25 percent, petty trade 0.12 percent, tailoring and transport 0.06 percent respectively, and other 0.12 percent.

For much of rural villages in the three regions of southern Nigeria, farming is still the primary source of livelihood. Changes in the scale and nature of rural-urban interactions and their relevance for the livelihoods of different groups are therefore largely related to transformations in the agricultural sector which has not occurred. Rather, a combination of factors, ranging from government policies (for example, land tenure systems and agricultural policies) to village-level characteristics (for example, population density and natural resource features), inter-household differences (for example, those between wealthier and vulnerable households, and those between migrants and indigenous residents), and intra-household differences (between genders and between generational groups) all combine to affect agriculture.

This section of the analysis explores what local informal networks or CBOs/groups which are present within the sample areas in the three regions and investigates the level of participation and benefits accruing from membership in these organizations. The research examined the perceived benefits of participation in these groups, and measures the amount of horizontal integration (groups, i.e., religion, ethnicity) and vertical integration (different social groups, i.e., ethnic mixing) within them. The section also seeks to evaluate individuals and households head membership, participation and involvement in indigenous CBOs and to explore whether a smoothing effect on livelihood security in rural areas exists from such membership. The overall result shows that the rural dwellers participate actively in indigenous CBOs as a coping strategy.

The distribution of various types of indigenous organizations among rural poor people indicates that the choice of different names for CBOs is for the purpose of clarity, identification, and ease of classification. An example of this is a credit union commonly referred to as *esusu* among market women's organization. The propensities for collective action in CBOs' approaches are informally designed to recognize the attributes and potential contributions of all, irrespective of age, gender, or class; and to exploit local opportunities for collaboration which exist for mutual gain. The Southwest region shows an aggregate distribution of CBOs of 40.1 percent, Midwest region 11.1 percent, and Southeast region 48.8 percent of the common indigenous CBOs found across the three regions.

The results from the survey cutting across all the villages surveyed shows that 97 percent of individuals belong to separate networks of relationships based on his or her neighborhood, ethnic group, region, religion, age, and gender. Each of these groupings operates with different norms and levels of mutual obligation or expectation, and generates different levels of generalized trust towards others within or outside the grouping. For example, in Laogun-Araromi village, Ede, Osun State, the women's group in the village prioritized their life chances on members' ability to contribute towards the education of their children. The characteristic feature of all the indigenous organizations was resource mobilization through different forms of co-operation through labor sharing, credit, bulk purchase, contribution of cash and other related materials.

Membership may be restricted or unrestricted. In unrestricted associations membership may cut across age, sex, and occupational or socio-economic status, while in restricted associations, membership is based on age, occupation (such as farmers or traders), or other socio-economic criteria. More than 70 percent of such organizations identified in the southern region were restricted; farmer's organizations predominated, which may be due to the fact that farming is, or is perceived as, an important economic activity in rural villages. Prospective members of CBOs must be recognized as honest, well-behaved, and respectable. Over half of the organizations required that at least two members attest to the character of any prospective member. Individuals without visible means of livelihood are encouraged to join, since one of the aims of the organization is for mutual assistance/benefits.

The levels of involvement from analyzed data based on the type of organization shows that youth organizations represented 52 percent of active members, 35 percent nominal members, 11.6 percent in executive position, and women's groups with 50 percent being active members, 40.6 percent nominal members, and 9.4 percent in executive position. Also, market organization has 50.6 percent nominal members, 37.1 percent as active members, and 12.4 percent in the executive rank.

The importance of CBOs is particularly instructive for understanding the plight of rural poor people, minorities, and marginalized groups who construct these networks of association for survival. CBOs' networks are basically strategies for survival based on a symmetrical pattern of mutual expectations through bartering and exchange of trust in the sense of borrowing, working together (labor), marketing, bulk purchase, and other local survival mechanisms centered on networks within, between, and beyond the communities.

The income bracket category between members' and non-members' income bracket ranges from less than ₦1,000 per annum to ₦50,000 and above. In the first category, the following percentage distribution was obtained for membership: (less than ₦1, 000 per annum) 0 percent, (₦1,000-5,000 per annum) 11 percent, (₦5,000-10,000 per annum) 32.8 percent, (₦10,000-20,000 per annum) 18.1 percent; (₦20,000-30,000 per annum) 12.3 percent, (₦30,000-50,000 per annum) 20.5 percent, and (₦50,000 and above per annum) 5.2 percent. Non-members show a decline in income as categories increase while there were no members in the category of less than ₦1,000 per annum in the income bracket when compared to members in the following range (less than ₦1,000 per annum) 10.4%, (₦1,000-5,000 per annum) 25%, (₦5,000-10,000 per annum) 52.1%, (₦10,000-20,000 per annum) 10.4%, and (₦20,000-30,000 per annum) 2.1%.

There is a statistically significant difference between membership income bracket and non-members income bracket, especially with those with strong sense of involvement. But the numbers of members' income bracket decrease as the income bracket levels increase from ₦20,000 to ₦50,000 and above. The income distribution levels show that many respondents who are members of CBOs and who had a level of social commitment towards their organizations stand better chances of increased income from their livelihood activities.

The research shows that membership of CBOs, based on traditional norms of solidarity and reciprocity, are key elements in household livelihood strategies and community cohesion through the various activities commonly executed between and among members. Farm input (38.83 percent) ranked highest among the activities of CBOs compared to others such as sales (22.16 percent), training (17.04 percent), community development activities (11.54 percent) and bulk purchase (6.98 percent). Together, these activities through indigenous CBO networks ensure sustainable levels of livelihood security and provide a safety net for the most vulnerable groups.

The financial benefit through CBOs' activities with well-functioning local institutional arrangements and localized livelihoods systems differs in economic gains as the major difference in collective benefits between members and non-members of CBOs depends on their management patterns. The benefits from collective association suggest that stimulating participation among members of CBOs such as women's organizations and other indigenous groups may improve rural poor livelihood security and also promote access to livelihood assets and communal values.

Conclusion and Implication for Policy

This research has provided insights into the various ways that CBOs, rooted in culture and traditional knowledge, could generate and influence policy change and public action on livelihood security. The thin line between livelihood security and livelihood insecurity lies in the balance between different institutional forms (formal) and indigenous organizations (informal) approaches to developing livelihood strategies on which the practices of household food security policies are creatively designed by and for the poor through the application of indigenous knowledge.

For many rural poor individuals and households in rural southern Nigeria, the means to sustainable livelihoods are scarce due to lack of access to various capital assets. The lack of access by individuals alone is an indication that CBOs have a role to play, on the one hand, in maintaining traditional safety nets for the less economically privileged through the "user-contribute" risk-sharing game and, on the other hand, in improving the functioning of networks of working together in areas of traditional financing and labor sharing as a means to livelihood security. The majority of these organizations of the rural poor rely more on networks of solidarity to secure livelihoods.

The linkages between indigenous knowledge and livelihood security are totally influenced by economic decisions of the poor and the lack of improved economic opportunities, and how individuals, households, and communities respond to livelihood opportunities. The network of relationships in traditional rural societies through cultural elements and indigenous knowledge strengthens group members and communal ties to forge indigenous cultural actions which stimulate mutually beneficial interactions among groups and members. Policy solutions that are effective, sustainable, equitable, and efficient are therefore required for creative and flexible combinations of cultural and CBO knowledge to livelihood security. Many development programs have emphasized the importance of local participation. The emphasis on local participation came after a long history of program failures. The efforts of the poor themselves, as individuals who strive to improve their own livelihoods, often with the assistance of family and friends, is by far the most common strategy for livelihood security for rural poor. Members agree to work together to achieve objectives that have been collectively identified and are important to their livelihoods. In most cases, non-members also benefit from the extensive network of relations who are members.

This research has revealed that several indigenous beliefs and practices contribute to livelihood security management through the activities of CBOs which help to overcome the barriers of access, literacy, language, cultural differences, and physical isolation. These characteristics provide CBO members with livelihood security tools used to inform, secure access to resources, and provide education for members about livelihood security strategies. Overall, the use of CBOs in rural villages is crucially conditioned by local culture and social systems which are key characteristics that underpin CBOs' initiatives. Other characteristics such as participation, tradition, indigenous knowledge, and social capital, which are peculiar tools for CBOs' success, are often undermined and unexplored in policy development for rural poor.

The challenge ahead, therefore, will be to find a level playing field, and an acceptable compromise between the dynamics of rural livelihood systems and developing a tractable conceptual system that is known to, and flexible to meet the needs of, the rural poor. The following suggestions should be taken into consideration in household and livelihood security policy formulation.

- Building the organizational capabilities of CBOs, suitably adaptive to rural poor livelihood practices;
- Recognition of social and cultural capacity associated with transformation processes and increment in group performance through enhanced access and abilities to meet livelihood needs;
- Explore the complementary synergies that exist between formal and informal institutions to create innovative pathways for poverty reduction;
- There is a need to review the political dimensions of economic decision-making and their positive or negative impact on achieving social development goals in rural areas as well as on the efficacy of macroeconomic policies on CBOs; and
- Greater public investment in the rural sector is required. Governments should provide transport and marketing infrastructure. Because poor producers are often located in marginal areas poorly served by roads, they face difficulties in gaining access to markets and inputs.

Finally, it is important to note that CBOs' activities necessarily empower rural poor in gaining access to strategies that help secure livelihoods security. Although networks may indeed empower individuals and help build and maintain CBOs' activities, there is evidence to suggest that the character of members also plays a role in terms of value, norm, trust, levels of involvement, and members' contributions.

These findings hold implications for both contingency and long-term models of the relationship between group network structures and livelihood security. However, the result suggests that integrative structures through the activities of CBOs yield higher access to assets and capitals of production. Unfortunately, little inquiry exists at the intersection of formal structure and the informal relationships uncovered via social network analysis. The output of this research will enable the development of close links between local government authorities, state government, federal government, and NGOs to develop a coherent rural livelihood security policy framework that promotes rural and urban poor people's food and livelihood security.

References

Agarwal, B. (1991). Social security and the family: Coping with seasonality and calamity in rural India. In E. Admad, J. Dreze, J. Hills, & A. Sen (Eds.), *Social security in developing countries*, pp. 17–24. Oxford: Clarendon Press.

Bourdieu, P. (1993). The forms of capital. In J.G. Richardson (Ed.), *Handbook of theory and research for the sociology of education,* pp. 241-258. New York: Greenwood.

Carter, M. (1997). Environment, technology and the social organization of risk in West African agriculture. *Economic Development Cultural Change*, 45(3), pp. 557-590.

CBN. (1998). *Statistical bulletin*, 9(2).

CBN. (2001). *Economic and financial review*, 39(2).

Crowley, E. (1993). Guinea-Bissau's informal economy and its contributions to economic growth. Report to the United States Agency of International Development and the Government of Guinea-Bissau, Agency for International Development Contract 657-0025-C-00-3078-00. Bissau: USAID.

Devereux, S., & Fishe, M. (1993). An economic analysis of group-lending programs in developing countries. *The Developing Economics,* 31(1), pp. 102-121.

Ellis, F. (2000). *Rural livelihoods and diversity in developing countries*. Oxford: Oxford University Press.

Federal Office of Statistics. (1999). *Poverty profile for Nigeria 1986-1999*. Lagos: Federal Office of Statistics.

Feld, S. (1981). The focused organization of social ties. *American Journal of Sociology*, 86(5), pp. 1015–1035.

Food and Agriculture Organization (FAO). (2002). Towards earth summit. (Social Briefing Number 2). Rome: Food and Agriculture Organization of the United Nations.

IFAD. (2005). Achieving the millennium development goals: Rural investment and enabling policy discussion. Panel Discussion Paper IFAD Governing Council—Twenty-Eighth Session, 16-17 February, 2005.

Louch, H. (2000) Personal network integration: Transitivity and homophily in strong-tie relations. *Social Networks*, 22(1), pp. 45–64.

Marsh, R., (2003). *Working with local institutions to support sustainable livelihoods*. Rome, Italy: Rural Development Division, FAO.

Narayan, D., & Pritchett, L. (1999). Cents and sociability: Household income and social capital in rural Tanzania. *Economic Development and Cultural Change*, 47, pp. 871–897.

Narayan, D., & Ebbe, K. (1997). *Design of social funds: Participation, demand orientation and local organizational capacity*. (World Bank Discussion Paper 375). Washington, D.C.

Nweze, N.J. (1991). The role of women's traditional savings and credit cooperatives in small-farm development. In C.A. Oguta (Ed.), *Issues in African rural development*, pp. 234-253. Little Rock, AR: Winrock International Institute for Agricultural Development.

Olowu, D., Ayo, B.D., & Akande, B. (1991). *Local institutions and national development in Nigeria*. Ile-Ife: OAU Press.

Platteau, J-P. (1991). Traditional systems of social security and hunger insurance: Past achievements and modern challenges. In E. Ahmad, J. Drèze, J. Hills, & A. Sen (Eds.). *Social security in developing countries*, pp. 161-2. Oxford: Clarendon Press.

Rao, V., & Walton, M. (2004). Culture and public action: An introduction. In V. Rao & M. Walton (Eds.), *Culture and Public Action: A Cross-Disciplinary Dialogue on Development Policy*, pp. 56-84. Palo Alto, Calif.: Stanford University Press.

Ratner, S. (2000). The informal economy in rural community economic development. (TVA Rural Studies Program/Contractor Paper 00-03). Retrieved on March 10, 2005, from < http://www.rural.org/publications/Ratner00-03.pdf >.

Rosenzweig, M.R. (1988). Risk, implicit contracts and the family in rural areas of low-income countries. *The Economic Journal*, 98(12), pp. 1148-70.

Thi-Dieu-Phuong, G.N. (1998). *Food insecurity and the evolution of indigenous risk-sharing institutions in the Sahel*. Unpublished doctoral dissertation, the Ohio State University.

Udry, C. (1990). Credit markets in Northern Nigeria: Credit as insurance in a rural economy. *World Bank Economic Review*, 4, pp. 251-270.

UNAIDS. (2004). *2004 Report on the global AIDS Epidemic*. Geneva: UNAIDS.

UNDP (United Nations Development Programme). 2001. *Human development report: Nigeria 2000/2001*. Millennium Edition. Lagos.

UNEP/CBD. (2003). Composite report on the status and trends regarding the knowledge, innovations and practices of indigenous and local communities relevant to the conservation and sustainable use of biodiversity. (UNEP/CBD/WG8J/3/INF/1). Washington D.C.: United Nations Environmental Protection.

Van Duuren, B. (2004). *Consultancy on institutional analysis in Cambodia, for the FAO Netherlands Partnership Programme (FNPP), Food security sub-theme 9: Enhancing the livelihoods of the poorest*. Rome: FAO.

World Bank. (1996). *Nigeria: Poverty in the midst of plenty. The challenge of growth with inclusion*. (A World Bank Poverty Assessment, Population and Human Resources Division Report No. 14733). Washington D.C.

World Bank. (2000). *World development report 2000/2001*. Washington, D.C.: The World Bank.

Zeller, M., Sharma, M., Henry, C., & Lapenu, C. (2001). *An operational tool for evaluating poverty outreach of development policies and projects*. (Discussion Paper No. 111). Washington, D.C.: IFPRI.

CHAPTER TWELVE

TRADE LIBERALIZATION AND EMPLOYMENT IN NIGERIA[1]

OLAYINKA IDOWU KAREEM

This chapter examines the effects of globalization measured by trade liberalization on employment generation in Nigeria. Globalization is a multidimensional concept that encompasses economic, political, social, and cultural aspects of human endeavor. It finds that openness of the economy and liberalization of customs and excise duties tend to enhance job creation. However, the liberalization of exchange rate and import duties enhance the level of unemployment through high cost of exports. Thus, the present trade liberalization is not employment enhancing. Hence, the chapter suggests a regulated trade liberalization policy that protects the domestic producers for some period before totally opening the Nigerian borders for international competition. The implication of this is that Nigerian economy and Africa at large have not been fully integrated into the global economy, and adequate integration would depend on the rate at which the continent can be structurally and technologically transformed.

Introduction

The concept of globalization is multi-dimensional, as it encompasses political, social, economic, and cultural aspects of human endeavor. Different meanings have been given to the concept of globalization depending on the way each author perceives it. However, the consensus is the freedom or non-barrier to goods and services across the border. This is also known as liberalization. Liberalization is the breaking of barriers to the exchange of things, be it economic, cultural, political, or social. The economic liberalization dimension to the issue of globalization deals with freedom in the movement of goods and services across the borders of the trading countries. This means that the barriers have been broken to allow for the exchange of trade among trading parties. It is this free movement of tradable goods and services among countries that is known as trade liberalization.

However, this issue of globalization has generated three schools of thought. The first is those that believe that globalization is the best thing that could happen to this world (Adewuyi, 2001; Omar, 1990). These benefits include access to modern technologies that are not available domestically, exchange of fruitful ideas, and access to goods and services at a relatively cheaper rate to the domestic economic. It encourages specialization and competitiveness, enhances modernization, access to latest information, and frontier of knowledge. They argued that all these put together would enhance the economic activities in any country and thereby accelerate economic growth and development. The second school believes that the advent of globalization has really brought a lot more havoc than good to any economy (Asobie, 2001; Igudia, 2003). They argued that globalization tends to marginalize developing countries, particularly Africa, given the continent's level of development (Magubane & Zeleza, 2003). Also, it encourages dumping of goods and services to countries that are not competitive, especially those in the developing world. Also, it erodes one's copyright privileges as people can use one's work without giving adequate credence or acknowledgment. It is also seen as encouraging the oppressor over the oppressed. The oppressors in this case are the developed countries while the developing countries are the oppressed. It is also observed that it discourages local production of goods and services, given that most developing countries' goods cannot compete favorably with those of the advanced nations. Then, the domestic industries would be forced to go out of business, thereby leading to massive retrenchment and thus increasing unemployment levels in the country. Due to these facts, some policy makers and analysts in the developing countries have been going against the globalization of their economies based on the facts that it has the potential of increasing the level of unemployment, aggravating poverty, and then creating crises within the country (Asobie, 2001; Alao, 2007).

Furthermore, the last school of thought opines that globalization can have positive or negative effect, depending on the way each country introduces or accepts it (Ajayi, 2001; O'Rourke & Williamson, 2000). Their argument is based on the fact that while some countries have gained, others have not. For instance, the Asian Tigers[2] gained due to their own way of introducing globalization, which involves adequate transfer of knowledge and technology that made their products able to compete favorably in global market. But in several other developing countries, the reverse is the case as most of their domestic industries were not protected, thereby declining due to international competition, which then lead to reduction in employment levels.

Therefore, given the aforementioned, the question that arises is, Does globalization reduce the level of employment in developing countries? This question leads us to the objective of the chapter, which is to determine the effect of globalization on employment using Nigerian data. Apart from the above section, the review of literature shall be done in the second section. Section three presents the theoretical framework, while the fourth section talks about unemployment/employment in Nigeria. Section five deals with the model and the empirical findings are given in section six. The last section concludes and gives policy implications.

Literature Review

There is no consensus definition of globalization in the development literature. The concept of globalization means different things to different people. Most economists take globalization to mean the closer integration of economies through trade and the flow of factors. This allows a lot of interpretations on how it could be measured. Some economic analysts believed that globalization is indicated by the relative commodity prices between trading nations.

According to O'Rourke and Williamson (2000), it is the convergence of relative prices that is known as the central manifestation of globalization. While some used growth rate of trade and factor (but capital rather than labor) flows to measure globalization, others take it to be economic liberalization, which enhances closer economic interactions, and even some set of analysts gave a narrower definition to globalization as being the organization and governance of global production systems (Lall, 2002). Adewuyi (2003) takes globalization to mean the process of both vertical and horizontal integration that involved an increased volume and variety of transnational transactions. Omar (1990) conceives globalization to mean the integration of the domestic economies via financial and trade interactions, leading to the collapse of barriers to trade that makes the domestic economics to be influenced by the policies of other products through trade and investments. Igudia (2003) defines globalization as the union of countries of the world where the national economies are opened and the economic activities were integrated with those of the international community, thus representing a global village.

However, economic geographers take globalization as the shifts in the location of economic activity consequent upon shrinking economic distance. Outside the discipline of economics, globalization has been defined in a variety of ways, in which some take it to be synonymous with capitalism, multinational corporations, and big business.

Globalization simply entails the liberalization of the political and economic aspects of human life in any country. The trade liberalization aspect of globalization would be the focus of this chapter as it has a significant impact on the domestic economy, although it is agreed that export-oriented economies have performed better than the import-oriented economies in terms of standard of living, wages, and employment (Herzer et al., 2004).

This does not say whether or not globalization has been good for growth and employment in developing countries. The secret behind the Asian Tigers' export success did not rest on passive liberalization, but that of building domestic capacities and leveraging international markets and resources (Mathews & Cho, 1999). There is sharp contrast between these countries' experiences and those of many other countries that liberalized their economies without eventually achieving comparable growth in exports, incomes, or employment. In other words, there is an important missing link in the conventional approach to globalization and employment. The forces of globalization that are external, i.e., shrinking economic distance, mobile resources, and the like, only provide opportunities for employment generation. The level at which poor countries utilize these opportunities or not depends largely on their ability to mount policies geared toward competitiveness; these policies are often at variance with the liberalization associated with globalization, that is, the removal of government from investment, technology flow, as well as international trade.

According to Stiglitz (1990) and Lall (2001), it is a well-acknowledged fact that many successful so-called Asian Tiger economies did not liberalize their trade and FDI policies, but rather used widespread interventions in capital, technology, and trade flows to enhance and promote competitiveness. Their trade interventions provided a domestic base for building proficiency in export activities and in reaping scale economies while FDI interventions were used to strengthen the local technological base. Their export orientation was critical to the success of these interventions, as it provided the competitive spur needed to force the development of capabilities in protected industries (Lall, 2002).

Theoretical Framework

It is appropriate to apply trade theory to globalization and job creation given the fact that many analysts take globalization to be the rise in exports and imports consequent upon trade liberalization. This narrow definition allows them to test with standard trade theories the impact of greater trade on the labor intensity of production in the static comparative setting that characterizes most such theories. The relevant theory is the Heckscher-Ohlin (H-O) model that was put forward by Heckscher and Ohlin (1933). The model deals with two factors of production—labor and capital—under the assumptions of perfectly competitive markets and identical production functions with freely available technologies across countries. This model shows that a rise in trade raises the demand for labor–intensive products in poor, labor–surplus countries. This is commonly taken to mean that in H-O all markets clear with macroeconomic equilibrium and full employment throughout, a rise in trade can only cause an inter-sectoral shift towards labor-intensive activities (so, higher wages), not greater employment.

Fitzgerald and Perosino (1995) note that the H-O model unambiguously predicts the direction of change of aggregate and sectoral employment and factor prices. Output increases in the exportable sector and decreases in the importable sector as instantaneous adjustment takes place along the production possibilities frontier. As the exportable sector is more labor-intensive than importable, the change in the composition of employment increases the aggregate demand for labor and reduces for capital. Consequently, the equilibrium real wage rises and capital rental falls. Aggregate employment does not increase because labor supply is rigid, but the increase in wages encourages producers to adopt more capital-intensive techniques in both sectors.

New trade theory, which was exemplified by Grossman and Helpman (1990), takes technological differences, scale economies, and externalities into account. This theory makes use of more realistic assumptions than the H–O; it does not produce unambiguous predictions for employment. To a large extent, the specific pattern of comparative advantage is indeterminate, and opening up to trade does not show how factor use will change. Once scale, agglomeration, externalities, and the like are introduced into the trade model, there arises the possibility of multiple equilibrium. Thus, market might clear at a low level or low growth equilibrium where developing countries specialize under free trade in low-technology, slow-growing activities. If, however, they can mount a concreted strategy to develop the skill and technology base necessary, they could arrive at a higher-level equilibrium. In such conditions, the impact of liberalization on employment depends on which equilibrium is reached, which depends in turn on government policy.

Unemployment/Employment Trends in Nigeria

Unemployment has been seen as a great problem to global economic development. In recent years, both developed and developing countries have witnessed the problem, though the developed countries have been curtailing the rate of their unemployment (Kareem, 2006). But, in developing countries, especially that of Africa, and Nigeria in particular, unemployment has been on a spiral increase which has culminated into reduction in household income and standard of living, thus, increasing the level of poverty.

Employment generation has been seen as a means of alleviating poverty, increasing the level of economic activities, and thereby translating into economic growth. Employment can be defined as a situation where someone within the labor force bracket willing and able to work engaged in a satisfactory economic activity, or would otherwise be unemployed. There are many types of unemployment in the literature ranging from frictional, to seasonal, cyclical, and structural unemployment. The International Labor Organization (2001) identified unemployment among the youth in Africa and Nigeria in particular as a major socio-economic problem.

Furthermore, according to Ariyo (2006), the level of employment is the avenue for any human being to make a decent living. The statistics of unemployment in Nigeria between 1990 and 2004 is given in Figure 12.1 below. The statistics show that unemployment in Nigeria has been on the high side, ranging from 30 percent in 1990 to 34 percent in 2004. It could also be seen that unemployment rate in Nigeria has been consistently high even though it may show some decline, which is worrisome despite the inflow of foreign capital into the country.

Figure 12.1: Unemployment Rate in Nigeria (%)

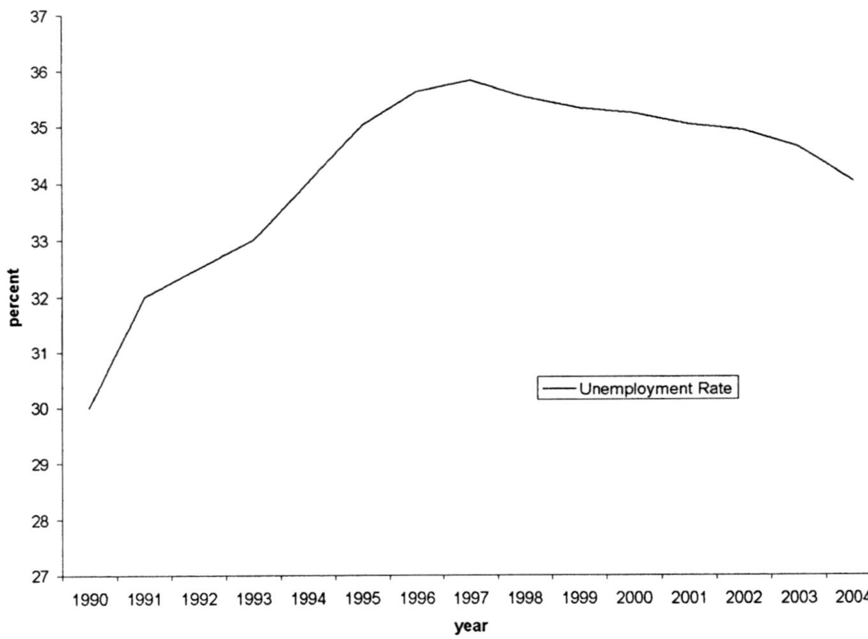

Source: World Development Indicator (2007)

On the contrary, the inflow of foreign private capital to Nigeria in 1990 was about N10.5 billion, and by 2000, it has gotten to over N16 billion. In 2004, inflow of foreign capital has increased to over N20 billion (see Figure 12.2 and Figure 12.3 below). These statistics show that Nigeria has been experiencing increases in the inflow of foreign capital to the economy; however, this has not been translating into an increase in employment to the generality of the people. Given this, we are tempted to ask, What kind of foreign capitals are brought to Nigeria?

The simplest answer to this question is that most of these foreign investments or capital that were brought to Nigeria came with their manpower and technical expertise, which gives little opportunity for the majority of Nigerians to be gainfully employed and at the same time, did not allow the transfer of technology to the domestic economy. For instance, in the extractive industry, especially the oil and gas sector of the Nigerian economy, most of the technical expertise that is used in the operations are provided by foreigners. The issue of domestic contents that have the potentials of creating many employments are not considered.

Figure 12.2: Total Foreign Private Capital in Nigeria (in millions of Naira)

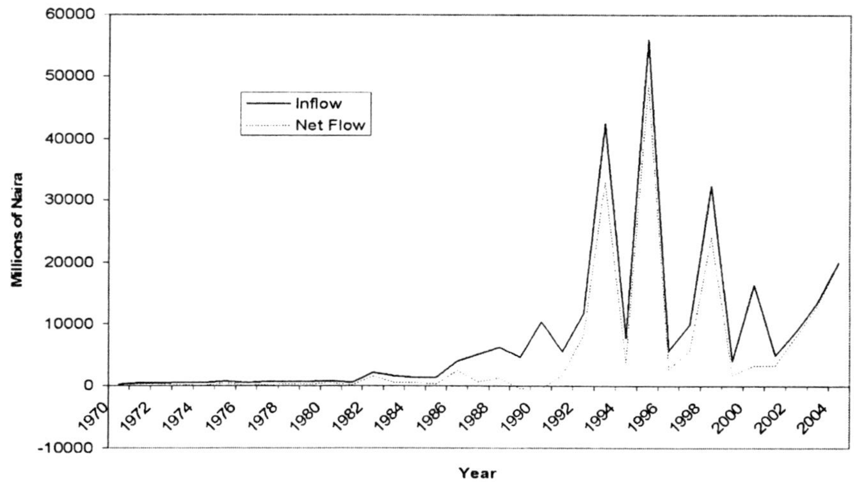

Source: Central Bank of Nigeria Statistical Bulletin (2006)

Figure 12.3: Total Unemployment Rate and Inflow of Foreign Capital

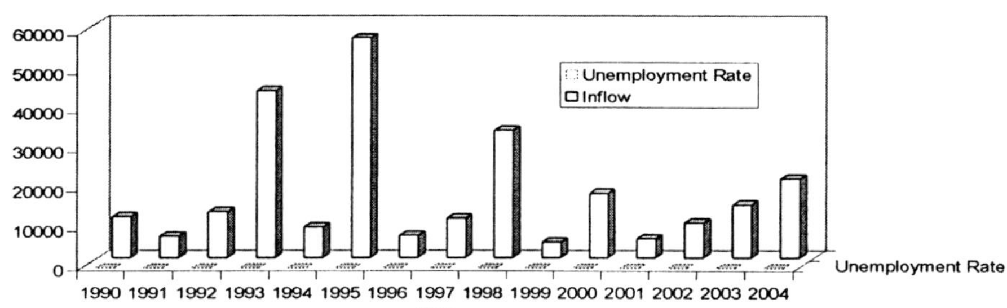

Source: World Development Indicator (2004)

Methodology

This chapter set up an econometric model to test the long-running relationship between globalization (measured by trade liberalization) and employment. We used import duty (IMPD), custom and excise duty (CED), exchange rate (EXC), and level of openness (OPN) to measure trade liberalization, while the labor force participation rate was used as an index of employment. We used annual time series from 1970 to 2004. The sources of these data are from the National Bureau of Statistics (NBS), CBN Statistical Bulletin, and World Development Indicator (WDI).

What we shall first do under the methodology is to specify the multiple regression model that shows the effect of globalization on employment. This chapter draws from that of Riddel and Schwer (2003) which tries to determine the relationship between employment growth and innovative capacity. Therefore, this chapter specifies the following multiple regression equation using annual data for the natural logarithm of the variables:

$$\text{InLFPR} = \alpha_0 + \alpha_1\text{InCED}_t + \alpha_2\text{InIMPD}_t + \alpha_3\text{InOPN}_t + \alpha_4\text{InEXC}_t + \mu_t \text{ ------- } (1)$$

Where LFPR is the labor force participation rate, CED is the custom and excise duty, IMPD is import duty, OPN is the level of openness in the economy, while EXC is the exchange rate. α_0 is the constant and $\alpha_1, \alpha_2, \alpha_3, \alpha_4$ are the coefficients, while μ_t is the stochastic or error term.

Theoretically, there is no exact consensus on the relationship that might exist when an economy is liberalized (economic globalization) and the employment rate. While some policy makers argue that liberalization would bring about a reduction in the level of employment, especially when the domestic firm's products cannot compete favorably with the imported ones. Others believe it will enhance the level of employment in the domestic economy as the producers of the imported products would be encouraged to start producing the imported products locally, which will generate employment.

Prior to testing for the direction of causality between the time series, the first step is to check the stationarity of the variables used in the models. The purpose of this test is to establish whether the time series have a stationary trend, and, if non-stationary, to show order of integration. The Augmented Dickey Fuller (ADF) unit root test shall be used to test the stationarity of all the time series that will be used in this chapter. ADF equation goes thus:

$$\Delta y_t = \propto y_{t-1} + x_t' \delta + \beta_1 \Delta y_{t-1} + \beta_2 \Delta y_{t-2} + \dots + \beta_p \Delta y_{t-p} + V_t \quad (2)$$

Where x_t is the exogenous regressor, such as intercept and time trend, while α, β and δ are the parameters to be estimated and V_t is the error term that is assumed to be the white noise. The null hypothesis for the unit not is that H_0: $\alpha = 1$ and the alternative hypothesis is H_1: $\alpha < 1$.

However, due to the probability of structural changes that might have occurred in the time period covered by the chapter, the ADF test might be biased in identifying data as being integrated even if there are structural changes. In order to control for this shortcoming that might arise from the ADF test, we make use of another unit root test called Phillips-Perron (PP) that is developed by Perron (1997). According to Herzer et al. (2004), this test evaluates the time series properties in the presence of structural changes at unknown point in time and, thus, endogenizes this structural break. The specification goes thus:

$$\overline{t_{\propto}} = t_{\propto}\left(\frac{\gamma_0}{f_0}\right)^{\frac{1}{2}} - \frac{T(f_0 - \gamma_0)\left(se(\hat{\propto})\right)}{2f_0^{\frac{1}{2}}s} \qquad (3)$$

Where $\hat{\propto}$ is the estimate, and $t_{\propto}$ is the t–ratio of $\propto, se(\hat{\propto})$ is the coefficient standard error, and s is the standard error of the regression test. Also, γ_0 is a consistent estimate of the error variance, while f_0 is the estimate of the residual spectrum at frequency zero.

Thus, after testing for the stationarity or otherwise of the time series, the next step is to test whether these time series can be used together to give meaningful results in the long run, and this is derived through the cointegration test. This chapter shall be using the Johansen cointegration test, which was developed by Johansen (1995) rather than that of Engle-Granger (1987). The reason for this is that Engle-Granger usually estimates the regression equation and tests the residuals for stationarity, which might be biased. Apart from that, it assumes one cointegrating vector in the systems with more than two variables, and lastly it assumes arbitrary normalization of the cointegrating vector. Given these shortcomings of the Engle-Granger cointegration test, we specify the full information maximum likelihood (FIML) cointegration approach developed by Johansen (1995). This approach is based on the vector autoregressive model *(VAR (p))* given as follows:

$$y_t = A_1 y_{t-1} + \cdots + A_p y_{t-p} + Bx_t + \ell_t \qquad (4)$$

Where y_t is a κ-vector of non-stationary *I(1)* variables, x_t is the d-vector of deterministic variables, and ℓ_t is a vector of innovations. The VAR can be re-written letting $\Delta y_t = y_t - y_{t-1}$

$$\Delta y_t = \prod y_{t-1} + \sum_{i-1}^{p-1} \tau_i \Delta y_{t-1} + Bx_t + \ell_t \qquad (5)$$

where

$$\prod = \sum_{i-1}^{p} A_i - 1, \quad \tau_i = -\sum_{j=i+1}^{p} A_j$$

This approach asserts that if the coefficient matrix $\prod$ has reduced rank $\tau < \kappa$, then we can have $\kappa \times \tau$ matrices $\propto$ and β each with rank r such that $\prod = \propto \beta'$ and $\beta' y_t$ is I (0). Given this, r is the number of cointegrating relations, i.e., the cointegrating rank, and each β column is the cointegrating vector. It should be noted that the element of $\propto_s$ are called adjustment parameters in the vector error correction (VEC) model, while the unrestricted VAR is used to estimate the above $\prod$ matrix.

Furthermore, another test involved the treatment of error term in the test above as equilibrium error, thus it uses this error term to tie the short-run behavior of the InLFPR to its long-run value. This test is called error correction model (ECM), which was popularized by Engle and Granger (1987). The specification goes thus:

$$\Delta InLFPR_t = \alpha_0 + \alpha_1 InCED_{t-1} + \alpha_2 InIMPD_{t-1} + \alpha_3 EXC_{t-1} + \alpha_4 InOPN + \alpha_5 ECT_{t-1} + \ell_t$$

(6)

Where Δ is the first difference and ECT_{t-1} is the error correction term lagged by one period while ℓ_t is the error term.

The Granger causality approach shall be used to test the direction of causality between globalization and employment in Nigeria. This approach tests whether one variable, say *x*, causes another variable, say *y*, so as to ascertain to what extent the current value of *y* can be explained by its previous values alone and to check whether the inclusion of the lagged values of *x* can improve the explanation. Granger (1969) asserts that *y* is said to be Granger caused by *x* if *x* helps in the prediction of *y*.

In other words, *x* Granger causes *y* if only its lagged values are statistically significant. This approach is preferred to the correlation method that is sometimes used in the literature, given the fact that correlation does not necessarily imply causation in any meaningful sense of the word. There are several magnificent correlations, which are simply spurious or meaningless in econometric analysis.

We specify the Granger causality equation of the form:

$$Y_t = \alpha_i + \sum_{i=1}^{n} \alpha_i X_{t-i} + \sum_{j=1}^{n} \beta_i Y_{t-j} + U_t \text{----------} (6)$$

$$X_t = b_i + \sum_{i=1}^{n} \lambda_i X_{t-i} + \sum_{i=1}^{n} \delta_j Y_{J-1} + U_{2t} \text{-----------} (7)$$

Where the Y and X represent employment and globalization, respectively. It is assumed that the disturbances U_{1t} and U_{2t} are uncorrelated. The F-statistic is used for the joint test of the hypothesis that:

In equation (6) $\alpha_1 = \alpha_2 = \text{- - -} = \alpha_n = 0$ and $\delta_1 = \delta_2 = \text{- - -} = \delta_n = 0$ in equation (7).

Empirical Results

We begin our empirical analysis by showing the degree of association between trade liberalization (as measured by CED, OPN, IMPD, and EXC), and employment through the multiple regression analysis. Table 12.1 depicts the result of the ordinary least square (OLS), and it shows that statistically significant positive relationships exist between labor force participation rate (InLFPR) and custom and excise duty, as well as level of openness in the economy. This means that the more the level of liberalization of custom and excise duty, the higher would be the level of employment in the country. That is, as government puts its hands off the custom and excise duties, it will allow free flow of goods and services, including technology that would then increase the level of economic activities in the country and thereby increase the level of employment and income. Also, if the country throws its borders open, there will be inflow of investments, which will increase the level of domestic productivity and thereby translate to higher employment rate. As it could be seen in Table 12.1 below, a negative relationship exists between exchange rate, import duties, and employment.

The reason is that as the country liberalizes exchange rate and import duty, imported products become less expensive which encourages more imports, and the export sector will witness low productivity as well as the domestic industries since they cannot compete favorably with foreign products, which is due to their marginalization in global trade. This will lead to retrenchment or layoff of staff that would aggravate the unemployment rate, which often leads to crises of different kinds. The autonomous variables show that if the country does not globalize—that is, restrict inflow and outflow of goods and services—there will still be an increase in the employment level given the value of the constant, which is 3.7405. The implication of this is that even if Nigeria did not embrace globalization as it is, which has made the country dependent on the advanced countries, the country will still be better off.

From Table 12.1, the degree of responsiveness of job creation to custom and excise duties as well as openness is 0.0175 and 0.0152, respectively. This indicates that for every 1 percent liberalization of CED, there will be about 1.8 percent job openings, and also for every 1 percent increase in openness of the country's border, there will be 1.5 percent rise in the level of job creation in the country. However, the responsiveness of job opportunities to 1 percent exchange rate liberalization is a reduction in the level of job openings by 0.1 percent, though it is statistically insignificant. But, for every 1 percent import duty liberalization, there will be a statistically significant 2.9 percent reduction in the level of job creation.

The coefficient of determination (R^2) indicates that about 88 percent of the changes in the level of employment in the country are caused by the indices of globalization. The joint significance of the model, F-statistic, which is 52.2179, shows that the model is statistically significant to the chapter and can really explain the reason for the changes in the level of job openings in the country.

Given this result, it is necessary to test its reliability—that is, whether it is not a spurious regression. This we have done through the Augmented Dickey-Fuller (ADF) and Phillips-Perron (PP) stationarity test.

Table 12.1: Multiple Regression Result

Variable	Coefficient	T-statistic	Prob	$R^2 = .8781$
C	3.7405	133.5304	0.0000	Adj $R^2 = 0.8613$
InLCED	0.0175	2.1287	0.0419	S.E = 0.0095
LnEXC	-0.0013	-0.4441	0.6602	F.Stat = 52.2179
InIMP	-0.0297	-4.1523	0.0003	Prob(F-Stat) = 0.0000
InOPN	0.0152	2.9811	0.0058	D.Watson = 1.8505

Source: Computed

Table 12.2: ADF Test

Variable	Level	First Difference	Second Difference	Integration Order
InCED	-2.2957	-7.2812	-	I(1)
InEXC	-2.2874	-5.5375	-	I(1)
InIMPD	-2.2983	-4.7021	-	I(1)
InOPN	-2.4118	-3.7854	-	I(1)
InLRPR	-0.2992	-1.6806	-5.7075	I(1)

Source: Computed

Note: The 5% critical value for ADF Statistic approximately is -3.5530, while -3.557 and -3.6220 are for the first and second difference, respectively.

Table 12.3: Phillips-Perron Stationarity Test

Variable	Level	First Difference	Second Difference	Integration Order
InCED	-2.2339	-7.2654	-	I(1)
InIMPD	-1.8064	-4.6691	-	I(1)
InOPN	-2.4463	-6.5431	-	I(1)
InEXC	-2.2516	-5.6267	-	I(1)
InLRPR	1.7845	-1.6041	-5.8565	I(1)

Source: Computed

Note: The 5% critical value for ADF Statistic approximately is -3.5530, while -3.557 and -3.6220 are for the first and second difference, respectively.

Table 12.4: Johansen's Cointegration Test

Hypothesis	Trace Test Statistic	
Null Alternative	Statistic	critical value 5%
R = 0 r - 1	97.9778	87.31
R≤1 r =2	64.6981	62.99
R≤2 r = 3	39.1917	42.44
R ≤3 r = 4	20.6221	25.35
R<4 r = 5	8.8728	12.25

Source: Computed

Table 12.2 above shows that all the time series that were used in this chapter are stationary at their first difference—that is, they are integrated of order one, i.e., I(1) variables, except that of InLFPR that is integrated of order two, i.e. I(2). We got the same result for the Phillip-Perron stationarity test, which then indicates that there is no influence of structural break in the model (see the diagram of the variables trend at the appendix). Thus, given the fact that most of these variables are I(1) variables, we need to know whether using them together in the model would yield reliable results through the cointegration test.

Table 12.4 also above shows the result of the Johansen cointegration test. It shows that the time series are above the critical value of 5 percent at two levels, meaning that we have two co-integrating vectors (or equations) at that level of significance. Since the variables are cointegration, then there would be no loss of information, implying that there exists a long-run relationship between globalization and the level of job creation.

The parsimonious results confirm what we got in the multiple regression above that the short-run changes in InCED and InOPN have a statistically significant positive effect on job creation as measured by InFPR, while InIMPD and InEXC have a significant negative effect on InLFPR. Thus, the coefficient of ECT(-1) that is the degree of adjusted shows that about -0.7536 of the differences between the actual and the long-run, or equilibrium value of job openings (InLFPR) is eliminated or adjusted each period (see Table 12.5). However, the speed of adjustments from the short-run disequilibrium to equilibrium in the present period is 75 percent, and it is statistically significant, which justifies the use of the error correction model in the chapter.

Furthermore, it is appropriate to know the direction of causality between globalization and employment. The Granger causality test results shed light on this, by using the lag specification as obtained from the EVIEWS.

Table 12.5: Parsimonious ECM

Variable	Coefficient	T-Statistics	Prob	R^2 = .9989
C	3.7319	1256.89	0.0000	Adj R^2 = 0.9986
InCED (-1)	0.0186	23.9627	0.0000	S.E. = 0.0009
InIMPD (-1)	-0.0303	-44.949	0.0000	Akaike = -11.0611
INOPN (-1)	0.0162	32.6606	0.0000	Schwarz = -10.7405
InEXC (-1)	-0.0017	-3.3997	0.0023	F.Stat. = 3733.846
InEXC (-2)	0.0012	2.2566	0.033	Prob(F.Stat) = 0.0000
ECM (1)	-0.7536	59.3493	0.0000	

Source: Computed

Table 12.6: Pairwise Granger Causality Test

Null Hypothesis	Obs	F-Statistic	Probability	Decision
InCED does not Granger cause InLFPR	32	1.1707	0.3254	Accept
InLFPR does not Granger cause InCED		4.0301	0.0294	Reject
InEXC does not Granger cause InLFPR	32	5.0476	0.0137	Reject
InLFPR does not Granger cause InEXC		2.5067	0.1003	Accept
InIMPD does not Granger cause InLFPR	32	0.9230	0.4095	Accept
InLFPR does not Granger cause InIMPD		4.7866	0.0166	Reject
InOPN does not Granger cause InLFPR	32	2.6639	0.0879	Accept
InCED does not Granger cause InOPN		1.4148	0.2604	Accept

Source: Computed

In Table 12.6 above, the result shows that for the Granger causality between InCED and InLFPR, the causality is from InLFPR to InCED, i.e. InLFPR → InCED. This is, custom and excise duty does not Granger cause job creation, but job creation Granger cause custom and excise duty. The second hypothesis test shows that exchange rate Granger cause job creation (InLFPR), while job creation does not Granger cause exchange rate, that is, InEXC → InLFPR. This means that there is unidirectional causality from InEXC to InLFPR. The Granger causality between InIMPD and InLFPR indicates that there is unidirectional causality from InIMPD to InLFPR, i.e. InMPD → InLFPR. This means that it is import duty that Granger cause import duty. While for the causality between InLFPR and InOPN, we found that there is independent causality among them. This indicates that as job creation does not Granger cause openness so also openness does not cause job creation.

The interesting thing to note from these results is that the two variables, InCED and InOPN, that have positive relationship with job creation Granger did not cause it, while those that have negative relationship, InIMPD and InEXC, Granger caused job creation. This means that the globalization (trade liberalization) indices that have more influence on job creation level in Nigeria are the exchange rate liberalization and that of import duty liberalization. Thus, globalization through trade liberalization as practiced in Nigeria has adverse effect on the level of job creation in the country, given the fact that most of the industrial products cannot compete favorably with their imported counterparts. The same thing can also be said of other countries in Africa, because many of the countries on the continent cannot compete favorably with their foreign counterpart, which makes them inferior partners in global trade.

Conclusion and Policy Implications

The principal objective of this chapter is to determine the effect of globalization job creation in Nigeria. Econometric techniques have been applied in order to determine this relationship. The literature shows that different arguments have been put forward on the impact of globalization on the level of employment in any country. Some believe that the relationship is positive, while others argue that it is negative. Though, globalization (as measured in this chapter as economic liberalization) has it pros and cons, this chapter tends to find out what is its effect on the job creation level in Nigeria.

Given the econometric analysis used in this chapter, we found out that globalization has been hampering on the level of job creation in the country, though we have two very important variables that gave this indication, exchange rate and import duty. But the outcome of our analysis shows that the effect of exchange rate is not significant, while that of import duty liberalization is the most significant that hindered the job creation level. This is reasonable because if there is increase in the liberalization of the import duty, there would be inflow of all sorts of products in the country, thereby turning the economy into a dumping ground. This will greatly affect the productivity level of domestic industries and in turn the level at which the economy can create jobs. If jobs are not provided for the citizenry, it might aggravate crises through youth restiveness, and this could be seen in the Niger Delta area of the country.

Thus, this chapter concludes that globalization as measured by trade liberalization is not job creation/employment-enhancing given the current economic situation in the country. Therefore, caution should be made to the rate at which the country is going by its trade liberalization policy, if it is to achieve a rise in the level of job creation. This could also be inferred for other African countries, since the continent is greatly marginalized in global trade.

The policy implication of our results is that if care is not taken, the productivity of the domestic industries might be falling, which will affect the rate of job openings, income, poverty, and the country's gross national product. Therefore, to correct this likely problem(s) of globalization, Nigeria, and by extension Africa, should make efforts to regulate the kind of trade liberalization policy they would adopt, especially pertaining to import duty, so as to bring the desired outcomes. Thus, we recommend regulated trade liberalization for the country.

Notes

1. I want to thank Mrs. Fatima Olanike Kareem and our son Farouq Olamide Kareem for their assistance, contributions, and understanding.

2. This refers to the highly industrialized economies of Hong Kong, South Korea, Singapore, and Taiwan. These countries recorded exceptionally high growth rates and rapid industrial development in the early 1960s and 1990s.

References

Adewuyi, A.O. (2001). Can Nigeria benefit from globalization? Constraints, opportunities and challenges. A paper presented at the 44th Nigerian Economic Society (NES) Annual conference, Ibadan, Nigeria.

Adewuyi, A.O. (2003). Impact of macroeconomic policy reforms on wages and employment: Evidence from Nigeria's manufacturing sector. *African Journal of Economic Policy (AJEP)*, 12, December.

Ajayi, S.I. (2001). What Africa needs to do to benefit from globalization. *Finance and Development*, 38(4), pp. 1-22.

Alao, A. (2007). *Natural resources and conflict in Africa: The tragedy of endowment.* Rochester, NY: University of Rochester Press.

Ariyo, A. (2006). Development financing of underdevelopment. An inaugural lecture delivered at the University of Ibadan, Ibadan, Nigeria, September.

Asobie, H.A. (2001). Globalization: A view from the south, *Annals of the Social Sciences Academy of Nigeria*, (13), pp. 16-32.

Dunning, J.H. (1992). The global economy, domestic governance, strategies and transnational corporation: Interaction and policy implication. *Transnational Corporation* 1(3), pp. 1-18.

Engle, R.F., & Granger, C.W.J. (1987). Co-integration and error correction: Representation, estimation and testing. *Econometrica*, 55, pp. 251-276.

Fitzgerald, E.V.K., & Perosino, G. (1995). *Trade liberalization, employment and wages: A critical approach.* (Queen House Working Paper, No.87).

Ghose, A.K. (2000). Trade liberalization and manufacturing employment. *ILO Employment Paper*, 3(5), pp. 1-17.

Granger, C.W.J. (1969). Investigating causal relation by econometric and cross-sectional method. *Econometrica*, 37, pp. 424-38.

Grossman, G.M., & Helpman, E. (1990). *Innovation and growth in the global economy.* Cambridge, MA: MIT Press.

Gujarati, D.N. (1995). *Basic econometrics*, 3rd ed. New York: McGraw-Hill Press.

Heckscher, E. & Ohlin, B. (1933). *Interregional and international trade*. Cambridge: Harvard University Press.

Herzer, D., Nowak-Lehmann, F., & Siliverstovs, B. (2004). Export-led growth in Chile: Assessing the role of export composition in productivity growth. Retrieved May 10, 2009, from www.igi.wiwi.uni-goettingen.de.

Igudia, P. (2003). Globalization and economic development: Nigeria's experience and prospects. Paper presented at the 44th NES Conference, Ibadan, Nigeria.

ILO. (2001). *World employment report 2001: Life at work in the information economy* Geneva: International Labour Organisation.

Johansen, S. (1995). *Likelihood-based inference in cointegrated vector autoregressive models*. New York: Oxford University Press.

Kareem, O.I. (2006, November). Globalization and employment in developing countries: The Nigerian experience. The conference proceedings of the 46th annual conference of Nigerian Economics Society (NES), Calabar, Nigeria.

Lall, S. (2001). *Competitiveness, technology and skills*. Cheltenham: Edward Elger.

Lall, S. (2002). The employment impact of globalization. QEH Working Paper Series 93, pp. 1-22.

Magubane, Z., & Zeleza, P., (2003). Globalization and Africa's intellectual engagements. In M.B. Steger (Ed.), *Rethinking globalism*, pp. 165-177. Lanham, MD: Rowman & Littlefield Publishers, Inc.

Mathews, J.S., & Cho, D.S. (1999). *Tiger technology: The creation of a semiconductor industry in east Asia.* Cambridge: Cambridge University Press.

Musa, M. (2000, May). Meeting the challenges of globalization. Paper presented at the plenary session of the AERC meeting of International Monetary Fund, Nairobi, Kenya.

Nelson, C.F., & Plosser, C.I. (1982). Trends and random walks in macroeconomic time-series—Some evidence and implications. *Journal of Monetary Economics,* (2), pp. 139-162.

O'Rourke, K.H., & Williamson, J.G. (2000). When did globalization begin? (NBER Working Paper, no.7632). Massachusetts: National Bureau of Economic Research.

Omar, C. (1990). The policy challenges of globalization and regionalization. (Policy Brief, no.11). Paris: OECD Development Centre.

Perron, P. (1997). Further evidence on breaking trend functions in macroeconomic variables. *Journal of Econometrics,* 80(2), pp. 335-385.

Riddel M., & Schwer, R.K. (2003). Regional innovative capacity with endogenous employment: Empirical evidence from the U.S. *The Review of Regional Studies*, 33(1), pp. 73–84.

Stiglitz, J. (1990). Some lesson from the east Asian miracle. *The World Bank Research Observer*, 11 (2), pp. 11-34.

World Development Indicator. (2007). *WDI – CD-ROM of the World Bank.*

CHAPTER THIRTEEN

GLOBALIZATION, POVERTY, AND THE FAILURE OF STATES IN AFRICA: IS THERE A CONNECTION?

OLALEKAN EMMANUEL OBADEMI

This chapter attempts to connect three issues: globalization, poverty, and state collapse. It focuses on globalization and the obvious endemic poverty in some African countries as it relates to trade, migration, and technology transfer, and examines how these have led to the failure of nation-states on the continent. As much as one cannot downplay the benefits of globalization in the light of evidence from countries like China, India, Malaysia, and so on, evident as significant reduction in poverty levels occasioned by enhanced access to markets and factor mobility among others, we must not lose sight of the dangers of cultural and institutional homogenization due to globalization. In addition, unbalanced trade relationships, imported terrorism, and other social vices are negative sides of globalization. In the concluding part of this chapter, relevant recommendations are made that can help shape global policy thrusts of developed nations and the less developed ones in order to maximize and spread the gains of globalization.

Introduction

The word globalization has been defined by many people and organizations. These definitions have emphasized different issues. Globalization is defined by the OECD (1993) as the process by which markets and production in different countries are becoming increasingly interdependent due to the dynamics of trade in goods and services and the flows of capital and technology. Globalization has also been defined by the World Bank as the enhancement of worldwide interdependence and the general awareness of deepening global connections. It is the growing integration of economies and societies. It is the growth of worldwide networks of interdependence including the large-scale operation of finance and business on a world scale irrespective of national borders.

Globalization entails the dismantling of international trade barriers, investment regulations, foreign exchange controls, and removing barriers to labor mobility. It is instructive to point out that though the word globalization has recently gained popularity in its usage, the features that characterize globalization had been prevalent at different periods of world history.

As reported in a World Bank Report (2002), the first wave of what is referred to as modern globalization was between 1870 and 1914 with significant migration of people from Asia, Africa, and Latin America to Europe and North America. This first wave of globalization resulted in the relocation of 10 percent of the world population permanently. One striking feature of globalization is the migration of people from one location to another. The second wave of globalization was between 1950 and 1980, characterized by mobility among citizens of Europe, Japan, and North America as a consequence of increased economic opportunities in these countries.

It is interesting to note, however, that the recent wave of globalization which started in the early 1980s has a momentum that surpasses the aforementioned waves. This momentum is not unconnected with the breakthrough recorded in information and communication technology that has turned the world to a global village. New technology has shrunk distances.

The momentum of the recent globalization has been accentuated also by the increasing regionalization of different parts of the world. It is on record that the Maastricht Treaty with the completion of the European Single Market propelled the vision of the United Europe that facilitated the idea of a unified currency known as the Euro.

On the African continent also, the emergence of the African Union being the result of the reorganization of the Organisation of African Unity has helped in advancing the new wave of globalization. Even within the African and Asian continents, sub-regional organizations like the Economic Community of West African States (ECOWAS), the South African Preferential Treatment Trade Area (PTA), and the Association of South East Asian Nations (ASEAN) have resulted in massive movement of people and capital across national borders. Regionalization essentially is the mid-way dimension of the move towards globalization.

Though there is the view that regionalization being pursued by different geographical blocks is one way nations within the same block try to maximize the benefits inherent in globalization, it has nonetheless energized the wave of globalization. On the whole, globalization has been enhanced and is still being driven by some forces and phenomena among which are competitive advantage, technological change, market forces, environmental factors, reduced transportation and distributional cost, distributed risk, the media, and the spread of the English language.

Globalization has diverse economic, political, social, and cultural effects on all nations of the world, though in varying degrees. The popularity of economic globalization is traceable to the emergence of the global economic order heralded by an economic conference held in Bretton Woods, New England. It is important to say that there is the suspicion that all the effects of globalization will in one way or another contribute to the failure of states if they are not properly managed.

The Benefits of Globalization

Scholars who support the current wave of globalization have highlighted the benefits of globalization, which cannot be denied. These benefits include:

a. more efficient resource allocation or what is generally referred to as allocative efficiency;
b. the possibility of the development of financial markets;
c. increased flow of capital to developing countries;
d. the prospects of increased international trade;
e. enhanced access to global markets for the sale of goods and services;
f. enhanced political understanding among nations of the world; and
g. poverty reduction.

The issue of poverty reduction as a major benefit of globalization has taken center stage because all the benefits of globalization should ultimately add up to a better standard of living most especially since the definition of poverty now embraces far more than economic or monetary considerations to include issues of having a political voice, equitable distribution of social amenities, better access to markets, etc. Many researchers have laid emphasis on how well globalization has resulted in poverty reduction.

Researches have shown that globalization has resulted in poverty reduction in China, India, and Malaysia. The number of extremely poor people in open economies of Asia otherwise known as the new globalizers has declined by 120 million between 1993 and 1998 (World Bank, 2002). This is evident as significant increases in access to education, better health, and better employment opportunities, among others, have been recorded. It is also in literature and affirmed in the World Bank Policy Research Report in 2002 that as a result of globalization, developing countries' exports have risen significantly by almost 80 percent between 1980 and 1998 (World Bank, 2002).

This positive result seems to be consistent with the effects of the first wave of globalization which took place from 1870 to 1914 and had the resultant effect of exports being doubled to 8 percent from an earlier figure while foreign capital tripled relative to income in developing countries of Africa, Asia, and Latin

America. With the latest wave of globalization the more globalized developing countries have succeeded in increasing their per capita growth rate from 3 percent in 1970s, to 4 percent in 1980s, to 5 percent in the 1990s.

A notable aspect of the benefits of globalization as it concerns poverty reduction is the issue of remittances by migrants. Remittances from migrants who moved from developing countries to developed economies have helped in improving the welfare of their people in their countries of origin since they have the privilege of earning better income in their new locations.

Studies have shown that migrants from Mexico earning $31 per week at home started earning $278 per week on relocating to the United States of America. Consequent upon the new wave of globalization, there has been a rise from 25 percent to 80 percent in labor-intensive manufactures from countries such as India, Indonesia, Turkey, Morocco, and China. In addition there has been an increase in the export of services from 9 percent to 17 percent.

Globalization, Debt, and Poverty

Globalization was earlier seen generally as beneficial because of its possibility of fostering greater interdependence among nations and facilitating freer flow of international trade, capital, information, and competition. However, this is not absolutely true in the real sense of it, judging from the balance of evidence. The increasing debt situation of many developing countries especially in Africa has given reason for serious concern. Consequently, there have been hues and cries over whom and which countries globalization will ultimately benefit.

There have been those that believe and affirm that globalization expressed as a global marketplace tend to widen inequality among nations. At issue is the fact that unfair competition and inequality existing in the lopsided trade relationship have caused the situation of "unequal partners, unequal rewards," and have also led to the precarious debt condition in many developing countries. There is the widespread view that Africa's contemporary socio-political and economic distress is accentuated by the current globalization regime which has also been aggravated by the aggressive international imperialism of trade and money.

The control of global resources and of the international produce markets, price fixing, and significant subsidy of the rich nation's domestic products have continued to ensure the underdevelopment of Africa. The case is such that whether it is farm produce, fossil fuels, solid minerals, Africa has always had to play catch-up and second fiddle and thus recording unfavorable balance of payments and subsequently a high debt overhang. As a consequence of this scenario, Africa has always had the lowest share of global wealth.

The malfunctioning of the global system and institutions has resulted in a situation whereby, while world trade for countries in Europe, the United States, China, and Japan are increasing, it is declining for African countries. This translates into uneven development evident as a continuous rise in the living standards of the rich at the expense of many African countries.

Currently in 2009, about one-fifth of the world population lives on less than a dollar per day, and the bulk of people in this category are in Africa. Globalization that has expressed itself in regional integration in most parts of the world has adversely affected poor countries and their people. The rate of collapse of businesses in the first few years of integration due to competition has always resulted in the loss of jobs. Studies in Colombia, Chile, and Morocco after liberalization showed a high rise of "churning" entry and exit of firms with the resultant effect of high labor turnover.

On the global scene, the reduction in tariff by developing countries ought to improve trade relations between them and developed nations but this is not usually so because many developed countries still put up barriers to limit the entry of products from less-developed countries. Globalization tends to promote and protect the idea of global standards, which may work against the welfare of developing countries. Worse still is the fact that when people from the developing countries migrate to the developed ones, the economic opportunities open to them as jobs and investment are discriminatory and below their skills, hence they are often under-employed and may not be able to send reasonable remittances to their dependents in their home countries. The negative effects of the globalization of finance has become obvious with the loss of jobs in Africa arising from the global financial crisis that started in the Unites States of America that has been transmitted to different nations of the world. The weakness of supervision in Africa has made its impact more severe as evident in the crash of the prices of quoted stocks.

Table 13.1: External Debt of Selected Countries ($ Million)

Country	1990	2003
Burundi	907	1,310
Chad	528	1,499
Cote d'Ivoire	17,251	12,187
Ethiopia	8,630	7,151
Nigeria	33,439	34,963
Republic of Congo	10,259	11,170
Sierra Leone	1,196	1,612
Somalia	2,370	2,838
Sudan	14,762	17,496

Source: World Bank, *World Development Indicators,* 2005.

This disadvantaged position of most African countries has resulted in continuous increase in the figure of their human poverty index as well as the debt profile (see Table 13.1, Table 13.2, and Table 13.3). The debt problem made it difficult for most of these countries to have resources sufficient enough for the provision of basic social services. The figures of the external debt of some of these countries and other associated issues highlighted below are quite instructive.

Table 13.2: External Debt as Percentage of GNP

Country	External Debt as a % of GNP
Congo	365.8
Cote D'Ivoire	251.7
Mozambique	443.6
Sierra Leone	159.7

Source: World Bank, *Annual Report*, 1997

Table 13.3: Regional Poverty Estimates (people living on less than $1 a day) (millions)

Region	1981	1984	1987	1990	1993	1996	1999	2001
China	634	425	308	375	334	212	223	212
East Asia & Pacific	796	562	426	472	415	287	282	271
South Asia	475	460	473	462	476	461	429	431
Sub-Sahara Africa	164	198	219	227	242	271	294	313

Source: World Bank, *World Development Indicators*, 2005.

As a result of poverty, marginalized countries in the globalization trend stand the risk of internal conflict. For example, Quy-Toan Do and Lakshmi Iyer (2007a) examined civil war in Nepal and found that poverty is the biggest determinant of whether a district will experience conflict. This is quite true also for Sudan, Ethiopia, and Somalia, among many other African countries. They estimate that from 1996 to 2004 that a 10 percent increase in poverty is associated with 24 additional conflict-related deaths in a district. In contrast, variables measuring social divisions such as caste polarization or linguistic fractionalization do not have a significant association with conflict intensity, suggesting that support for conflict comes from economically deprived areas and not mainly from social divisions.

Since 1945, over 70 poverty-induced civil wars have broken out in different parts of the world resulting in about 20 million deaths and displacing over 65 million people. In the same vein, Collier and Hoeffler (2004) stated that controlling other factors, higher dependence on primary commodity export, which is a major feature of most poor African countries, increases the risk of conflict very substantially. Citing cross-country studies by scholars, including Collier and

Hoeffler (2004), Fearon and Laitin (2003), and Mignel et al. (2004), Do and Iyer (2007b, p. 2) found that poorer countries face a greater risk of civil war.

Table 13.4: People Living on Less Than $2 a Day (%)

Region	1981	1984	1987	1990	1993	1996	1999	2001
China	88.1	78.5	67.4	72.6	68.1	53.4	50.1	46.7
East Asia & Pacific	84.4	76.6	67.7	69.9	64.8	53.3	50.3	47.4
South Asia	89.1	87.2	86.7	85.5	84.5	81.7	78.1	77.2
Sub-Sahara Africa	73.3	76.1	76.1	75.0	74.6	75.1	76.1	76.6

Source: World Bank, *World Development Indicators*, 2005.

Globalization, Crime, and War

Understandably, a significant feature of globalization is the migration of people from one location to the other, and incidentally this has not been lacking in the various waves of globalization. As at year 2006, the number of people living outside their country of birth was estimated to be over 180 million or 3 percent of the world population (World Bank, 2006).

This movement has serious impact in the form of social, economic, cultural, and political challenges it poses on the source and destination countries. On a positive note, Yang and Martinez (2006) found that an increase in remittances leads to a reduction in migrants' household poverty in the Philippines as it has done in many other migrants' countries. However, in the destination countries, it has induced social and civil unrest due to the resistance often put up against migrants by nationals of the destination countries with regard to migrants' unhindered access to social and economic benefits.

Another dimension to the issue of crime and war is that more often, rich terrorists recruit poor and vulnerable people to join in the execution of their terrorist acts with promise of financial gains. This has played itself out in Somalia, Ethiopia, and Sierra Leone. Also the reduction in barriers, which is a key issue in globalization, has led to easier acquisition of arms and ammunitions gotten at very cheap rates due to the activities of unscrupulous businessmen and smugglers.

In addition, the increased connections between nations have resulted in the movement of hard drugs from one part of the world to the other with its attendant consequences. The ease at which funds can be transferred from one part of the world through electronic means being a major future of globalization has further increased the crime rate even in developing economies.

While it is true that at some point in time globalization has resulted in the rise of developing countries' exports, this has not translated into better standards of living for the people of these countries due to official corruption in high places. Interesting though quite unfortunate, corrupt government officials and businessmen have accomplices in developed countries. The result of this is capital flight while the nations shortchanged are denied the needed resources that would have been used to move their economies forward. In some instances, many interventions in form of aids to developing countries are not delivered but redirected back to the developed economies, and in cases where they are delivered, they are usually not delivered in full.

As a consequence of globalization, there has been an increase in foreign-induced crisis in Africa in countries like Niger Republic, Cote d'Ivoire, Chad, Ethiopia, Sierra Leone, and even Liberia. Another angle to the problem caused by globalization is that in order to reap the benefits of globalization which benefited land owners in Ethiopia and Congo, there were sharp contests for available lands resulting in conflicts. The lopsided land ownership, though traced to many years of misrule, has continued to be a reason for continuous crisis in these countries.

Globalization, Poverty, War, and Failure of States

Although the pains of World War I and World War II are behind us, the lessons of those experiences should not be forgotten if global peace is to be achieved. Taking into consideration the first wave of globalization between 1870 and 1914 with the migration and mass relocation of people from one place to the other, there was a quest for territorial expansion by different emerging nations that built up into conflicts and killings, which became full-blown in the years of World War I.

The issues that led to World War II between the period of 1939 and 1945, among which is the dispersal and migration of Jews to different parts of the world, are quite significant. History has it that the migration of the Jews from the Middle East to countries in Europe, where they started making economic progress and expansion to the displeasure of people in their host countries, contributed to the fueling of the crisis that resulted in World War II, though there were other reasons linked to the expansionist tendency of the then German government.

In order to adequately discuss the issue of globalization, poverty, fragility, and the failure of states, it is imperative to define and explain the concept of state fragility and state failure. The United States Agency for International Development defines a fragile state or failed state as that characterized by a growing inability or willingness to assure the provision of basic services and security to their population. Fragile states are also defined as those whose government cannot and will not deliver core functions to the majority of its people including the poor.

The World Bank defines a fragile state based on its own internal country policy and institutional assessment exercise affirming that fragile states have the peculiar features of having a significant number of poor people. They are those that create a negative spillover evident as conflict, instability, and refugees' flow to their neighbors. Nation-states that are unable to perform certain minimal functions for the security and well-being of their citizens are generally classified as failed states. These states often have weak institutions, high debt profile, high poverty rate, and as such, many of them fall under the Low Income Countries Under Stress (LICUS). Now as it relates to Africa, many conflicts have been linked to clashes between migrants and local nationals in countries like Ethiopia, Sierra Leone, and Rwanda.

From the figures earlier presented on the tables above and taking a good look at the features of fragile and failed states and the fact that many of the countries highlighted had at one time or another been classified as a fragile state and in some cases failed states, one cannot help but see the linkage between globalization, poverty, and state failure.

Apart from poverty, there are, however, other factors that encourage crisis in developing countries. For example, in Sudan there has been continuous resistance to the effects of cultural change that globalization is putting up. In many other African countries, including Nigeria, there is the subtle resistance to cultural and institutional homogenization that globalization portends. While a segment of the society tries to embrace Western civilization and education, another segment resists vehemently the influence of Western civilization and education thereby causing social tensions that have in many cases snowballed into major conflicts. For example, there were reported cases of parents withdrawing their children from the conventional schools to Arabic schools in some parts of Nigeria at a time before the intervention of the federal and state governments.

As reported by the World Bank, sometimes a foreign culture is seen as a threat to local cultures and societies do often seek to protect their culture due to some suspicion. In the light of the historic scramble for Africa by developed nations, there is the need for some caution.

Other dimensions to this are that, as a consequence of globalization, many African nations have suffered and are still suffering unbalanced trade relationships, loss of jobs due to the collapse of small domestic enterprises as a result of competition, and inequality in the distribution of income. There are evidences that growing integration has sometimes led to heightened inequalities within countries and these in turn have fueled social and political crises that have resulted into full-blown wars. For example, in Uganda and Nigeria, while integration has led to increased economic growth, income inequality has widened the gap between the rich and the poor.

This scenario is one of the things that has fueled crisis in the Niger Delta region of Nigeria, and which has further been complicated by the frequent oil spillage, gas flaring, and general environmental pollution rendering many Nigerians poor through their being denied the privilege of farming and fishing. Though bedeviled by a negative consequence of weak government institutions in many African countries, the positive effect of globalization is that the improved healthcare facilities have led to overpopulation and associated social vices.

Conclusion: Curtailing the Negative Effects of Globalization

It may not be too far from the truth to say that globalization may have done more harm than good to many African countries and other developing countries in other parts of the world, judging from the arguments put up in the earlier part of this chapter. The question now is, How do we curtail the negative effects of globalization especially with reference to Africa?

First of all, consider the loss of jobs arising from business collapse as a consequence of globalization, and also consider the fact that this loss of jobs may not be a short-run effect as some have claimed. Those who lose their jobs may not easily be able to get needed skills to benefit from emerging opportunities, so there should be policies of social protection such as insurance, pension funds, and social safety nets to help the unemployed. In addition, taking a look at it from the angle of environmental pollution, there is the need for environmental regulations to be enforced through WTO sanctions, while the core actions stipulated by the Kyoto protocol aimed at addressing global warming should be enforced also.

The responsibility of curtailing the negative effects of globalization does not leave out the government of African countries. There is the need for the governments of African countries to put in place appropriate and workable policies coupled with the strengthening of institutions that will adequately support growth. Creating an enabling environment for businesses to thrive is germane, and doing this may involve issues like giving tax holidays, subsidy to local firms, contract enforcement, protection of property rights, well-functioning bureaucracy, and regulations and good governance. This is important because the quality of government policies to a large extent has a link with how well a particular country can access the benefits of globalization. It is common knowledge that macroeconomic instability occasioned by corruption and associated crisis have undermined the rate of integration of African countries into the global economy.

References

Caglar, G., & Maurice, S. (2007). International migration: Economic development policy. Retrieved July 9, 2007, from http://econ.worldbank.org.

Calvo, S., & Reinhart, C. (1996). Inflow of capital to developing countries in the 1990s. *Journal of Economic Perspectives*, 10(2), pp. 125-128.

Collier, P., & Dollar, D. (2002). Aid allocation and poverty reduction. *European Economic Review*, 26

Collier, P., & Hoeffler, A. (2004). Greed and grievance in civil war. *Oxford Economic Papers*, 56, pp. 563-595.

Collier, P., & Hoeffler, A. (2002). On the incidence of civil war in Africa. *Journal of Conflict Resolution*, 46(1), pp. 13-28.

Collier, P., Hoeffler, A., & Pattillo, C. (2001). Flight capital as portfolio choice. *The World Bank Economic Review*, 15(1), pp. 55-80.

Do, Q., & Iyer, L. (2007a). Poverty, social divisions, and conflict in Nepal. World Bank Policy Research Working Paper 4228.

Do, Q., & Iyer, L. (2007b). Geography, poverty and conflict in Nepal. Harvard Business School, Working Paper No. 07-065.

Fearon, J. and Laitin, D. (2003). Ethnicity, insurgency and civil war. *American Political Science Review*, 97, pp. 75-90.

Miguel, E., Satyanath, S., & Sergenti, E. (2004). Economic shocks and civil conflict: An instrumental variables approach. *Journal of Political Economy*, 112(4), pp. 725-753.

OECD. (1993). *Annual report: Trends in international migration.*

Torres, M., & Anderson, M. (2004). *Fragile states: Defining difficult environment for poverty reduction* (UK-DFID PRDE Working Paper No. 1), London.

UNDP. (2000). Human poverty report: Overcoming human poverty.

World Bank (2006). *World Bank policy research report.*

World Bank. (2002). *Globalization, growth and poverty: Building an inclusive world.* Oxford University Press.

World Bank. (2005). *World Bank development indicators.*

Yang, D., & Martínez, C.A. (2006). Remittances and poverty in migrants' home areas: Evidence from the Philippines. In Ç. Özden & M. Schiff (Eds.), *International migration, remittances, and the brain drain*, pp. 81-121. New York: Palgrave Macmillan.

SECTION IV

CRISIS: HOT SPOTS AND CONTESTATIONS

CHAPTER FOURTEEN

A CROSS-REGIONAL ANALYSIS OF AFRICAN CONFLICTS IN THE AGE OF GLOBALIZATION

AGBO UCHECHUKWU JOHNSON

Within the last two decades, millions of people have been killed in wars in Africa. Millions have died from diseases and epidemics generated by wars. Many have also been raped or had body parts amputated. From the Mano River Union to Darfur to Rwanda, these conflicts have remained endemic. Most often, these conflicts characterized as ethno-religious, identity-driven, and intra-state politics are mainly anchored on competition for shrinking economic spaces in the face of worldwide market economy. We argue that the fallout from the end of the Cold War played a significant role in the crises as industrialized nations are consolidating and monopolizing the wealth of the world in the name of globalization. As a result of the marginalization of Africa, identity has become a tool for competition in order to gain undue advantage by one group over another. This study investigates the identity context and marginality in African conflicts. The paper concludes by stating that identity has been employed as a mobilization tool to access socio-economic and political space by marginalized groups.

Introduction

The last two decades in Africa can be called the age of civil wars. It reached its apogee in the genocide in Rwanda in 1994. Sall (2001, p. 9) observed that "as many as 20 countries in Africa have experienced civil wars or other forms of violent conflict in the past two decades. The Rwandan genocide was an exceptionally tragic episode." Civil war is any armed conflict that involves (a) military action internal to the metropolis; (b) the active participation of the national government; and (c) effective resistance by both sides (Small & Singers, 1982). Civil war as a concept therefore centers on the internality of the war to the territory of a sovereign state and the participation of the government as a combatant (Sambanis, 2004).

While genocide requires that acts be perpetrated against a group with an aggravated criminal intent, namely, that of destroying the group in whole or in part, the degree to which the group was destroyed in whole or in part is not necessary to conclude that genocide has occurred. That one of the acts in the definition was perpetrated with a specific intent suffices. In other words, the intent which is peculiar to the crime of genocide need not clearly be expressed. The intent may be inferred from a certain number of facts such as the general political doctrine which gave rise to the acts possibly covered by the definition, or the repetition of destructive or discriminatory acts. The intent may also be inferred from the perpetration of acts which violate the very foundation of the group, acts which are not in themselves covered in the list in Article 4(2) which are committed as part of the same pattern of conduct (United Nations, 1948).

There is no doubt that the Mano River Union, Darfur, and Rwanda conflicts have benefited from the two definitions. They are civil wars and also genocidal in nature. Although some of the conflicts in Africa have been going on for several decades, the fall of the Berlin Wall (and invariably the ascendance of globalization) signaled a major change in the nature of conflicts and in the attitudes and motivations of the actors involved. The root causes of the violence associated with the conflicts might not always be the same as the mechanisms that sustain a given conflict. It is also important to identify trigger factors and factors of escalation or de-escalation of each conflict (Sall, 2001, p. 10). It was in this direction that Stedman (1991, p. 374) stated that crises and conflicts in Africa, especially at the national and sub-national levels, could be seen to revolve around the four important issues of identity, participation, distribution, and legitimacy. Of the four issues raised, identity has been more pronounced in African conflicts in the age of globalization. Nationally, sub-nationalists have been competing for participation, distribution, and legitimacy. This paper investigates the identity, context, and marginality in Africa's conflict, drawing from the Mano River Union, Darfur, and Rwanda.

Globalization and Identity in African Conflict

Globalization is an ideology of worldwide integration from the nation-state to the global system. However, it is obvious that all the players are in the game but not equal in the game. The weaker ones are being dictated to by the more powerful, and they are confronted by rules, situations, and conditions that are not in their interest (Nnoli, 1998). The other side of globalization is that it is also about the operation of social movements that are not bound by the state or by capital.

Religious (ethnic and other identities) movements, for example, are creating their global spaces and operating in total disregard of the interest of states, capital, and imperialism. The information superhighway is creating possibilities of the invention of meaning and action that are not controlled or predetermined (Ibrahim, 1998, p. 44). To understand these issues, we have to look at the dominant ideology in the world today. Globalization has transported capitalism to every corner of the world. In addition, everywhere it stops, it plants competition. In the developing nations with weak economies, capitalist competition took different forms. One of the forms is identity. Identity has become a tool for competition by one group against another in order to gain undue advantage.

The relationship between identity and competition is interesting because it represents a link between social interactions and individual cognitions, and this can contribute to our understanding of processes that are framing ethnic identification in our society (Lubbers, Molina, & McCarty, 2007). The terms "identity" and "ethnic identity" have a strong political economy dimension. Political actors in their contest for state power use these words. Two theories are commonly used to explain identities, namely: social identity theory (SIT) (Tajfel & Turner, 1986) and identity theory (IT) (Stryker & Serper, 1982). Both theories state that people have repertories of identities (both personal and social) and that the identity that becomes salient varies according to the social environment. SIT alludes to categories of social environment, and IT to social network as environment. The point, as Imobighe (2005) observed, was,

> [T]o satisfy their needs, human beings must of necessity interact with, and in the process make demands on their environment, their society and fellow human beings. In the process of such interactions, conflict could arise due to the incompatibility of the goals they pursue, or incompatibility of the means they are using in pursuing their chosen goals. Often times, it is difficult to establish the precise causes of conflicts largely because conflicts are social phenomena involving human beings and are not necessarily given to a given scientific explanation. (p.1)

Whichever direction the theorizing moves, the issue is that identity problems are more pronounced when competition becomes tougher. The economic realities of capitalism violating human security in its chess of capital and profit gave rise to negative forms of identity politics and their explosive consequences. The binary categories that emerged include Sikh/Hindu and Muslim/Hindu in India; Pathan/Muhaji in Pakistan; Tutsi/Hutu in Rwanda and Burundi; Christian/Muslim, Hausa/Igbo, settler/indigene in Nigeria; Muslim/Christian and Arabs/Blacks in Sudan; Sinhala/Tamil in Sri Lanka; (xenophobia in South Africa and Cote d'Ivoire against foreign economic migrants, and contempt for foreigners/non-Christians by nationalists respectively); and in numerous cases, the nationalists versus the terrorists/rebels. What it does mean seems to be that whatever the issue might be, each group constructs a discursive practice that is antagonistic to that of the other (Ibrahim, 1998, p. 43). As Annan (1997, p. 8) stated,

> [T]his particularistic and exclusionary form of identity politics has intensified in recent years within and among nations—it is responsible for some of the most egregious violations of international humanitarian law and in several instances, of elementary standards humanity—negative forms of identity politics are a potent and potentially explosive force. Great care must be taken to recognize confront and restrain them lest they destroy the potential for peace and progress that the new era holds in store. (p. 8)

The human agency of a given identity may be (or is) a function of the dominant language of politics of the "significant other" (Adesina, 2000). Indeed, the significant other was what turned the Mano River Region, Darfur, and Rwanda into identity conflicts.

The Political Economy of the Mano River Union Conflict

Liberia

The Mano River Union (MRU) was established in 1973 by Liberia, Sierra Leone, and Guinea with the objective of achieving economic integration amongst the member countries. The Union aimed to establish a Customs Union amongst member states, but rather than achieving the aim, it has been bedeviled by intractable conflicts beginning from the early 1990s (Agbu, 2006). The 1990s was a most dramatic period in the history of West African sub-region, with civil wars in Liberia and Sierra Leone leading to the loss of hundreds of thousands of human lives. Several thousand more were mutilated and scattered into refugee camps (Ka, 2001). The Liberian conflict was fertilized by politics of exclusion, which translated to economic empowerment of one group over the other.

Liberia was established in 1822 as refuge for freed American slaves. The country has existed as an independent republic since 1847. The long history of Liberia's independence would have worked in her favor to develop a modern nation-state in Africa, but this failed as the Americo-Liberians (ex-slaves) made themselves the dominant class against the indigenous groups of Liberians. Therefore, power was captured by the Americo-Liberians who enthroned a one-party state. The True Whig Party's monopoly of power permitted it to maintain control over all other forms of organization within the republic. Americo-Liberian political elites recognized the dangers inherent in the exposure of the tribal people (native) to Westernization, industrialization, and urbanization through the open-door policy. They hoped not only to avoid the dangers, but also to put the open-door policy to work in perpetuating the supremacy of the Americo-Liberian ruling class (Liebenow, 1970).

The control of the Americo-Liberian-led True Whig Party in politics, economics, and civil society was total. The President's son, William V.S Tubman Jr., was appointed the President-General of the Labour Congress of Industrial Organization of Liberia. Recruitment of new political leaders came from low-class Americo-Liberian families, and that of the tribal population takes place at a much slower rate. Also, marriage among the Americo-Liberians was as much a political act as it was a social and economic one, which establishes more than a bond between two individuals. It also interrelates as a series of corporate groups to whom the parties to the marriage may turn for political alliance, information regarding changes in the political climate, and access to the spoils available in the state (Liebenow, 1970).

The military establishment was also firmly under the control of the True Whig party. Patronage prevailed over professionalism in the appointment of officers, and the enlisted men within the Liberian Front Force, who were mainly drawn from the tribal people of the country, who were considered as stooges. The enlisted men were held in awe by the people in the interior. Because of the license, the government permitted them to rip off the tribal villages in order to compensate for their low pay and their exclusion from the officers corps. The tribal villages were also excluded from development in order not to expose them to good life and education, which may later threaten the domination of the (ex-slaves) Americo-Liberians.

This socio-economic and political oppression prevailed throughout the era of Presidents Tubman and William Tolbert, which prepared the ground for the Liberian crisis. For more than a century, the country was dominated politically and economically by descendants of freed slaves otherwise referred to as "Americo-Liberians" (Berman & Sams, 2000).

In 1980, Army Master Sergeant, Samuel Doe, led a bold coup d'état in which President William Tolbert was killed. Because of a widespread dislike for the minority Americo-Liberians elite, this coup was warmly welcomed by a large segment of the Liberian population. However, it was not long before Doe increasingly became oppressive and unpopular. He surrounded himself with members of his Krahn ethnic group at the expense of the others. His ruthlessness and incompetence made him feared and reviled (Berman & Sams, 2000). The style of governance which Doe adopted generated an ethnic power struggle to capture state power. It also became glaring for the indigenous ethnic groups outside the Krahn power cult that Doe leadership was not different from the Americo-Liberian hegemony since he cannot even press for the common interest of all or better still, the oppressed indigenous groups under former Americo-Liberian leadership.

This generated ethnic competition for power, which was demonstrated by the 1985 attempted coup which Doe assumed to have been led by Mano and Gio officers. The Armed Forces of Liberia (AFL) killed as many as 3,000 Mano and Gio civilians (Howe, 1997), as deterrence for other ethnic groups to fall in line and accept Doe's oppressive rule. Instead of deterring other groups, however, it created a fertile ground for armed rebellion which Charles Taylor (his former ally) led. Charles Taylor therefore used the Mano and Gio ethnic groups that had been subjected to severe repression to launch a guerrilla war against the Doe regime. The prosecution of the guerilla campaign by the National Patriotic Front of Liberia (NPFL) and other factional groups that emerged to root out Doe, was successful because there was already an army of the deprived and oppressed who were waiting for leadership to be provided.

Sierra Leone

Sierra Leone is located on the southwest coast of Africa. It is sandwiched between Guinea and Liberia. The British colonial administration divided Sierra Leone into two distinct political areas: the colony (26 square miles) and the protectorate (27,540 square miles). One feature of the colony was the existence among its population of a community known as Creoles numbering over 25,000 who settled there as repatriated slaves in the late eighteenth century and the first half of the nineteenth century (Kilson, 1970).

The early contact of the Creoles with Western culture offered them the opportunity to have education, enabled them to attain a measure of wealth and influence in commerce, and colonial civil service. In this connection, the Creole community also gained political ascendance in Sierra Leone in spite of their small numbers (Agbo, 2006).

Sierra Leone is a multi-ethnic country. In terms of its ethnic composition, this is rather varied. In the South and Southeast are mainly the Mendes, Sherbros, Vais, Kissis, and Kono; in the North, the Temmes, Limbas, Kurankos, Mandingos, Susus, and Yalunkas. In the Western area, with the capital Freetown, there are visible intermixes among the various group over the generations, blurring the linguistic cultural distinctions of any one group, especially the Creoles (Boas, 2001, p. 713).

The civil war in Sierra Leone began in March 1991. The Revolutionary United Front (RUF) led by Foday Sankoh was predominantly formed by political exiles to overthrow Joseph Momoh's one party rule and to restore multiparty democracy in the country (Agbo, 2006, p. 33). Zach-Williams (2001) argued that the Sierra Leonean conflict had hardly any ethnic or religious dimension, usually common in many other civil wars. However, the Mende and Creoles and to some extent the Kono are the dominant groups. Zach-Williams (2001) further contended that the traditional structure of antagonism in the war was very complex. Again, it appeared that the use of violence as a means of achieving political and economic power was deeply rooted in the Sierra Leonean political culture.

Kabbah (1999) stated that the intimidation of the general public by successive dictatorial regimes, the high level of literacy, high unemployment, poverty, lack of social programs for the youth, and the failure of the judicial system killed loyalty and any sense of belonging in the state. All these created a deep-seated cynical attitude towards government, politics, politicians, and the public administration apparatus.

What various regimes in Sierra Leone denied the people were freely given to the masses through violence by RUF. Lamenting the situation in Sierra Leone Penfold (1998) contended that

> [T]he tragedy of Sierra Leone is that her people are among the poorest in the world, while the country is among the richest. The reasons for this are entirely man-made. Other countries in the world are poor because of natural disasters, few resources, unfertile territory or bulging populations. Not so in Sierra Leone. God bless this land with an abundance of resources. Just a relatively few people are responsible for the misery and hardship suffered by so many. (p. 1)

When the NPFL and RUF were formed, a lot of jobless young people joined the movement because it promised to give them hope, power, and a new meaning in life. Both movements had a common program and vision. Their magic concept of building power was to reward supporters and build a base of political power (Reno, 1997). Taylor and Sankoh knew that the Mano River States of Liberia and Sierra Leone have failed the people, and worked on their psychology of political economy.

The National Patriotic Front of Liberia (NPFL) and RUF became vehicles for personal enrichment, and the diamond mining areas and other natural resources location became their prime target. Young people with little schooling were particular targets in both movements' recruitment efforts. They were molded quickly not to share a political belief or ideology, but instead to participate in resource extraction, the mining and trading of diamonds, the monitoring and taxing of trade across the border, and the looting of household property (Ewinstein, 2005).

The House Divided in Sudan: Darfur Crisis

The Darfur region forms what is known as western Sudan. The region has a dense population of 5.4 million people of various ethnic groups. Prominent among these ethnic groups are the Zaghawa, who are non-Arab nomads who inhabit the northernmost zone which is part of the Libyan Sahara. The area has other minority ethnic groups. The Eastern and Southern zones of Darfur are populated by Arab sub-clans (the Rezeigat, Habbaniya, Beni, and Halba) who are cattle herders. The central area of the region is mainly inhabited by the Furs from which the region got its name, Darfur: Land of the Fur (Ihekire, 2007, p. 10).

The people of Darfur are mostly farmers and animal herders who depend on the same arid environment for natural resources. The civil war in southern Sudan began in the early 1980s. It was fought between the Sudan People's Liberation Movement (SPLM) and government forces for over 20 years. A comprehensive peace accord between the government of the Sudan and the SPLM was reached, which ended the crisis. The Darfur crisis sprang up to change all the progress made in achieving peace in Sudan. Darfur is home to a complex mix for which the tribe remains a key identifying factor. There are a minimum of 36 main tribes, but some sources cite as many as 90 by including sub-divisions or clans. This mix is composed of two major black groups, Arabs and non-Arabs, the latter known locally as "zurga." Centuries of coexistence and intermarriage have reduced distinctions of the cultural identification or non-identification with the Arab world as members of both groups are dark-skinned. Except for the Zaghawa, who specialize in herding camels, the indigenous black African groups depend on subsistence farming and animal husbandry, while groups of Arab extraction live on camel herding in northern Darfur (Abraham, 2004).

The open rebellion in Darfur, which resulted in many casualties and the displacement of hundreds of thousands of people, erupted in early 2003. This happened when the two loosely allied rebel groups, the SPLM/Army (SPLM/A) and the Justice and Equality Movement (JEM), attacked government military installations. The resolve of the two movements was predicated on the political and economic marginalization of the region. The groups also complained about an alleged 20-year campaign by the government to recruit militias of Arab origin in Darfur and Chad. Further, they pointed out that the militia of Arab extraction known as the "Janjaweed" had been receiving greatly increased government support to clear civilians from areas considered disloyal (Abraham, 2004, p. 523). The Darfur conflict is being debated in the international community whether what the Janjaweed carried out there in the name of civil war constitutes genocide or not. The issue is that the war took a racial dimension and not a religious one, since over 90 percent of Darfur people are Muslims. The matter is that the issues involved in the civil war in Darfur are deep and wide ranging. The conflict has three facets. One is the tension between government-aligned forces and the rebels, while the second one is between government militia and civilians. The third one involves the conflict within the Darfur communities themselves (Abraham, 2004, p. 524).

The conflict in Sudan had its seeds sown by the colonial government because until 1956, the southern part of Sudan was completely cut off from the north until independence. They did not allow people from the North to go to the South, neither did they allow people from the South to go to the North. So with that policy of trying to separate the two parts of the country, they sowed the seeds of this conflict (Editorial: *Daily Trust*, October 29, 2002 p. 2). In this vein Ihekire (2007, p. 11) contends that

> [T]he ongoing conflict in Darfur has its roots in both remote and immediate causes. The remote cause can be traced to independence in 1956, when power was bequeathed to a small Sudanese group of Arab elites in the Khartoum area of the country. This sowed the seeds of racial discrimination, politics of exclusion and exploitation and the institution of politics which undermined the rights and privileges of the people. (p. 11)

After independence also, the national government in power committed a lot of mistakes, as the South was kept a step behind the North especially in economic development, education, and health care (Khalil, 2002). In this manner, the national government led by the Arabs in the North marginalized the Darfur people. To redress this, they formed the Darfur Development Movement in 1966 and started to redress the deep-rooted political and economic marginalization of the region by successive Sudanese governments since independence. The situation was compounded in 1984 when Arab herdsmen were forced by near-famine conditions caused by drought to migrate southward in search of water and pasture for their animals. These migrations were responsible for clashes between the migrating Arab nomads and non-Arab farming communities and have been partly responsible for the violence (Ihekire, 2007, p. 11).

The violent conflict in Darfur is, therefore, the outcome of mismanaged socio-economic and political issues in Sudan by the power elites in the North, especially the Arabs. The key to understanding the escalating ethnic violence in Darfur is also the concept of "Dar" (the tribal homeland). Historically, the indigenous groups and earlier settled Arab migrants each had their own Dar. The major tribes voluntarily agreed to settlement of other groups and accorded them a recognized administrative status (Abraham, 2004).

Politics set in when the economic space for both groups started narrowing down considerably. Yousef Takana listed three traditional, resource-based conflicts between 1968 and 1976, five between 1976 and 1980, and 21 between 1980 and 1998. In these conflicts, he attributed the rapid escalation of violence to the absence of development efforts in the region and the shortcomings of government administration, including its deliberate weakening of the "native administration systems that had for generations helped Darfur's tribes regulate their affairs" (Abraham, 2004).

Instead of the government of the Sudan envisaging the direction these sporadic conflicts were moving, it decided to play ethnic politics. Government manipulation of the ethnic fabric of the region gradually produced an alarming shift in the nature of the conflict, with ethnicity becoming a major mobilizing factor. Traditional forms of conflict gave way to ethnic-engineered conflict. Ethnically driven conflicts that emerged in the late 1980s were sustained and exceptionally fierce, with ethnic solidarity helping to draw in additional parties. Fighters began identifying themselves more broadly as "Arab" or "non-Arab" for the first time in the 1987-1989 conflict between Fur and the Arabs (Abraham, 2004).

The government reaction, therefore, was to contain the non-Arabs with Arab government militia, Janjaweed, instead of addressing the economic issues that gave vent to the rebellion. The scramble for these limited natural resources and non-recognition of the collective grazing rights of the people led to innumerable inter-ethnic conflicts. Added to all these are the problems of political marginalization and lack of socio-economic development, which has been entrenched in the region over the years. These factors escalated the violence, which already existed among the different ethnic groups.

At the root of much of the conflict is competition over fertile land and water, exacerbated by desertification in Northern Sudan and the drought that has affected Darfur on and off since the 1970s. Nomadic groups of all origins from the Northern semi-desert belt have been pushed southward in search of grazing lands and water. The regular presence in Darfur's agriculturally rich central belt of the nomads and their herds has caused friction with farmers. Ecological decline and lack of development in the entire region have combined to impoverish Darfur people of all ethnic backgrounds (Abraham, 2004).

These created the SLA/A, JEM, NMRD and Sudan Federal Democratic Alliance (SFDA) as parties to the conflict in Darfur. The salient feature of this conflict is that it developed

> [A] subaltern identity that also had the potential of being either exclusive or inclusive. The two meanings were not only contradictory but came from the experience of two different insurgencies. The inclusive meaning was more political than racial or even cultural (linguistic). The racial meaning came to take a strong hold in both the counter-insurgency and insurgency in Darfur. The Save Darfur campaign's characterization of the violence as "Arab" against "African" obscured both the fact that the violence was not one-sided and the contest that was critical precisely because it was ultimately about who belonged and who did not in Sudanese politics. The depoliticization, naturalization and ultimately, demonization of the nation "Arab" as against African has the deadliest effect, whether intended or not, of the save Darfur campaign. (Mamdani, 2007, p. 6)

Rwanda: Genocide and Identity

The Rwandan genocide has been contextualized severally but the identity context remains a little-discussed issue. Identity competition revolves around the consideration of ethnicity, culture, race, and religious affinity. These predominate and influence decision making and mobilization for political power in order to allocate resource-based identity (Iwara, 2006). Ethnic identity is only one expression of the myriad of identities exploding in Africa. Identities, ethnicity, religion, clan, caste, etc. are multiple and are located in memories that are deeply entrenched in a rich blend of history and myth (Ibrahim 1998, p. 43). Armed with different theories on race inequality fashionable at that time in nineteenth century Europe, the colonizer deliberately falsified the sociological reality of Burundi and Rwanda by affirming high and loud that the ethnic components in the country were fundamentally different and on this basis it manufactured the Hamitic myth whereby the Mututsi (Tutsi) was superior, came from "outside," was dominant, a conqueror, physically imposing, more intelligent, cunning, profound, and arrogant. In short, a

> [B]lack European made to govern and lord over the others. While the Muhutu (Hutu) was negro and, like all other negroes, a big child and all children are superficial, being light, impulsive, etc. The Bantu farmer had a stocky build and was naturally created to serve blindly and obey the "Tutsi lord." (Grahame et al., 1999, p. 89)

The historical overview shows the complexity of the history of Rwanda which should not in any way be reduced to a conflict between the Hutu and the Tutsi, as history also shows us the essentially planned character of an ethnic antagonism. The role of the Rwandan elite class in that process during the German protectorate and especially during the Belgian colonization and the first and the second republics was primordial. That divisionist policy was, however, favored by contradictions that were remotely based on identity but were, in reality, directly social and political (Gasana et al., 1999). This history of identity authored by colonialism was sustained by the post-independence political elite. As Eteng (2006) observed,

> Ethno-nationalism denotes the crystallization of socio-nationalism consciousness among members of an ethnic group which regards itself both as a distinct, identifiable objective group in-itself, as well as a group for itself a community interest relative to other ethnic groups. An ethnic group manifests such consciousness of communal nationalism, when in the context of nation-wide competitive and conflictual socio-economic, political, and cultural contacts with other ethnic formation, delimits its geographical and cultural pan-ethnic space, organizes and mobilizes members in socio-cultural political associations through which it articulates its ideology and world view, its interest and value preferences, and its strategies for accessing political power and available materials benefits and opportunities, and from which its draws physical, material and human resources when and where necessary. (p. 46)

In Rwanda, shortly after independence, the Hutu-led administration decided that the Hutu/Tutsi identity should be spelled out on identity cards, and by implication, should supersede the national identity. From that moment, being Tutsi meant less rights, more persecution, exile, etc. In 1994, it was the reference to the identity card that determined those who were to be victims of genocide (Ibrahim, 1998). President Habyarimana's regime instituted the violence which led to the April-June 1994 genocide. The regime witnessed a rise in regional and ethnic discrimination through a policy known as regional and ethnic equilibrium. It established a quota for ethnic groupings and regions proportional to their representation in the population as far as access to education and to jobs in public administration and the private sector was concerned. The Hutu from the North, the region which the regime claimed had been historically discriminated against, gave themselves the lion's share (Gasana et al., 1999, p. 158).

The Tutsi (15 percent of the population) saw themselves awarded a quota of 90 percent on this basis and many of them were satisfied with the share due to the cessation of harassment—even if they found themselves excluded from political and senior posts in the administration and in the army. The Hutu from the South and from the central parts of Rwanda were ousted from their dominant positions by the Hutu from the North (Gasana et al., 1999, p. 158).

What this policy entails was that the government of Rwanda officially created two worlds in one state. The inclusive and exclusive, oppressors and oppressed, insiders and outsiders (exiled). This was against the tenet of capitalist globalization which encouraged free competition not on an ethnic basis but on the basis of skills. But those who were favored saw nothing wrong with the system. Under this situation violent conflicts became inevitable. With the opportunity provided by ethnicity for those in power and political positions, ethnic rivalry and conflicts were promoted. In the same vein, Ayoade (2005) stated that

> [A]part from the opportunistic application of ethnicity, it is also the handiest explanation of failure, but never of success. Nobody who succeeds to secure a job (political power) through the manipulation of the ethnic machine never owns up to its contributions. However, unsuccessful candidates are often too quick to attribute failure to ethnicity. It is therefore a paradox that unsuccessful candidates acknowledge efficiency of ethnicity in inter-ethnic competition while successful candidates (insiders) continue to deny its role. (pp. 1-2)

Today, the Tutsi are in power, and they have banned the two words "Tutsi" and "Hutu" from public discourse. But since only one group is in power, nothing has changed, only the identity of the victim. In essence, if the state cannot provide security for members of the community and it cannot provide public goods, other actors cannot but step in (Ibrahim, 1998, p. 44). The process of identification and differentiation is driven by emotion. Identification is aimed at protecting and advancing the interest of the ethnic group thus exhibiting some form of self-preservation and self-perpetuation. Obviously, the condition for ethnicity is that at least two ethnic groups must be contending for resources (Ayoade, 2005). Indeed, the conflict in Rwanda as in most African situations, arose as a result of groups contending for space to appropriate resources.

Identity and Marginality in African Conflict

To begin with, even though conflict is inevitable, violent conflicts can be avoided if those who control state power decentralize governance and allow the resources of the state to be equitable. In this connection, exclusionary politics led to conflict and if not properly managed will further lead to violent conflict. It also follows that most African states are pluralistic, and as such, breed identity consciousness in pursuit of competition for available resources in the state. In the absence of other channels of resource accumulation and distribution, the soul of African states becomes important to the political elites.

The state in Africa is everywhere, and its power appears boundless. There is hardly any aspect of life in which the state does not exercise power and control. That makes the capture of state power singularly important (Ake, 1996, p. 23). In this power contest, the elite struggle for political power by mobilizing regionalism, racism, and ethnicity. The faction that gains power also relies on these to establish hegemony and to perpetuate its controls on state power (Jega, 2000). Historically, identity-based politics have been significant in struggles for political power and control of the state. The state has, historically, shaped and conditioned the arena for competition over scarce societal resources and for expanded accumulation (Jega, 2000). The first issue is the control of political power and its instruments such as the armed forces and the judiciary. The second is the control of economic power and resources. Both are powerful instruments that are used to influence the authoritative allocation of resources to groups and individuals (Ibrahim, 2000).

The groups or individuals that capture state power hardly allow the opportunity to slip out of their hands. As repression increases, there is a marked increase in the rate of the decomposition and/or disarticulation of effective state authority and legitimacy, and the coercive apparatus of the state becomes terroristic in its actions, rather than playing its expected role as the organ state building. This situation provoked the intensification of different forms of identity mobilization and consciousness (ethnic, regional, communal) and even conflagration (Ibrahim, 2000). The most important question, therefore, is the perception and fear of domination by a group (especially those that are not favored by the power equation). Violent ethno-regional conflicts therefore, are usually linked to the perceptions of group domination in the absence of channels for articulating demands (Osaghae, 1992, pp. 219-220). In such situations, therefore, ethnicity becomes a strategy of competition in which ethnic identity is deployed in the campaign for support. In such a campaign, the affected person or group of persons equate personal interests with group interest in such a way that the group sees itself as endangered by the loss of the position. In fact, the most important ingredient of ethnicity is how to successfully transform personal into group interest. In a way, it sounds strange because the individual personifies the group. In reality, however, once the individual achieves his or her goal, the group becomes irrelevant until the need arises again. Such occasions, however, serve to keep the group alive (Ayoade, 2005, p. 2).

Conclusion

In the framework of identity problems in this study, it is clear that without understanding the political economy of conditions in Africa in the age of globalization, we cannot understand the underlying variables in identity conflicts in Africa. From Mano River Union, to Darfur and Rwanda, overwhelming evidence abounds that the conflicts were engineered substantially by the economic conditions in which the people found themselves. They became pawns in the hands of the political elites in power. Instead of governance addressing development issues for common interests, it degenerated into a cult of identity that excluded others. The creation of two worlds in the state along ethnic lines by political leaders exacerbated identity conflict in Africa.

The Mano River Union, Darfur, and Rwanda conflicts were fertilized by the inclusion–exclusion binary. The ethnic characterization and stereotypes of identities that feature in the conflicts are by-products of competition for state resources. The parochial identities that emerged in the conflict became tools of mobilization and appropriation in a plural society.

Pluralism can, however, be turned to advantage when an environment of healthy competition is created. When ethnic groups compete for production rather than consumption, a rational situation of national development is created.

But where each attempts to reap benefits without contributing to the distribution pool, what is distributable will continue to diminish and competition (along identities) will be unhealthy (Ayoade, 2005).

References

Abraham, K. (2004). *Sudan: The politics of war and peace*. Washington, D.C.

Adesina, J.O. (2000). Adjustment and the transformation of labour identity: What's new and does it matter? In A. Jega (Ed.), *Identity transformation and identity politics under structural adjustment in Nigeria*. Upsalla: Elanders Gotab.

Agbo, J.U. (2006, January 12-14). Democracy, the state and conflict management in Africa: A critical assessment of Mano river region. Paper presented at the Zaria Conference on Humanities in Africa in the 21st century: Prospects and Challenges. Ahmadu Bello University, Zaria.

Agbu, O. (2006). *West Africa's trouble spot and the imperative for peace-building*. Dakar: CODESRIA Monograph Series.

Ake, C. (1996). The political question. In O. Oyediran (Ed.), *Governance and development in Nigeria: Essays in honour of professor Billy Dudley*. Ibadan: Agbo Areo Publishers.

Annan, K. (1997). Facing the humanitarian challenge: Towards a culture of prevention. *New Nigeria,* editorial, April 9.

Ayoade, J.A.A. (2005, April 13). Ethnic and national development. Paper presented at the National Seminar on the Role of Attitudes in Nigeria's Development, Abuja, Nigeria.

Barbara, H. (2003). No lessons learned from the Holocaust? Assessing risks in genocide and political mass murder since 1955. *American Political Science Review* 9(1), pp. 2-3.

Berman, E.G., & Sams, K.E. (2000). *Peacekeeping in Africa: Capabilities and culpabilities*. Geneva: UNIDIR.

Boas, M. (2001). Liberia and Sierra Leone dead ringers? The logic of neopatrimonial rule. *Third World Quarterly*, 22(5), pp. 697-723.

Diplomatic Focus. (2002). *Daily Trust*, October 29.

Eteng, I.A. (2006). Ethnicity, ethno-class relations and crisis of Nigerian enduring "national question" and political instability. In D. Oni, S. Gupta, T. Omoniyi, E. Adegbija, & S. Awonusi (Eds.), *Identity politics and social conflicts*. Lagos: CBAAC.

Ewinstein, J.M. (2005). Resources and the informational problem in rebel recruitment. *The Journal of Conflict Resolution*, 49(1), pp. 598-624.

Gasana, E., Butera, J., Byanafashe, D., & Kareikezi, A. (1999). Rwanda. In A. Adedeji (Ed.), *Comprehending and mastering African conflicts: The search for sustainable peace and good governance*. New York and London: Zed Books.

Grahame, J.S., Makoraka, C., Nditije P., & Sindayizeruka, O. (1999). Burundi. In A. Adedeji (Ed.), *Comprehending and mastering Africa conflict*. London: Zed Books.

Howe, H. (1997). Lessons of Liberia: ECOMOG and regional peace keeping. In E. Micheal et al. (Eds.), *Nationalism and ethnic conflicts*. Cambridge: MIT Press. http://pambazuka.Org/en/category/feature/40135.

Ibrahim, J. (1998). Ethnicity and identity in south Asia and Africa. In *Globalization and social science in Africa*. CODESRIA Bulletin. Dakar, Senegal, numbers 3 and 4.

Ibrahim, J. (2000). The transformation ethno-regional identities in Nigeria. In A. Jega (Ed.), *Identity transformation and identity politics under structural adjustment in Nigeria*. Upsalla: Elanders Gotab.

Ihekire, C.R.U. (2007, December 11-13). Conflicts in Sudan. A paper presented to the Association of Senate, Shoora and Equivalent Councils in Africa and the Arab World (ASSECAA), The Committee on Peace and Conflict Resolution, National Assembly, Abuja, Nigeria.

Imobighe, T.A. (2005, January 13). Exploring the conflict management potentials and capacity of the AU peace and security council. Paper presented at the one day National Conference on the Africa Union and the Future of the Africa Continent, Nigerian Institute of International Affairs, Lagos, Nigeria.

Iwara, A.U. (2006). Identity politics, globalization and socio-political engineering in Nigeria. In D.S. Oni, T. Gupta, E. Omoniyi, E. Adegbija, & S. Awonusi (Eds.), *Identity politics and social conflicts*. Lagos: CBAAC.

Jega, A. (2000). The state and identity transformation under structural adjustment in Nigeria. In A. Jega (Ed.), *Identity transformation and identity politics under structural adjustment in Nigeria*. Upsalla: Elanders Gotab.

Ka, S.N. (2001). Sierra Leone history and civil war. *Daily Observer*, January 12.

Kabbah, T.A. (1999). Unity now. *Independent Observer*, 1(3), p. 1.

Khalil, A. (2002). Diplomatic focus. *Daily Trust*, 22(2), p. 2.

Kilson, M. (1970). Sierra Leone. In J.S. Coleman, & C.G. Robert, Jr. (Eds.). *Political parties and national integration in tropical Africa*. Los Angeles: University of California Press.

Liebenow, G. (1970). Liberia. In J. S. Coleman, & C. G. Robert, Jr. (Eds.), *Political parties and national integration in tropical Africa*. Los Angeles: University of California Press.

Lubbers, M.J., Molina, J.L., & McCarty, C. (2007). Personal networks and ethnic identifications: The case of migrants in Spain. *International Sociology*, 22(6), pp. 721-722.

Mamdani, M. (2007). The politics naming: Genocide, civil war, insurgency. Pambazuka. Retrieved June 11, 2009 from,

Nnoli, O. (Ed.). (1998). *Ethnic conflicts in Africa*. Dakar: CODESRIA.

Osaghae, E. (1992). *Managing ethnic conflicts under democratic transition in Africa*. Ibadan CREDU.

Penfold, P. (1998). Corruption and abuse of power. *Weekend Independent Observer*, Freetown, October 17, p. 1.

Reno, W. (1997). War, markets and the configuration of West Africa's weak states. *Comparative Politics*, 29(4), pp. 490-510.

Sall, E. (2001). Conflict in Africa: Post conflict transition, the state and civil society. *News from the Nordic Africa Institute*, p. 9.

Sambanis, N. (2004). What is civil war? Conceptual and empirical complexities. *The Journal of Conflict Resolution*, 48(6), pp. 814-858.

Small, M., & Singer, J.D. (1994). International and civil war data. *Journal of Peace Research*, 45(6), pp. 765-782.

Stedman, S. (1991). Conflict and conflict resolution in Africa: A conceptual framework. In F. Deng & A.B. Zack-Williams (Eds.), *Conflict resolution in Africa*, pp. 374-383. Washington, D.C.: The Brookings Institute.

Stryker, S., & Serper, R.T. (1982). Commitment, identity salience and role behaviour: Theory and research example. In W. Ickes & E. S. Knowles (Eds.), *Personality, roles and social behaviour*, pp. 199-218. New York: Springer Verlag.

Tajfel, H., & Turner, J. C. (1986). The social identity theory. In S. Worchel & W.G. Austip (Eds.), *Psychology of intergroup relations*. Chicago: Nelson-Hall.

United Nations. (1948). Convention on the prevention and punishment of the crime of genocide. New York, 9 December.

Zack-Williams, A.B. (2001). Sierra Leone: The political economy of civil war, 1991-1998. *Third World Quarterly*, 20(1), pp. 143-162.

CHAPTER FIFTEEN

GLOBALIZATION, IDENTITY POLITICS, AND THE ESCALATION OF IFE-MODAKEKE CRISIS

OLAJIDE O. AKANJI

This chapter argues that globalization contributed to the transformation of Ife-Modakeke crisis from a minor intra-ethnic problem of the mid-nineteenth century to an issue of global concern by the twenty-first century. The various dimensions the crisis had assumed in the course of the years, the chapter argues, underscore the centrality of the process of globalization in it. Specifically, the chapter claims that the volatility of the recent phase (1997-2000) of the crisis was due to the availability of foreign munitions and the activities of Diaspora hometown associations. These two factors, the study infers, are engendered by forces of globalization. Hometown associations, such as the Modakeke Progressive International, mobilized support and resources towards the communal crisis in Nigeria. The associations equally provided propaganda space through the Internet and funds for the home communities. This, the chapter contends, facilitated the procurement and use of sophisticated weapons and foreign munitions, which protracted the crisis and worsened its lingering human cost.

Introduction

This chapter analyzes the interface between globalization and the Ife-Modakeke crisis. Globalization is assumed to be capable of engendering socio-economic development; in the same way, it is considered to be central to the problem of violent crises. It is around the question of violent crises, which often manifest at ethnic, sub-ethnic, religious, and political levels, that the issues of human rights and citizenship in Nigeria revolve. The Ife-Modakeke crisis is an age-old problem in Yorubaland of southwestern Nigeria. Several attempts have been made to analyze the problem. This accounts for a substantial body of scholarly works on it. Yet, the fluidity and volatility of the crisis in recent times has continued to demand that new perspectives be used to examine it. This chapter thus seeks to engage what can be called the Ife-Modakeke phenomenon (i.e., the Ife-Modakeke crisis) from the perspective of the role of globalization. By so doing, it attempts to redefine the Modakeke phenomenon as one that is much more expansive and complex than it is often portrayed in the literature.

Apart from the introduction and conclusion, the chapter is divided into three sections. The first section undertakes an historical overview of the pre-1997 phase of the crisis. The second and third sections focus respectively on the analysis of the nature of the recent (1997-2000) phase of the crisis and the role of globalization in it.

Ife-Modakeke Crisis: A Pre-1997 Overview

The crisis involving the Ife and Modakeke people is among the protracted sub-ethnic crises in Nigeria. The crisis dates back to the eighteenth century history of in-and-out migration in Yorubaland. The Yoruba ethnic group, to which the Ife and Modakeke people belong, is an omnibus group comprising of many sub-ethnic identity groups. Among these sub-ethnic groups are the Oyo, Ife, Egba, Egbado, Ijebu, Ijesha, Ekiti, Akoko, Ondo, (Ajayi & Akintoye, 1980, p. 281) and Igbomina (Aleru, 2006). Historical accounts revealed that a dynamic and highly impactful in-and out-migration, occasioned by wars, trade, festivals, marriages, natural disaster, and others, occurred among the various Yoruba sub-ethnic groups in the pre-colonial days. In spite of this fluid inter-group relationship, the numerous sub-ethnic groups maintained their separate and distinctive identity. It is in this context that the genesis of Ife-Modakeke relationship, which initially was cordial, is to be understood.

Generally speaking, the literature on inter-group relations in Yorubaland, and Nigeria in general, concurred that the Modakeke people are the descendants of the people displaced by the collapse and disintegration of the old Oyo Empire in the eighteenth century (Johnson, 1921; Akinjogbin, 1992; Albert, 1999; Akanji; 2008; Oyeniyi, 2006). The displaced people, records showed, were primarily Yoruba people of Oyo descent—i.e., they were of Oyo sub-Yoruba ethnic group. The displaced Oyo people were, however, scattered into other sub-Yoruba ethnic groups, such as the Ife and the Egba (Johnson, 1921, p. 13). This was the genesis of the contact between the Ife and the Modakeke. This suggests that Modakeke people are not Ife (though both are Yoruba); they are traditionally Oyo people (i.e., they belong to the Oyo sub-ethnic group). However, the displaced Oyo people who domiciled at Ife, after years of settlement in Ife territory, adopted the name Modakeke as a mark of identity. Initial relationship between the two groups, records showed, was peaceful, as evidenced by several cases of inter-group marriages.

Communal bitterness, animosity, and hostilities, however, ensued between the two groups (Ife and Modakeke) over a number of issues, including the loss of a settlement called Ibadan (initially considered by the Ife as an outpost of Ife kingdom) by Ife warriors to some displaced Oyo warriors resident in the settlement around the late eighteenth century. The hatred generated by the loss of Ibadan reverberated all through the Ife Kingdom, where many of the displaced Oyo people had settled and were living peacefully. The hatred, with time, snowballed into open armed confrontations. For instance, the two communities engaged in a bitter war twice in 1849. This was followed by a period of relative peace, which lasted till 1880. Between 1881 and 1886, the two communities resumed hostilities against each other. This was during the civil war that engulfed the entire Yorubaland from 1877 to 1893 (Albert, 1999, p. 147; Akanji, 2008, pp. 204-205; Johnson, 1921, p. 232).

It took the intervention of the British imperial power to mediate a truce and bring the war to an end in 1886. An aspect of the truce emphasized the relocation of Modakeke community from Ife territory. Modakeke community was to be relocated to nearby Oyo communities, particularly to Ode-Omu, by 1886. This directive was however ignored. It was not until 1909, after the British occupation and colonization of Yoruba land and other ethnic groups, that the relocation clause in the truce was implemented. Nevertheless, British colonialism in Yorubaland, albeit Nigeria in general, contributed to the continuation and sustenance of the Ife-Modakeke crisis. One aspect of British colonial rule can be identified as having impacted on the crisis.

Principally, the colonial economic policy was instrumental to the re-emergence of Modakeke community back in Ile-Ife between 1919 and 1923, and the consequent resuscitation of the old communal hostility from 1946 onwards. This was because the colonial economic policy was such that emphasized the need for the colonies to be self-supporting. This, however, did not imply that the policy was aimed at building the economic capability of the people; rather, it was geared at removing the financial burden of administration from the colonial government. Part of the economic policy was the introduction of a compulsory tax system. Alongside the tax system was the monetization of the offices of the traditional chiefs. Both the tax system and the monetization of the offices of the traditional rulers were sequel to the adoption of the indirect rule political system of government, which turned traditional rulers/chiefs into stipendiary staff of the colonial government. Given this system, traditional chiefs and rulers were paid monthly income from the tax generated from their domains. This implies that the value of each traditional chief/ruler's monthly income was determined by the number of taxable adults, and by implication, the human population in their domain. This, however, was contrary to ancient custom and practice among the Yoruba people, where traditional rulers/chiefs lived primarily on proceeds from their farms, freewill gifts to the crown, tributes from the vassals, and war booties, among others.

A consequence of this policy was that traditional rulers/chiefs had to devise ways to enhance the taxes generated from their domain; since their monthly incomes depended on it. This, going by archival records, partly explains why the traditional ruler of the Ife kingdom, Ooni Ademiluyi (1910-1930), acceded to the entreaties of the British District Officer in the Ife/Ijesha Division to allow the return to Ile-Ife of Modakeke people, who had earlier been dispersed from Ife kingdom to other Yoruba towns and cities in 1909 (National Archives, 1922a-c; National Archives, 1947). The Modakeke people thus returned to Ile-Ife and Ife territory between 1919 and 1923. The return of the Modakeke people to Ife territory between 1919 and 1923, however, resulted in the resuscitation of the old animosity between them and the Ife, as the relationship between the two groups was again fractured from 1946 onwards over the issues of payment of land rent (*ishakole*) and the right to land ownership (Akanji, 2007, pp. 82-86; Akanji, 2008, p. 207). But, unlike the pre-colonial history of the crisis, which was dominated by armed confrontations, the crisis during the long years of colonial rule (1893-1960) was characterized by periodic protests, litigations, display of collective obstinacy, and agitation for land rights, resource control, and internal self-determination.

The post-colonial phase of the crisis was characterized by the continuation of the above pattern of protestations and contestations, except that it was more of a quest to assert the right to internal self-determination, as inherent in the demands for autonomous local government by the Modakeke. The nature of the crisis between 1960 and early 1990 was therefore different from the colonial and pre-colonial accounts. For example, while 1960 to 1979 could be tagged a period of relative peace between the two communities, since there was no significant incidence of open intransigence (except for the controversies and legal tussles over the interpretation of the Land Use Decree of 1978), 1980 marked the onset and resuscitation of violent clashes and antagonism between them. The relative peace of 1960 to 1979 could be adduced to some factors: the immediate post-independence political turbulence in the country, which, first, culminated in the military intervention of 1966, followed by a period of military rule (1966-1979), and then the civil war (1967-1970).

Conversely, the return of democratic governance in October 1979 resuscitated the age-old crisis. This was due to the politicization and manipulation of issues relating to the two communities by the governing elites. For instance, violence erupted in 1981 between the two groups over the failure of the state government to grant territorial autonomy to Modakeke as allegedly promised by the ruling political party, the Unity Party of Nigeria (UPN) during its electioneering campaigns. The leadership of the ruling party was identified as a contributory factor in the failure of the state government to grant the request of the Modakeke (Ibidapo-Obe, 1981, p. 16). Similarly, the granting of an autonomous local government status to the Modakeke in 1983 by the National Party of Nigeria (NPN)-led state government (the political party that succeeded UPN after the 1983 election) smacked of political manipulation. As a result, the two communities were on edge all through the 1980s to the 1990s.

Ife-Modakeke Crisis, 1997-2000

The fragile relationship between the Ife and Modakeke in the 1980s deteriorated and degenerated into bitter communal war or simply put, a "communal holocaust," between 1997 and 2000 over the issue of autonomous local government status for Modakeke. The genesis of the "holocaust" is traceable to the Modakeke agitation for internal self-determination from Ife dominance, as evident in their demand for autonomous local government status in 1996. It was the politicization and manipulation of this issue that, however, provoked the orgies of violence that occurred from 1997 to 2000. The manipulation and politicization was evident in the way and manner the military government, under General Sani Abacha, and the political elite executed the federal government territorial restructuring (state and local government creation) policy. This is because, on the one hand, while the government conceded to Modakeke's request for an Ife East local government, it tacitly denied their request for the composition and location of the headquarters of the council. The Modakeke had requested and anticipated that the proposed Ife East local government would be headquartered in Modakeke and that this should comprise mainly of Modakeke and its villages.

On the other hand, the most visible evidence of political inconsistency and manipulation was the release, by the federal and state governments, of conflicting locations/names of the headquarters of the Ife East local government council. For instance, while the official press release of December 4, 1996, by the secretary to the federal military government, Alhaji Gidado Idris, and which was carried by all major national newspapers, named Enuwa, an Ife community, as the headquarters of the local government ("FG names new LGs," 1996, p.1). The federal government gazette, signed by the Head of State on November 18, 1996 (but which was released to the public on December 30, 1996) listed Modakeke as the headquarters of the council (FGN, 1996). Similarly, the federal government gazettes of March 2, 1997, and that of December 1, 1998, headquartered the Ife East local government in Modakeke (FGN, 1997; FGN, 1998; Akanji, 2007, p. 230). In the heat of the controversy generated by the conflicting reports, and to dampen tension, the state government named Oke Ogbo, a supposedly neutral community, as the headquarters of the council. This, however, was not accepted by the Modakeke, who considered Oke Ogbo an outpost of Ife. This question of an acceptable council headquarters laid the basis for violent confrontation in 1996, as both communities had good reasons to lay claim to the council headquarters. The situation degenerated and snowballed into full-scale hostilities in 1997, with horrendous human rights implications.

Globalization and the Recent Phase of Ife-Modakeke Crisis: The Nexus

The preceding analysis gives an unmistakable impression of a close connection between globalization and the Ife-Modakeke crisis; as evidenced in the role colonialism played in shaping the crisis in the late nineteenth century through to the mid-twentieth century. This section, however, examines the role of globalization in the recent phase of the crisis. This is sequel to such an assertion by Abiodun Alao, an expert in war and conflict studies, who noted that "the conflict benefitted from the effects of globalization, as both sides were alleged to have set up websites on the Internet to solicit for financial contributions for arms procurement from their respective indigenes in the diaspora" (Alao, 2007, p. 75). In the light of this, the chapter examines the role of diaspora hometown associations and the use of foreign munitions in the crisis.

Role of Hometown Associations in the Diaspora

The salience of civil society social networks, including hometown associations, ethnic, or tribal associations, cannot be overemphasized in the overall working and configuration of modern communities. This is due to the critical roles such networks play in fostering societal peace and mitigate inter-group violence. Ashutosh Varshney (2000), for example, argued that civil society social networks, both intra and inter-ethnic (organized and/or casual) played significant roles, albeit differently, in ethnic conflict. Olaniyi (2003, pp. 341-342) also noted that "social networks extricate and disentangle urban communities from ethnic chauvinism. Indeed, inter-ethnic social networks . . . constitute horizontal ties that halt contentious issues from degenerating into horrendous violence." It is in this context that the roles of hometown associations, established by the indigenes of Ife and Modakeke communities in the United States and the United Kingdom, are examined.

Hometown associations were established by Ife and Modakeke indigenes in the diaspora. Among the notable ones are the Ife Descendants Union, United States, Modakeke Progressive International, United States, and Egbe Omo Ife, United States, and Modekeke Progressive Union, the United Kingdom, with branches in Europe and the United States. A cursory look at these diaspora hometown associations reveals a number of salient facts. First, these associations had relationship with sister associations in Nigeria (or better put, they were branches of the parent associations in Ife and Modakeke communities in Nigeria). Second, these associations had active Internet presence. Third, the associations had organizational structures, which were either formal or informal. Fourth, they were non-profit, non-political organizations in nature. And lastly, their principal objective was the promotion of the socio-economic development of their respective communities in Nigeria. For example, the Ife Descendants Union (IDU) in Houston, in the United States, established in 2000, had as part of its objectives,

> To develop Ile Ife technologically, socially, and economically; . . . preserve the rich and diverse culture of Ile-Ife and improve the image of Ile Ife in the global arena. To serve as a vehicle for the promotion of economic development of Ile

> Ife by encouraging host and others to engage in mutually beneficial activities. (Ife Descendants Union, Houston)

Similarly, the Constitution of the Modakeke Progressive International, United States, declared the objectives of the association to include,

> To protect and develop Modakeke community in the USA. To foster friendship among Modakeke sons and daughters in the United state of America (USA). To play a leading role in the development of our town-Modakeke. (Modakeke Progressive International, Houston)

In the same vein, Egbe Omo Ife, Dallas, United States, decleared its objectives as,

> Our objectives are to promote the interest of Ile Ife indigenes; the ancestral home of all Yoruba in and outside of Nigeria, wherever they may be committed to the economic, cultural, educational and social development of Ile Ife . . . (Egbe Omo Ife, Dallas)

The above suggests that the Ife and Modakeke diaspora hometown associations can be categorized as social networks. But, contrary to Varshney and Olaniyi's theses, these diaspora hometown associations were one of the factors that escalated the recent phase (1997-2000) of the Ife-Modakeke crisis. In one way or the other, these offshore (diaspora) hometown associations played a critical role in the 1997-2000 phase of the crisis. The involvement of these associations added, however, a new twist to the age-long crisis. This is because never before the 1997-2000 incident was there any record of external (offshore) involvement in the crisis.

One significant, though rather negative, contribution of especially the Modakeke Progressive International, United States, was in creating a propaganda space through the Internet. The association maintained an active website through which it disseminated information about the crisis to the whole world. The information on the website, however, reflected the Modakeke version/side of the age-long struggle. Though the association claimed that the website was not a propaganda space, yet, it painted the Ife as the guilty party, the belligerent, and bellicose community. For example, commenting on the issue of *Ishakole* (royalty) (which was one of the issues that underpinned the crisis), the association stated that

> The payment of *Isakole* continued till March 29, 1978 when the Land Use Decree was promulgated by the Obasanjo regime. The Decree vested the ownership of all land in the state. All the citizens have as from that date become tenants of the state. Being habituated to living on other people's sweet, the Ife stoutly resisted the enforcement of the Decree . . . It is against this background that the fierceness and desperation with which Ifes are now pursuing their mad and unlawful ambition can be best appreciated. It is foreign to their culture to apply themselves to tasks capable of securing their tomorrow. It is, however,

> congenital and hereditary in them to seek to appropriate the product of other's labor. What a despicable and dishonorable way of life. (Modakeke Progressive International, Houston)

In another place, the association pointed out that

> We have lived side by side for more than a hundred and sixty years, they have not been able to integrate or assimilate us through natural processes. Now they are desperate to do it by force of arms. . . . They don't have the population. They don't have the material resources. They don't even have the goodwill, fellow-feeling or spirit of comradeship which are fundamental requirements for anyone who wants another person to associate or identify with him. They now resorted to force to realize their dream status of Lords and masters in a feudal enclave in which others will labor for them to live. It is this inhumanity, and indeed bestiality that we are resisting and continue to resist. (Modakeke Progressive International, Houston)

The website was no doubt a propaganda media by the Modakeke community in the diaspora, given the sly and provocative nature of its content. Through this medium, the Modakeke in the diaspora were encouraged and mobilized to support their kith and kin fighting the Ife between 1997 and 2000 in Nigeria. Thus, instead of engendering means to an early and amicable resolution of the crisis, the content of the association's website, which was inflammatory and critical of the Ife political elite, on the one hand, and the generality of Ife community, on the other, escalated it.

Another impact of the diaspora hometown associations in the crisis was in the provision of funds. Ife and Modakeke in the diaspora, through membership in hometown associations in the countries of their residence, contributed financially towards the cause of their communities in Nigeria. This was due to the existence, at the time, of community contributory scheme in both Ife and Modakeke communities in Nigeria. For example, the community contributory scheme was referred to as "*Owo menumo*" (i.e., a secret contribution) in Modakeke (Olawade, 2003), while among the Ife, it was carried out under the guise of development levy (Ajayi, 2003; Modakeke Progressive International, Houston). The scheme was, however, voluntary, but the fact that members of the two communities were convinced of the rightness of their communal cause made them to wholeheartedly participate in it. This scheme provided the means by which the combatants in both communities were fed and equipped, and the mercenaries among them were paid (Akanji, 2007, p. 225). It should, however, be noted that the community contributions scheme may not have been the only source of finance for the conflict. Ajayi (2003), for example, alleged that the Ife funded the crisis from the community contributory scheme and donations of money and materials by Ife indigenes home and abroad. He equally argued that Ife political elite used their positions and connection in government to import, under diplomatic cover, large quantity of arms.

Foreign Munitions

Another issue that escalated the recent phase of the crisis was the availability and use of sophisticated weapons. Foreign munitions, such as machine guns, AK 47 rifles, cartridge rifles, among others, were common features of the crisis between 1997 and 2000. This was attested to by the police commissioner in Osun State, Mr. Sunday Aghedo, who, though he initially denied the use of sophisticated and imported weapons outside of locally made weapons by the combatants, revealed that highly sophisticated weapons were being used (Akanji, 2007, p. 222). Similarly, the arrest in 1997 of a principal actor, from one of the warring communities in the raging crisis with large quantities of sophisticated arms, points to the presence and use of sophisticated foreign munitions in the crisis (Akanji, 2007, p. 222). The pertinent question this raises is: "How did such weapons get into the hands of the combatants?" A quick and simple answer to this is that, in the age of globalization, arms and ammunition do not have bounds any more. They can be easily procured, whenever the means and will to do so are available. But, beyond this, and given the connection the two communities had with the outside world through their hometown associations in the United States and United Kingdom, it is possible to deduce that the Diaspora hometown associations aided the procurement of foreign munitions. In the same vein, it would indeed be a misnomer not to link the availability of foreign, sophisticated munitions to the financial contributions of the Diaspora hometown associations to the "contributory schemes" in the two communities. Another way, however, to answer the question is to consider the allegations that the federal government of Nigeria supplied the Ife community with sophisticated weapons during the crisis. This allegation was based on the fact that some of the weapons seized by Modakeke combatants from Ife combatants bore the insignia of the federal government. This, on an objective note, could have been arms seized from some of the policemen dispatched by the government to the two communities during the crisis.

But, whichever way the issue is considered, the fact that sophisticated weapons were used in the communal crisis shows the centrality of globalization in it. This is because the process of globalization facilitates and enhances mobility and movement of people and materials, including weapons, across borders and space. This no doubt explains why the crisis, particularly between 1997 and 2000, was gruesome and with high human and material cost. The gale of arson that characterized the 1997-2000 crises was unprecedented, given the fact that there had not been any other time when the casualty rate was as high as that of the period. For example, in 1981, a total of about 20 people died; not less than 100 sustained injuries of one form or the other, while properties worth millions of naira were either burnt or looted (Ibidapo-Obe, 1981, p. 29). In 1983, the crisis resulted in the death of 7 people; 21 persons suffered varying degrees of injury, and many valuable properties were vandalized or destroyed (Omolowo, 1983, p. 1). However, though the 1997-2000 incidences lacked any official record of the statistics of the losses that attended it, a newspaper report put it as over 600 deaths and properties worth several millions destroyed (Akanji, 2009, p. 46). Similarly, the fact that the recent phase of the crisis lasted for four unbroken years attests to its unprecedented nature.

Conclusion

The foregoing analysis has attempted to situate the escalation of the Ife-Modakeke crisis within the context of globalization. Globalization, the chapter noted, engendered the formation of diaspora hometown associations by Ife and Modakeke people in the United States and the United Kingdom. These associations provided propaganda space and served as the conduit pipes for external funding of the crisis. In addition, the Diaspora hometown associations engendered the availability and use of sophisticated weapons and other foreign munitions in a crisis that was purely local in nature. These escalated the crisis and intensified the casualty rate. Besides this, British colonial activities among the Yoruba people, which started in 1893 and lasted all through to 1960, equally shaped the crisis. In all, the long drawn, protracted nature of the Ife-Modakeke crisis was no doubt a function of a number of factors, including the process of globalization. This partly explains why the crisis has remained knotty despite several interventions by governments, individuals, groups, and non-governmental bodies.

References

Ajayi, J.F., & Akintoye, S.A. (1980). Yorubaland in the nineteenth century. In O. Ikime (Ed.), *Groundwork of Nigerian history*, pp. 280-302. Ibadan: Heinemann Educational Books Ltd.

Ajayi, I.O. Personal communication, December 12, 2003 (O.O. Akanji, interviewer).

Akanji, O.O. (2007). *Migration, group rights and communal conflicts in Ife-Modakeke, Nigeria.* Unpublished doctoral dissertation, University of Ibadan.

Akanji, O.O. (2008). Identity-based conflicts in Africa: The case of Ife-Modakeke, Nigeria. In B. Zewde (Ed.), *Society, state and identity in African history*, pp. 201-221. Addis Abba: Forum for Social Studies (FSS).

Akanji, O.O. (2009). Group rights and conflicts in Africa: A critical reflection on Ife-Modakeke, Nigeria. *International Journal on Minority and Group Rights*, 16(1). pp. 31-51.

Akinjogbin, I.A. (1992). Ife: The years of travail, 1793-1893. In I. A. Akinjogbin (Ed.), *The cradle of race: Ife from the beginning to 1980*, pp. 148-170. Port Harcourt: Sunray Publishers.

Alao, A. (2007). *Natural resources and conflicts in Africa: The tragedy of endowment.* Rochester, NY: University of Rochester Press.

Albert, I. O. (1999). Ife-Modakeke crisis. In O. Otite & I.O. Albert (Eds.), *Community conflicts in Nigeria: Management, resolution and transformation*, pp. 142-183. Ibadan, Spectrum Books Ltd.

Aleru, J.O. (2006). *Old Oyo and the hinterland.* Ibadan: Textflow Ltd.

Egbe Omo Ife, Dallas. (n.d.). Egbe Omo Ife, Dallas, Texas, USA: The home of the cradlers. Retrieved June 10, 2009 from http://egbeomoifedallas.org.

Federal Government of Nigeria (FGN). (1996, December). *Official gazette* 83(72). (State Creation Transitional Provision) Decree no. 36. Abuja: Government Press.

Federal Government of Nigeria (FGN). (1997, March). *Official gazette* 84(7). (Local Government Basic Constitutional Transitional Provisions) Decree no. 7. Abuja: Government Press.

Federal Government of Nigeria (FGN). (1998, December). *Official gazette* 85(65). (Local Government Basic Constitutional Transitional Provisions) Decree no. 36. Abuja: Government Press.

"FG names new LGs" (1996, December 5). *The Punch*, pp. 1-2, 6.

Ibidapo-Obe, K. (1981) *Report of the judicial commission of inquiry into the communal disturbances in Oranmiyan central local government area.* Ibadan: Government Press.

Ife Descendants Union, Houston. (2000). I.D.U. Ile-Ife: Where the World Begins. Retrieved June 10, 2009, from http://ifedescendants.org.

Johnson, S. (1921). *The history of the Yorubas: From the earliest times to the beginning of the British protectorate.* Lagos: C.M.S Bookshop.

Modakeke Progressive International, Houston. (n.d.). Modakeke and Ife: How it all began. Retrieved June 10, 2009, from http://modakeke.org.

National Archives. (1922a). Re-migration of Modakeke: Correspondence about. In file no. 1929, Vol. 1, Oyo Prof 1. Ibadan.

National Archives. (1922b). Letter from Mr. Birch, the District Officer, Ibadan to the Senior Resident, Oyo Province 25-3-1922. In file no. 1929, Vol. I, Oyo Prof I. Ibadan.

National Archives. (1922c). Letter from W. A. Ross, Senior Resident, Oyo Province to the Secretary, Southern Province, Lagos, 16-10-1922. In file no. 1929, Vol. I, Oyo Prof I. Ibadan.

National Archives. (1947). Letter from the Modakeke Progressive Union, Lagos, to the Senior Resident, Oyo Province, 18 August 1947. In file no. 1929 Vol. II, Oyo Prof. 1, Ibadan.

Olaniyi, R. O. (2003). Ethnic conflict, segregation and civil society: Metropolitan Kano in contemporary time. In F. Laurent & I. O. Albert (Eds.), *Security, crime and segregation in west African cities since the 19th century*, pp. 333-352. Paris and Ibadan: Karthala and IFRA.

Olawade, T. Personal communication, October 25, 2003. (O.O. Akanji, interviewer).

Omolowo, U. (1983, July 21). Press statement by Oyo state commissioner of police. *Daily Times*, p.1

Oyeniyi, A. B. (2006). Problems of inter-group relations in Nigeria: Origin and causes of Ife-Modakeke conflict. In O. Akinwunmi, O. O. Okpeh, Jr., & J. D. Gwamna (Eds.), *Inter-group relations in Nigeria during the 19th and 20th centuries*, pp. 711-735. Makurdi: Aboki Publishers.

Varshney, A. (2000). Ethnic conflict and civil society: India and beyond. Paper presented at the 2000 research training workshop, Centre for Research and Documentation (CRD), Kano, Nigeria.

CHAPTER SIXTEEN

THE 2001 TIV-JUKUN ETHNIC CRISIS: THE "INDIGENE-SETTLER" FACTOR RECONSIDERED

MOSES T. ALUAIGBA

The Tiv-Jukun ethnic conflict remains one of the most prolonged and violent crises in Nigeria. Since its first episode in 1959, it has re-occurred in 1979-1980, 1990-1992 and 2001. The 2001 incident witnessed the worst human casualty and material loss. It has often been accounted for mainly by the "indigene-settler" factor superseded by earlier migration of the Tiv people to the present Taraba State. This chapter, however, argues that there were other core predisposing factors responsible for the 2001 crisis, including the involvement of the federal government in the crisis, politics, poor management of previous occurrences, and the impact of globalization. The chapter recommends constitutional amendment, implementation of the 10-point plan of action, guarantee of citizens' rights, punishment of perpetrators of violence, and compensation of victims as ways of permanently ending the conflict.

Introduction

Polarisation between ethnic groups and resulting conflicts between them as they compete for resources, political and economic power and other goals, has spawned negative consequences of tremendous proportions, of which genocide, ethnic cleansing and civil war are but a few examples (Stremlau, 1999, p. 1).

Nigeria, undoubtedly, is a multi-ethnic state (Bamishaiye, 1976, p. 71). Although there is no agreement among scholars on the exact number of ethnic groups in Nigeria, it is estimated that between 250 and 400 different nationalities make up the political entity presently identified as Nigeria (International IDEA, 2000, p. 90; Agbese, 2001, p. 135; Maduagwu, 2004, p. 36; Leith & Solomon, 2006, p. 4). These various ethnic formations, as diverse in terms of culture and language as they are, however, interacted at different levels in the pre-colonial era through trade, marriages, and even wars. These interactions prevailed until 1861 when the British systematically colonized the territory via suppression and finally created Nigeria through the historical act of the amalgamation in 1914. This creation was later to be described by Nigeria's foremost nationalists Obafemi Awolowo and Ahmadu Bello as "a mere geographical expression" and "the mistake of 1914" respectively (Maduagwu, 2004, p. 37). These statements right from the outset crystallized the burning problems inherent in the divergent emerging Nigerian state, with ethnicity being one of such core problems.

Most writers attribute the negative traits of ethnicity in Nigeria to the colonial experience which the country went through (Philips, 1984, pp. 153-155; Kankara, 1998, pp. 2-11; Odunuga, 1999, p. 221; International IDEA, 2000, p. 144; Leith & Solomon, 2006, p. 4). For example, Leith and Solomon argue that

> [a]s a result of boundary demarcation during the colonial period, Nigeria as political entity was created in 1914—a multi-ethnic nation consisting of more than 200 ethnic groups speaking over 250 languages. . . . Although these groups interacted with one another before the colonial era, they were not primordial societies, and the artificiality of the British-drawn boundaries contributed to the social construction of these ethnic groups, so much so that the creation of these 'tribes' [is] closely linked to the era of colonial rule. (2006, p. 4)

The International IDEA (2000) further underscores the point raised by Leith and Solomon (2006) above to the effect that it is on the basis of the institution of ethnicity in Nigeria by the British colonialist that the Nigerian ruling elite has capitalized on the circumstance to manipulate ethnicity in an attempt to preserve their interest, with ethnic conflicts as the resultant centrifugal consequences in the country. Indeed,

> The Nigerian political elite who inherited the powers of the colonialists at independence in 1960, continued this manipulation of ethnic differences for their own selfish interests. In the process . . ., the urban-based ethnicity of the past has now been reinforced by ethnic mobilization in rural areas, which pits ethnic communities against one another in an attempt to claim entitlements on ethnic basis. The Hausa-Kataf, Jukun-Tiv, Kuteb-Jukun, Hausa-Mambilla and Ogoni-Andoni blood-lettings are concrete examples of this. (International IDEA, 2000, p. 93)

The deduction arising from the foregoing is that at independence, Nigeria inherited a culture of ethnicity that produced an unending cycle of ethnic conflicts. These conflicts have not only been "a decisive factor in the country's political turbulence and instability" (Suberu, 1996, p. 12), they have impeded the process of national integration (Benjamin, 2002, p. 7) as well as "put a damper on further political and economic development" (Leith & Solomon, 2006, p. 4).

The Tiv-Jukun ethnic conflict is one of the many conflicts in Nigeria, but apparently is the most prolonged ethnic conflict predating even the birth of modern Nigeria (Alubo, 2006, p. 89). The uniqueness of the conflict stems from the fact that it remains "the most violent and well organized ever witnessed outside the Nigerian civil war" (Best, 1999, p. 86). The terrifying aspect of the Tiv-Jukun conflict is its propensity to unleash heavy human casualty and material loss on the two ethnic groups whenever the conflict occurs. Beginning in 1959, the Tiv-Jukun standoff has taken place severally in 1979, then in 1987, 1990, and 2001 (Bur, 2002, p. 10).

The 2001 Tiv-Jukun conflict stands out clearly as the most devastating episode of the crisis compared to its previous incidents. This is based on the carnage and material loss occasioned by the crisis (Okocha, 2001, p. 5) that attracted the attention of the international community. Various factors have been used in explaining the 2001 crisis, principal among which is the "indigene-settler" issue. What this chapter has attempted to do is to employ other equally very fundamental factors in explaining the 2001 Tiv-Jukun ethnic tragedy. Some other factors considered include the role played by politics in the conflict, poor management of previous occurrences, the involvement of government in the 2001 version of the conflict, as well as the impact of globalization, which created an enabling environment that fuelled the crisis.

Defining Ethnic Conflict

Ethnic conflict has been defined by Rosel (1995, p. 123) as "a conflict which result from real or perceived ethnic differences, which in their turn are enhanced, re-interpreted and politicized with the help of a new and dangerous doctrine—ethnic nationalism." Rosel further points out that there is always a tendency for such a conflict to degenerate into "an armed conflict . . . to the point where both parties reach the conviction that their opponent seeks their own total destruction and where—in a posture of defence—each will try to annihilate the adversary first" (1995, p. 124).

In an attempt to conceptualize ethnic conflict, Bangura (1995, p. 6) observes that "many ethnic conflicts erupt spontaneously, most need political entrepreneurs or mobilisers, a network of organizations, and a discourse or set of principles or ideas to activate them." He concludes that any time a conflict erupts, "there are usually two or more organizations competing, sometimes violently, for the loyalty of an ethnic group" (1995, p. 6). Cohen (cited in Leith

& Solomon, 2006, p. 3) conceives ethnic conflict as a situation that is determined by what he calls "self/other relationship." In this kind of relationship, there is subjective perception of identities anchored on self—interest that the groups involved seek to protect and satisfy at all costs; this provides an igniting force to propel a conflict.

No matter the notion attached to ethnic conflict, what is clear and must be borne in mind is that ethnic conflict is characterized by an instance in which two or more contending ethnic groups, on the basis of their ethnic differences and scarce resources, are entangled in a clash which could be violent in a bid to outwit each other in the course of preserving the interest of either of the groups involved. This conflictual relation in most cases results in catastrophe in terms of human and material losses.

Antecedents of the Tiv-Jukun Ethnic Conflict

There is no consensus on the genesis of the confrontation between the Tiv and Jukun ethnic groups. According to Torwel (2005, p. 5), conflicts of violent dimension between the Tiv and Jukun have occurred since 1953. To Bur (2002, p. 10), the first occurrence of the clash between the two groups started in 1959. On the contrary, Anifowose (2003, p. 52) states that violent conflict involving the Tiv and Jukun people was first recorded in 1977 in the Wukari area of the then Gongola State. However, what these divergent accounts indicate is that there is a long standing feud between the Tiv and Jukun ethnic nationalities.

Prior to the era of colonialism, the Tiv and Jukun groups enjoyed a harmonious inter-ethnic relationship (Alubo, 2006, p. 97; Avav, 2002, p. 14). The two groups lived with other ethnic groups such as Chamba, Kuteb, Ichen, Hausa, Fulani, etc. in what was later carved out as Wukari Federation. The coming of the British colonialists changed this cordiality between the Tiv and Jukun because the nature of colonial policy in the area favored the Jukun more than the Tiv (Anifowose, 2003, p. 50; Alubo, 2006, p. 96). This was more so given that the Jukuns were more receptive to the British colonizers while the Tivs vehemently resisted the British conquerors. Similarly, the Jukun had established formal political structure amenable to the British Indirect Rule system unlike the Tiv whose republican nature precluded any centralized government. The British therefore brought the Tiv and other surrounding ethnic groups under the authority of the Aku Uka perceived to be superior to other groups (Hagher, 2002, p. 10); naturally this planted a seed of discord among the Tiv and Jukun who were hitherto friends.

Anthropological records (see Asuni, 1999; Best et al., 1999) indicate that both the Tiv and Jukun migrated to Wukari in the present-day Taraba State of Nigeria. The peak of these migrations is shrouded in the criss-cross movement of various ethnic groups across the entire African continent in the eighteenth century. These movements underscore the dislocation of many ethnic groups in Africa who happened to have migrated in part or in total to other parts of the continent, thus emerging as either kingdoms or empires with varying histories of origin.

According to Denga (cited in Alubo, 2006, p. 89), the Tiv, a Bantu offspring, migrated from Central Africa via the Cameroons to their present abode in the Benue Valley in the eighteenth century. The migration of the Tiv who are traditionally farmers to this area was triggered by the search for fertile farmlands and expansion in their population. According to the Tiv account of the conflict, they first settled in "Waka" which was later renamed by the Jukun as Wukari (Best et al., 1999, p. 88); at the time of their settlement, the Jukun were still in the site of their ancient Kwararafa Kingdom, eighty-three kilometers north of Wukari. The Jukun only came to "Waka" on invitation by the already settled Tiv group and subsequently renamed and took control of the town. This claim of indigeneship of Wukari by the Tiv coupled with other accompanying emerging factors accounted for the recent violent conflicts between these two minority ethnic nationalities in the past four decades.

The Jukun, on the other hand, migrated from Yemen along with the Kanuri who settled in Lake Chad while the Jukun settled in the Benue Valley where they established the Kwararafa Kingdom that flourished up to the nineteenth century (Asuni, 1999, p. 2; Best et al., 1999, p. 87; Anifowose, 2003, p. 50). This Jukun kingdom thrived until it collapsed due to the activities of the invading Fulani Jihadists. With this fall, the Jukun shifted base to Peju and again from there, the capital was finally set up in 1840 in Wukari. The Jukun claimed that they were the original indigenes of Wukari while the Tiv were the settlers or newcomers because the Jukun out of generosity gave a portion of the land to the early Tiv immigrants to settle. However, due to the rapidly growing population of the Tiv, they started expanding their settlements to other Jukun towns and areas. In doing this, the Tiv renamed the new settlements using Tiv names. For example, "Tsokundi was renamed as Ayu, Chachanji changed to Peva, Rafin Kado to Genyi, Bako to Abako, Kante to Santyo, Wukari to Waka" (Best et al., 1999, p. 107). This created fear of domination among the Jukun; hence they embarked on the "rejukunization" process, a plan of re-conquest that has made bloody conflicts inevitable.

The 2001 Version of the Crisis

The 2001 Tiv-Jukun conflict was a replica of preceding episodes. In short, it has been seen as an offshoot of past contestations between the two groups over issues as land, acceptance of Tiv as indigenes of Taraba State, inclusion of the Tiv in Wukari Traditional Council, fears of domination over Jukun by Tiv and the issue of marginalization (Alubo, 2006, pp. 109-110). What set the 2001 crisis aside distinctively is the scale of brutality, human rights abuse, and high human casualty rate as well as the manner the disaster was ignored by the federal government under the then President Obasanjo (Human Rights Watch, 2002a).

The incident that immediately triggered the 2001 conflict began on June 13, 2001, when a Tiv farmer and Fulani herdsman engaged each other at Tse Ikyambe, a village co-habited by the Tiv, Fulani, Hausa, Etulo, and Sayawa ethnic nationalities. According to Hagher (2002),

> On that fateful day, . . . [a] Fulani herdsman, trespassed into the farm of Mr. Iortim Umande, a Tiv farmer. When challenged by the farmer, the Fulani herdsman drew his dagger and stabbed the Tiv farmer to death. This led to reprisals by the Tiv, and subsequently the Jukun took over and wage war of ethnic cleansing on the Tiv of Taraba State. (2002, p. 26)

There are conflicting chronologies of how the crisis unfolded based on self-exonerative accounts by both the Tiv and Jukun people; these varied accounts in slight details highlight the day-to-day narrative of all the events during the period of the inferno. Table 16.1 is the tabulated Tiv-Jukun side-by-side account of the crisis in 2001:

Table 16.1: Chronology of Events in the 2001 Tiv-Jukun Conflict in Taraba State

Date of Occurrence	Events	
	Tiv Account	Jukun Account
6/13/2001	Fulani herd trespassed into a Tiv man's farm. The incidence resulted in a fight and there was loss of life.	Fulani herd trespassed into a Tiv man's farm. The incidence resulted in some loss of life.
6/21/2001	———	Aku Uka called for a meeting to calm the tension between Tiv/Fulani.
7/2/2001	———	Fulani attacked Tor Danusa village, Donga Local Government Area (LGA).
7/3/2001	———	A staff of PH Construction Company was shot (Donga LGA) by Tiv.
7/6/2001	———	Meeting on Tiv-Fulani crisis.
8/13/2001	———	One Fulani man was killed, another injured by Tiv at cattle market, Katsina- Ala road, Wukari.
9/5/2001	Ikyaior was attacked and 14 people (12 Tiv, 2 Igbo) were killed.	Chonku village was attacked by the Tiv.
9/6/2001	Jootar was attacked and three people killed.	———
9/7/2001	Gboogboo was attacked and two people were killed.	———

Date of Occurrence	Events Tiv Account	Jukun Account
9/8/2001	Toho Abanyi village was attacked and two people were killed.	Three vehicles were burnt at Jootar along with passengers.
9/9/2001	_____	Governor Akume visited Jootar and ordered the military men to leave the area.
9/12/2001	_____	Jandekyura (Tiv village) was attacked by the Fulanis.
9/12/2001	_____	The Police reported that Tiv killed one of their officers at Jandekyura.
9/13/2001	Jandekyura was attacked.	Sondi was attacked by Tiv.
9/14/2001	Gur village near Jootar was attacked.	Fyayi village was destroyed by Tiv.
9/15/2001	Jukun attacked Vaase and a lunatic was killed.	Vaase village was attacked by Fulani.
9/17/2001	_____	Rafin Kada was attacked by Tiv.
9/20/2001	_____	Arufu, Ikwe, and Akwana were reported to have been burnt down by the Tiv.
9/25/2001	_____	Chinkai was attacked by Tiv, 1 killed, four injured.
9/26/2001	_____	Chinkai was attacked again by the Tiv.
10/1/2001	_____	Rafin Kada was attacked a second time by the Tiv, two boys killed, three injured, operation lasted for 4 hours and 25 minutes.
10/4/2001	_____	Dooshima village was attacked, and road block mounted by the Tiv was dismantled by a combined Fulani/Jukun/Hausa youths, Ibi LGA.
10/6/2001	_____	Abako (Tiv/Jukun village, predominantly Tiv) and the road block mounted by the Tiv dismantled.
10/7/2001	Abako attacked.	_____
10/10/2001	Nineteen soldiers were captured at Vaase by Tiv militia group. The soldiers were moved to Zaki-Biam and killed.	_____
10/13/2001	Dan Anacha in Gassol LGA was attacked.	Dan Anacha was attacked by the Jukun militia.
10/19/2001	Soldiers on a reprisal attack invaded Kyado.	_____

Date of Occurrence	Events Tiv Account	Jukun Account
10/22/2001	Soldiers attacked defenseless civilians at Gbeji and killed over 150 civilians.	———
10/23/2001	Zaki-Biam was razed, properties were destroyed, over 100 people killed, thousands fled to the hinterland.	———
11/15/2001	———	Nigeria Red Cross Society distributed relief materials to refugees in Wukari.
11/18/2001	———	One Fulani man was killed at Asaa (Jukun village) by the Tiv.
11/23/2001	———	One Mallam Wuryeba Adunga Yerima Ason was killed by the Tiv and his body dumped in a well by the Tiv.
12/5/2001	———	300 cows belonging to the Fulani were killed by the Tiv at Tsokundi.
12/9/2001	———	Three Jukuns were shot at Chinkai by the Tiv.
12/10/2001	———	One Fulani and one Jukun were shot at Nwuben by the Tiv.
12/17/2001	———	Chinkai was attacked by the Tiv, two people killed, four badly injured.
12/29/2001	———	Arewa Consultative Forum visited Wukari for fact finding.
1/6/2002	———	A woman was killed at Rafin Kada by the Tiv.
1/20/2002	———	Four people were shot at Bantage and a farm was set ablaze by the Tiv.
1/21//2002	———	A woman was hurt at Sondi by the Tiv.
2/12/2002	———	Five Jukun women were kidnapped by the Tiv.
2/12/2002	———	Two vehicles were bent at Tsokundi by the Tiv.
2/15/2002	———	Seven cows rustled at Chinkai by the Tiv.
2/16/2002	———	Thirty cows taken away from Yantukpa by the Tiv to Benue State, one pickup van was seized at Sondi by the Tiv militia
2/18/2002	———	A Fulani man killed and beheaded at Rafin Kada road by the Tiv.
3/7/2002	Refugees from Ibi LGA were repatriated back to Ibi.	———
3/14/2002	Refugees from Gassol LGA were repatriated.	———

Date of Occurrence	Events: Tiv Account	Events: Jukun Account
3/21/2002	Refugees from Wukari LGA were repatriated.	______
3/16/2002	______	Two Fulanis killed at Tsokundi road and over 40 cows killed too, seven herds of cattle were taken to Benue State. Also, a car was shot at Rafin Kada road by the Tiv.
3/26/2002	______	An Achaba (motorcycle) boy was killed by Tiv at Ikyaior village after conveying the Tiv home, the motorcycle was taken away.
3/30/2002	______	A Tiv militia in army uniform was caught at Gidan Idi.

Source: Compiled from Alubo, O. (2006). *Nigeria: Ethnic Conflicts and Citizenship Crises in the Central Region* (pp. 116-119). Ibadan: PEFS.

The pattern of perpetuating violence during the conflict was swift. Both sides made use of well-armed youth militia as well as retired military officers. According to Alubo, the violence that was unleashed on either side was characterized by:

- Burning of houses;
- Killings of the enemy;
- Stop and search operations through which the enemy is pulled from passing vehicles and summarily executed;
- Looting of property, including food and other farm produce;
- Stealing of domestic animals and/or their slaughter by militia groups;
- Molestation of women; and,
- Mass exodus to safety (2006, pp. 115-116).

The precise number of casualties from both the Tiv and Jukun sides arising from the 2001 crisis has not been ascertained compared to the 1990–1992 occurrences in which up to 6,000 people were reported killed (ISHR West African Committee, 2001, p. 6). Although as documented by ISHR West African Committee (2001, p. 8), 500 unarmed civilians were killed when the troops from the 23rd Armoured Brigade from Takum on October 23, 2001, raided Zaki-Biam and the villages of Vaase, Gbeji, Anyiin, and Jootar. This number of the dead excludes those killed by the Tiv and Jukun militants in various warring locations in Taraba and some parts of Benue States. Another source (see Alubo, 2006, p. 125) has it on record that 15 villages were raided by the army. With regard to refugees, the *Environment and Development Challenges News* (n.d., 1) account indicates that over 50,000 people were internally displaced by the conflict. The bottom line of all these records is that the conflict was a monumental calamity as both sides in the crisis suffered heavy human and material losses as well as social dislocation.

Factors Responsible for the 2001 Episode

A myriad of factors collaborated in exacerbating the 2001 Tiv-Jukun conflict. These factors are, however, not in themselves adequate explanatory frameworks for full analysis of the crises because of their attachment to deep-rooted controversies between the Tiv and Jukun in the past four decades during which the conflict has been witnessed at different periods. Some of these factors have been sketched below:

"Indigene-Settler" Factor

The "indigene-settler" factor is often explained as being central to the Tiv-Jukun conflict (ISHR West African Committee, 2001, p. 6; Avav, 2002, p. 27; Anifowose, 2003, p. 54; Alubo, 2006, p. 92). However, the "indigene-settler" issue alone is not sufficient enough in explicating the 2001 episode. The "indigene-settler" factor has become a bone of contention because, as it has been explained,

> Since the creation of states about two decades ago other ethnic groups especially in Taraba and Nasarawa States have viewed the Tiv as a threat. Consequently, they have been unwilling to share political power or natural resources with the Tiv whom they now firmly refer to as "settlers" "immigrants" or "non-indigenous." (ISHR West African Committee, 2001, p. 6)

It is in an attempt by the Jukun to re-claim their land from the non-indigenes the Tiv, and whenever a slight opportunity presents itself (as in 2001), it is capitalized upon to cause atrocious conflict.

Political Consideration

Politics played a major role in fueling the 2001 episode of the Tiv-Jukun conflict. According to Torwel (2005, p. 4), ". . . almost all the violent conflicts involving Tivs and Jukuns occurred within political electioneering periods since 1953." The introduction of party politics in Nigeria has always pitched the Jukuns against the Tivs, and the two have always belonged to different political parties since 1954 (Asuni, 1999, p. 2). And due to the numerical strength of the Tiv, candidates supported by the Tiv or of the Tiv origin have always won elections against their Jukun counterparts. For example, in the 1956 Federal Elections into the National Assembly, the Nigeria Peoples Congress (NPC) Jukun candidate lost to the United Middle Belt Congress (UMBC) Tiv candidate.

In 1983, when Alhaji Bamanga Tukur won the governorship election in the former Gongola State, he attributed the victory to the support given to him by the Tiv and went ahead to appoint a Tiv man, Dr. Samuel Tor Agbidye, as commissioner to the chagrin and surprise of the Jukuns (Best et al., 1999, p. 95). In the 1987 local government elections in Wukari local government, the Tivs supported Alhaji Danladi Shehu, a Hausa man, to defeat the Jukun candidate. Subsequently, a Tiv man was appointed deputy chairman of the local government. Former governor of Taraba State, Jolly Nyame also appointed Hon. David Orbee Uchiv as his special adviser. The rising political influence of the Tiv in Taraba politics has deepened Jukuns' fear of political domination by the Tiv. In 2001, there was therefore a ". . . planned and deliberate effort to exterminate [the Tiv] people from Taraba" (Hagher, 2002, p. 197); this bred enough velocity needed by the crisis to produce the kind of inferno witnessed in 2001.

Poor Management of Previous and the 2001 Episodes

The lackluster attitude of government in handling past Tiv-Jukun crises encouraged perpetrators of the atrocities during the 2001 case knowing fully well that they would go unpunished in the long run. Government had never been firm in punishing culprits in the past; similarly the non-compensation and rehabilitation of victims of earlier crises leaves the wounds inflicted on them unhealed. For example, the 10-point agreement reached between the federal government and Taraba state government meant to ensure peace after the 1990–1993 crisis has never been implemented (Anifowose, 2003, p. 54), the Tivs are still calling for its execution. As for the victims of the 2001 conflict, it was on July 5, 2007 (six years after the crisis), that an Enugu High Court headed by Justice Lewis Allagoa ordered the federal government to pay ₦41.8 billion as compensation to the victims of the Zaki-Biam massacre (Anza, 2007, p. 46). Also, in the case of the 2001 crisis, the partial "poor and insufficient handling of the situation . . . [and] the Nigerian military involvement on the side of the Jukun" (Torwel, 2005, p. 2) made the other party to the conflict, the Tiv, to ensure ". . . the effective and decisive defence of [their] territories and people. . ." (Hagher, 2002, p. 195). This exceedingly fueled the crisis.

Involvement of Government

The involvement of the federal government in the 2001 conflict is well documented (ISHR West African Committee, 2001; Human Rights Watch, 2002a; Human Rights Watch, 2002b; Human Rights Watch, 2002c; Torwel, 2005; Environmental & Development Challenges, not dated). On October 10, 2001, 19 soldiers were captured at Vaase by Tiv militia and subsequently killed in Zaki-

Biam. In an attempt to trace the killers of the 19 slain soldiers, on October 23, 2001, soldiers from the 23rd Armoured Brigade of the Nigerian army based in Yola, Adamawa, invaded the four villages of Anyiin, Zaki-Biam, Gbeji, and Tse-Adoor utilizing heavy weapons such as tanks, armored personnel carriers, and rocket-propelled grenade launchers. According to reports, the "soldiers were under specific orders from the government of President Obasanjo and his Defence Minister General Yakubu Danjuma . . ." (ISHR West African Committee, 2001, p. 2) to carry out the operation. This overt intervention of government-controlled army in the conflict against one side to the crisis, the Tiv, regrettably led to the Tivs' suffering heavy casualties. This no doubt exacerbated the crisis.

Impact of Globalization

Many analysts (for example, see Cohen, 2001, p. 75; Holton, 2000, p. 140; Snow, 2008, p. 147; UNDP Report, 2001, p. 345; Woods, 2001, p. 389) of globalization have highlighted their objection to the phenomenon because of its excruciating consequences on developing societies. Apart from the economic distortion in developing countries occasioned by the dismantling of national economic boundaries thus accelerating interconnectedness and giving way to free flow of capital, products, and services, globalization has produced variegated forms of insecurity in the world today. Insecurity of individuals and their communities is compromised because of the advantage the unrestricted illegal trade in arms, drugs, and women the globalized economy offers. This pesky development ". . . is contributing to the violence and crime that threatens neighbourhoods around the world" (UNDP Report, 2001, p. 345). This scenario of violence and criminality is typified by the carnage that transpired during the 2001 Tiv-Jukun conflict. Due to the free flow of weapons into Nigeria from neighboring countries, both the Tiv and Jukun groups accessed these arms with ease. The willful use of these weapons during the crisis gave it the attribute as one of the most violent inter-group conflicts Nigeria has ever experienced since independence.

Recommendations

The resolution of conflicts involving ethnic groups is a herculean task that is odious. However, in the case of the last Tiv-Jukun conflict that occurred in 2001, the following recommendations are made:

a) Constitutional amendment: The constitutional review proposed by the National Assembly and billed to take off in 2008 must ensure that Chapter III, Sections 25, 26, and 27 of the 1999 Constitution which deals with citizenship must be amended to be unambiguous on the issues of citizenship and indigeneship in Nigeria. The constitution must state clearly the fact that every Nigerian is a citizen in whatever part of the country he/she lives irrespective of place of birth and must be accorded full rights as an indigene of the place. This will surely reduce, if not eradicate, the prevalence of ethnic conflicts (such as the 2001 Tiv-Jukun conflict) based on the dichotomy between who is an indigene and who is a non-indigene among Nigerians.

b) Implementation of the 10-point plan of action: After the series of crises between the Tiv and Jukun from 1990 to 1993, the federal government intervened to adjudicate. A 10-point plan of action was the major output of the intervention and in it, the governments of Taraba and Benue States were to provide equal opportunities in employment to all indigenes devoid of ethnic or indigeneship consideration. This plan has not been implemented by these states. If it is implemented, it will serve as a long-term, if not a permanent solution to the long-standing dispute between Tiv and Jukun inhabitants of these states by diluting sentiments amongst the two groups.
c) Guarantee of citizens' rights: The two states should guarantee citizenship rights to all their inhabitants. The federal government must compel the two states of Taraba and Benue involved in the conflict to guarantee citizenship rights to all their inhabitants. Rights that relate to life, property, jobs, etc. should be given to all Jukun residents in Benue just as the same should be given to Tivs living in Taraba.
d) Punishment of perpetrators: Perpetrators of violence during the 2001 conflict must be identified and prosecuted through the law courts, and if found guilty must be punished accordingly. This will serve as a deterrent to others with a similar intention to foment trouble in the future to refrain from doing so.
e) Compensation: The federal government should devise a mechanism of compensating all the victims of the 2001 crisis. This will ameliorate the psychological trauma such surviving victims experienced, and it will tremendously foster faster reconciliation among the communities that were involved in the conflict.

Conclusion

Conflict is undoubtedly inevitable especially in human relations. The ability of a given society to develop mechanism(s) of settling conflicts whenever they erupt among groups that make up such a society without recourse to violence determines how matured that society is. It is also a measure of the level of advancement the society has reached in overcoming the excesses of primordial sentiments in its fold. Nigeria has contended with the problem of ethnic conflicts since independence without any headway in sight towards permanently eliminating the dreadful social ill.

The Tiv-Jukun conflict with particular reference to the 2001 episode discussed in this chapter is one of the conflicts in Nigeria whose solution still remains elusive. Already tens of thousands of lives have been lost in the conflict as well as properties valued at millions of naira. Even those who survived the crisis have either been dislocated or totally disorganized in life. Inter-communal relations have gone sour and have been poisoned with hatred. It is difficult for development to be nursed both at the individual and societal levels under this kind of scenario. Government, in tune with best practices around the world, must always be impartial in handling conflicts of this nature. For the Tiv and Jukun people, they must recognize that time has come for them to permanently sheathe their swords and to know that better, modern mechanisms of resolving conflicts through negotiation and consensus building abound and must be utilized in an age when such problems benefit from new skills and approaches.

References

Agbese, P.O. (2001). Managing ethnic relations in a heterogeneous society: The case of Nigeria. In J.M. Mbaku, P.O. Agbese, and M.S. Kimenyi (Eds.), *Ethnicity and governance in the third world*, pp. 125-48. Aldershot, England: Ashgate.

Alubo, O. (2006). *Nigeria: Ethnic conflicts and citizenship crises in the central region.* Ibadan: Programme on Ethnic and Federal Studies.

Anifowose, R. (2003). The changing nature of ethnic conflicts: Reflections on the Tiv-Jukun situation. In T. Babawale (Ed.), *Urban violence, ethnic militias and the challenge of democratic consolidation in Nigeria*, pp. 48–56. Lagos: Malthouse Press.

Anza, P. (2007). ₦41.8 billion compensation for victims of Zaki-Biam massacre. In *Newswatch*, 46(4), pp. 46-47.

Asuni, J.B. (1999). Searching for peace in Africa. Retrieved May 8, 2006, from http://www.conflictprevention.net/page.php?id=40$formid=73$action=show$survey id=55.

Avav, T. (2002). *Refugees in own country (The Tiv-Jukun crises) 1990-93.* Abuja: Supreme Black Communications.

Bamishaiye, A. (1976). Ethnic politics as an instrument of unequal socio-economic development in Nigeria. In A.O. Sanda (Ed.), *Ethnic relations in Nigeria: Problems and prospects* (pp. 71-91). Ibadan: The Caxton Press.

Bangura, Y. (1995, May). The search for identity: Ethnicity, religion and political violence. Occasional Papers, No. 6, UNRISD, Geneva: The United Nations Research Institute for Social Development.

Benjamin, S.A. (2002). Conflict management in Nigeria's fourth republic. In *CRD Newsletter* January-March, pp. 7-8. Kano, Nigeria.

Best, S.G., Idyorough, A.E., & Shehu, Z.B. (1999). Communal conflicts and the possibility of conflicts resolution in Nigeria: A case study of the Tiv-Jukun conflicts in Wukari local government area, Taraba state. In O. Otite & T.O Albert (Eds.), *Community conflicts in Nigeria: Management, resolution and transformation*, pp. 82-117. Ibadan: Spectrum Books.

Bur, A. (2002). Communal crisis and its impact on community development. In A. Bur (Ed.), *Communal relations: Conflicts and crisis management strategies*, pp. 1-13. Makurdi: Aboki Publishers.

Cohen, S.E. (2001). Globalization and the boundaries of the state: A framework for analyzing the changing practice of sovereignty. *Governance: An International Journal of Policy and Administration*, 14(1), pp. 75-97.

Environmental & Development Challenges. (n.d.). NIGERIA: Resource aspects of communal clashes. Retrieved May 24, 2006, from http://www.edcnews.se/Research/Nigeria-Tiv.html.

Hagher, I. (2002). *Beyond hate and violence: Understanding the Tiv struggle for citizenship rights and social justice in Nigeria.* Ibadan: Caltop Publications.

Holton, R. (2000). Globalization's cultural consequences. *Annals of the American Academy of Political and Social Science*, 570, pp. 140-52.

Human Rights Watch. (2002a). Nigeria: President ignoring gravity of military massacre. Retrieved May 23, 2006, from http://hrw.org/english/docs/2002/04/19/nigeri3864_txt.htm.

Human Rights Watch. (2002b). The government response to events in Benue. Retrieved May 23, 2006, from http://www.hrw.org/reports/2002/nigeria/Nigeria0402=06.htm.

Human Rights Watch. (2002c). Military revenge in Benue: A population under attack. Retrieved May 23, 2006 from http://64.233.161.104/search?q=cache:r6fii7OkIXQI.:hrw.org/reports/2002/nigeria/Nigeria.

International IDEA. (2000). *Democracy in Nigeria: Continuing dialogue(s) for nation building.* Stockholm: International Institute for Democracy and Electoral Assistance.

ISHR West African Committee. (2001). Genocide and Nigerian army massacre of Tiv civilians in central Nigeria. Retrieved March 3, 2006, from http://www.ishr.org/sections-groups/wac/tiv.htm#top.

Kankara, M.M. (1998). *Ethnicity and tribal sentiment in Nigeria: An update.* Zaria: Bakuwa Group of Companies.

Leith, R., & Solomon, H. (2006). On ethnicity and ethnic conflict management in Nigeria. Retrieved March 18, 2006, from http://www.eldis.org/static/DOC9642.html.

Maduagwu, M.C. (2004). An agenda for peaceful coexistence in a Democratic Nigeria. In O.M. Maduagwu & A.S. Mohammed (Eds.), *The challenges and prospects of democratisation in Nigeria*, pp. 26-45. Nigeria: Fulbright Association of Nigeria.

Odunuga, S. (1999). Nigeria: A victim of its own success. In A. Adedeji (Ed.), *Comprehending and mastering African conflicts, The search for sustainable peace and good governance*, pp. 221-135. London: Zed Books.

Okocha, C. (2001). Tiv/Jukun crisis: Century old fire, still burning. Retrieved October 27, 2008, from http://www.thisdayonline.com/archive/2001/12/08/20011208spe01.html.

Philips, C.S. (1984). Nigeria and Biafra. In F.L. Shiels (Ed.), *Ethnic separatism and world politics*, pp. 151-208. Lanham: University Press of America.

Rosel, J. (1995). Ethnic nationalism and ethnic conflict. *International Politics and Society*, 2, pp. 117-30.

Snow, M.D. (2008). *National security for a new era: Globalization and geopolitics after Iraq.* New York: Pearson Longman.

Stremlau, J. (1999). The evils of ethnic politics. Retrieved March 18, 2006, from http://www.sn.apc.org/wmail/issues/990326/NEWS52.html

Suberu, R.T. (1996). *Ethnic minority conflict and governance in Nigeria.* Ibadan: Spectrum Books.

Torwel, V. (2005). Framing political conflict in a multi-ethnic democracy: A critical analysis of the news of the 2001 Nigerian Tiv-Jukun conflict. Retrieved October 15, 2007, from http://www.uiowa.edu/jmc/graduate/conventions/march2005.html#torwel.

UNDP. (2001). Globalization with a human face. In D. Held, & A. McGrew (Eds.), *The global transformations reader: An introduction to the globalization debate*, pp. 341-47. Cambridge: Polity Press

Woods, N. (2001). Order, globalization and inequality in word politics. In D. Held, & A. McGrew (Eds.), *The global transformations reader: An introduction to the globalization debate*, pp. 387-99. Cambridge: Polity Press.

CHAPTER SEVENTEEN

PETROLEUM, THE ENVIRONMENT, AND THE ECONOMICS OF NATIONALISM IN THE NIGER DELTA

SHERIFF FOLARIN AND HENRY OKODUA

The Niger Delta conflict has come into global limelight for some time. The indigenes of the area have agitated over the sordid acts of ecocide and the absence of physical development. In recent months, several factors have added a dangerous twist to the crisis. They include organized militia formations, the most notorious of which is the Movement for the Emancipation of the Niger Delta (MEND); expanding nature militia operations, including their attacks of Niger Delta and non-Delta targets of national strategic importance such as the oil installations; the July 2009 attack of the Lagos Atlas Cove; and kidnapping of expatriates working in the oil fields. This chapter reviews the various dimensions and manifestations of the crisis and makes a number of recommendations.

Introduction

The Niger Delta crisis has, in very recent times, taken a much more dangerous dimension, underscoring the degeneration of the issue due to the failure of governments at all levels and other non-state actors, including the multinational companies (MNCs), to bring the crisis to an end. The emergence of militia and cult groups among the communities in the last three years points to the aggravation and deterioration, rather than resolution, of the conflicts. The government's seeming complicity and protection of the MNCs, using instruments of coercion to protect the foreign companies, has multiplied illegal means and instruments to fight the cause of "economic and social emancipation," as some militants claimed in February 2007 in an interview by Jeff Koniange of the American Cable News Network (CNN). This study examines the protracted Niger Delta crisis, exacerbated by oil, ecological, and socio-ethnic factors, and its implication for Nigeria's external relations. It does this by revisiting the many unresolved issues, including the Ogoni crisis, which explain the escalation of the crisis.

While social and relative deprivation is considered primary and environmental issues are looked at as the secondary causes of the problem in some studies (in some, it is reduced to political and some ethnic or communal), the impact of the Niger Delta problem on Nigeria's relationship with the international community is the only consideration in some others; efforts to situate the environmental issues and the eventual world attention are infinitesimal and insignificant, or almost non-existent. This chapter attempts to correct that by reexamining the activities of the oil companies which have created enormous ecological problems in the region, in addition to the abjection of the people, thereby leading to internal strife.

This study therefore considers the role of environmental issues in the Niger Delta crisis. The link between the environmental issues and conflict in the Niger Delta is established, while the role of government in the crisis, its protection of the multinational oil companies at the expense of its own people, and elimination of environmental activists including Ken Saro-Wiwa in mid-1990s, are discussed. However, the emergence of vicious militant groups, such as the Niger Delta Peoples Volunteer Force (NDPVF), Movement for the Emancipation of the Niger Delta (MEND), and their many incursions on the economic and resource base of the region which constitute a setback to Nigeria's economic development, coupled with the huge environmental crisis in the region, represent the economic cost of the phenomenon and also explain the international dimension of the crisis.

Backgrounds to the Niger Delta Crisis

The Niger Delta region covers an estimated area of 20,000 km^2 within wetlands of 70,000 km^2 formed primarily by sediment deposition. It is located on the south-south geographical region of Nigeria and has a population of about 20 million people made up of many ethnic nationalities. The region comprises of nine states which include Abia, Akwa-Ibom, Bayelsa, Cross River, Delta, Edo, Imo, Ondo, and Rivers. However, the core Niger Delta region includes the three states of Bayelsa, Delta, and Rivers. The Delta environment is made up of four major ecological zones which include: mangrove swamp forests, freshwater swamps, coaster barrier islands, and lowland rainforests. Thus, the well-endowed ecosystem of the Delta is simply incredible as it naturally can sustain more species of freshwater fish, economic trees, and a wide variety of crops than any other ecosystem in West Africa.

In 1956, Shell British Petroleum (now Royal Dutch Shell) discovered crude oil at Oloibiri, a village in the Niger Delta, and began commercial production in 1958. Today, there are 606 oil fields in the Niger Delta, of which 360 are on-shore and 246 off shore (EIA, *Nigeria Country Analysis Brief*, 2005). Nigeria is now the largest oil producer in Africa and the sixth largest in the world, averaging 2.7 million barrels per day (bbl/d) in 2006. Nigeria's economy is heavily dependent on earnings from the oil sector, which provides 20 percent of GDP, 95 percent of foreign exchange earnings, and about 65 percent of budgetary revenues (CIA World Fact Book, 2005, cited in Nwilo & Badejo, 2006).

The Niger Delta Crisis is unarguably related to environmental problems in the area which surprisingly is closely linked to the activities of its oil industry. The problem of oil spills, deliberate destruction of the mangrove to pave way for pipelines, disappearance of the aqua life again due to oil spills and frequent movements of heavy ships, etc. are common occurrences in the Niger Delta. Communities in the region had ventilated their grievances through political and constitutional means against the marginalization and environmental abuses of their soils and waters from independence (Seminitari, 2006). In more recent times, particularly from the 1990s, they had become more restive and violent in their protests against the activities of foreign oil companies, notably Royal Dutch Shell (Shell Petroleum Development Company). The 1990s witnessed the outburst of violence against transnational oil corporations, the government's seeming conspiracy with them, and the use of one ethnic group against another, or infiltration by transnational corporations TNCs/government of ethnic groups with black sheep, which bred grave intra- and inter-ethnic hostilities (Agbese, 2002).

The government's complicity in the crisis found manifestation in the deployment of heavily armed military personnel to fight and dislodge the militants; guard oil facilities, operations, expatriates and the MNCs (Ikpatt, 2001). In addition, oil companies have had to recruit jobless local youths to watch over oil interests, thus setting local people against themselves. The official reason given, however, was that the presence of heavy security would act as deterrence to aggressive communities from destroying oil installations. The rationale behind this was controversial as it also showed insensitivity to the fundamental causation of persistent conflict, namely abjection and denials.

Impact of Oil Industry on the Environment in the Niger Delta

Some of the major environmental concerns of the negative exploration activities of oil companies in the Niger Delta include oil spillage and gas flaring in the area. The net effects of these shortcomings have expectedly made life extremely difficult in the region. Nwilo and Badejo, (2006), in support of the foregoing, pointed out that since the discovery of oil in Nigeria in the 1950s, the country has been suffering the negative environmental consequences of oil development. Akpofure et al., (2000), cited in Nwilo and Badejo (2006), claim that when there is an oil spill on water, spreading immediately takes place, with the gaseous and liquid components evaporating.

Other studies have also shown that oil on water surfaces also interferes with gaseous interchange at the sea surface, and dissolved oxygen levels will thereby be lowered. This no doubt reduces the life span of marine animals. Microorganisms also degrade petroleum hydrocarbons after spillage (Atlas, 1981; Leahy & Colwell, 1990; Atlas & Bartha, 1992). Oil spill incidents have occurred in various parts and at different times along the country's coast. According to Nwilo and Badejo (2005), several major oil spills in the coastal zone were the GOCON's Escravos spill in 1978 of about 300,000 barrels, SPDC's Forcados Terminal tank failure in 1978 of about 580,000 barrels, and Texaco Funiwa-5's blowout in 1980 of about 400,000 barrels. Other oil spill incidents are those of the Abudu pipe line in 1982 of about 18,818 barrels, the Jesse Fire Incident which claimed about 1,000 lives, and the Idoho Oil Spill of January 1998, of about 40,000 barrels. The most publicized of all oil spills in Nigeria occurred on January 17, 1980, when a total of 37 million liters of crude oil got spilled into the environment. This spill occurred as a result of a blowout at Funiwa 5 offshore station. Nigeria's largest spill was an offshore well blowout in January 1980 when an estimated 200,000 barrels of oil (8.4 million U.S. gallons) spilled into the Atlantic Ocean from an oil industry facility, which damaged 340 hectares of mangrove (Nwilo & Badejo, 2005). Table 17.1 below provides a summary of oil spill incidences in Nigeria between the period 1976 and 2005. These are official figures which, in most cases, may not adequately report all incidents of oil spillage.

It is important to note here that spilled oil is most of the time lost to the environment. For example, Nwilo and Badejo (2006) pointed out that available records for the period of 1976 to 1996 indicate that approximately 6%, 25%, and 69% respectively, of total oil spilled in the Niger Delta area, were on land, swamp, and offshore environments. Also, between 1997 and 2001, Nigeria recorded a total number of 2,097 oil spill incidents.

It must be recognized that oil spillage is not new. In fact, oil spills have been part of the history of oil production globally. "And it is not peculiar to Nigeria. The only difference, however, is that in other climes, response by both governments and the oil companies are usually swift" (Nairaland.net, 2006). In addition, oil companies and the Nigerian government need to be concerned about the economic and environmental impacts of oil spills, and to swiftly deploy "spill containment facilities" whenever spills occur. These include "oil skimmers used to recover and eliminate oil spills, oil spill containment devices, emergency spill kits, crude oil sludge control systems, stem jet refrigeration, bio-remediation product distribution, chemical clearing solutions" (Nairaland.net, 2006).

Table 17.1: Record of Oil Spill Incidents in Nigeria, 1976-2005

YEAR	NO. OF OIL SPILLS	QUANTITY OF OIL SPILLED (BARRELS)	(%) OF QUANTITY OF OIL SPILLED	QUANTITY RECOVERED (BARRELS)	(%) OF QUANTITY RECOVERED
1976	128	26,157.00	0.84	7,135.00	27.28
1977	104	32,879.00	1.05	1,703.01	5.18
1978	154	489,294.00	15.67	391,445.00	80.00
1979	157	694,170.00	22.24	63,481.20	9.14
1980	241	600,511.00	19.24	42,416.83	7.06
1981	238	42,722.00	1.37	5,470.20	12.80
1982	252	42,841.00	1.37	2,171.40	5.07
1983	173	48,351.30	1.55	6,355.90	13.15
1984	151	40,209.00	1.29	1,644.80	4.09
1985	187	11,876.60	0.38	1,719.30	14.48
1986	155	12,905.00	0.41	552	4.28
1987	129	31,866.00	1.02	6,109.00	19.17
1988	208	9,172.00	0.29	1,955.00	21.31
1989	195	7,628.16	0.24	2,153.00	28.22
1990	160	14,940.82	0.48	2,092.55	14.01
1991	201	106,827.98	3.42	2,785.96	2.61
1992	378	51,187.96	1.64	1,476.70	2.88
1993	428	9,752.22	0.31	2,937.08	30.12
1994	515	30,282.67	0.97	2,335.93	7.71
1995	417	63,677.17	2.04	3,110.02	4.88
1996	430	46,353.12	1.48	1,183.02	2.55
1997	339	81,727.85	2.62		
1998	399	99,885.35	3.20		
1999	225	16,903.96	0.54		
2000	637	84,071.91	2.69		
2001	412	120,976.16	3.88		
2002	446	241,617.55	7.74		
2003	609	35,284.43	1.13		
2004	543	17,104.00	0.55		
2005	496	10,734.59	0.34		
Total	**9,107**	**3,121,909.8**		**550,232.9**	**22.80**

Source: Egberongbe, F.O.A, P. C. Nwilo, & O. T. Badejo, 2006 (based on data from Department of Petroleum Resources, Nigeria).

The other major negative consequence of oil exploration and exploitation is gas flaring. This is a practice whereby the associated gas accompanying the production of crude oil is burnt off so as to maximize the production of crude oil. However, the prevailing consensus worldwide regarding gas flaring is that it is wasteful economically and environmentally. The burning of gas by flaring leads to the emission of carbon dioxide, the main greenhouse gas.

Venting of the gas without burning, a practice for which flaring seems often to be treated as a synonym, releases methane, the second main greenhouse gas. It is therefore very disturbing to note that associated gas flaring continues unabated in Nigeria.

For instance, a report by Friends of the Earth (2005) shows that "more gas is flared in Nigeria than anywhere else in the world. Estimates are notoriously unreliable, but roughly 2.5 billion cubic feet of gas associated with crude oil is wasted in this way every day. This is equal to 40% of all Africa's natural gas consumption in 2001" (p. 13). The same report further disclosed that "the flaring of associated gas (AG) in the Niger Delta is a human rights, environmental and economic monstrosity."

Nowhere else in the world have communities been subjected to it on such a scale. It is estimated to cost Nigeria US $2.5 billion annually, whilst "the roaring, toxic flares affect the health and livelihoods of Delta inhabitants" (Friends of the Earth, 2005, p. 13). In terms of how much is flared, the Friends of the Earth (2005) report estimated that for the first 20 years or so of the industry, almost all the AG was flared: 2.1 billion cubic feet per day (bcf/d) or 92% in 1981, for example.

Gas flaring in Nigeria is widely believed to have contributed more emissions of greenhouse gases than all other sources in sub-Saharan Africa combined. The World Bank (2002) sums up the scale of Nigerian flaring as follows: "The most striking example of environmental neglect has been in the oil sector, where natural gas flaring has contributed more emissions of greenhouse gases than all other sources in sub-Saharan Africa combined" (p. 23).

Within the Niger Delta, there is a common but firm belief that gas flaring is damaging the health of the local people. This stems from the fact that flaring of AG from oil production facilities is like setting a match to a large container of petrol. The enormous heat they emit simply would not permit any life (plant and animal) around them to survive. Exposure to these pollutants impacts human health adversely. According to the United States Environmental Protection Agency (Friends of the Erath, 2005, p. 26): "Many scientific studies have linked breathing particulate matter to a series of significant health problems, including: aggravated asthma, increases in respiratory symptoms like coughing and difficult or painful breathing, chronic bronchitis, decreased lung function, and premature death" (p. 24). Also, according to the U.S. EPA: "It has been clearly established and accepted that exposure to benzene and its metabolites causes acute nonlymphocytic leukemia and a variety of other blood-related disorders in humans" (cited in Friends of the Earth, 2005, p. 27). Gas flaring is thus considered to be a likely cause of premature deaths and cases of leukemia in the Niger Delta.

One other well-established health-damaging consequence of gas flaring includes high incidences of acid rain, which the Delta residents have long complained about—particularly how their corrugated roofs have been corroded by the composition of the rain that falls as a result of flaring. The primary causes of acid rain are emissions of sulphur dioxide (SO_2) and nitrogen oxides (NO_x), which combine with atmospheric moisture to form sulfuric acid and nitric acid, respectively. Acid rain acidifies lakes and streams and damages vegetation. In addition, acid rain accelerates the decay of building materials and paints. Prior to falling to the earth, SO_2 and NO_x gases and their particulate matter derivatives, sulfates and nitrates, contribute to visibility degradation and harm public health. In the Delta, an oily hue is often observed on collected rain water (Friends of the Earth, 2005).

The report further added that the observation that gas flaring in the Niger Delta is causing acid rain is also backed by the U.S. government's Energy Information Administration, which states, "The continued process of gas flaring has not only meant that a potential energy source—and source of revenue—has gone up in smoke, but it is also a major contributor to air pollution and acid rain" (2005, p. 26).

Niger Delta Conflicts, Global Response, and Nigeria's External Relations

By 1970, about 300,000 barrels of crude oil had been spilled in the Niger Delta area (Earth Action, 1994). According to Shell, the spillage was an act of sabotage by the Biafran army as they were losing in the civil war (Shell, 1995). Shell figures also show that from 1985 to early 1993, 5,352 barrels of oil were spilled in 87 incidents in Ogoniland after their staff had been withdrawn (Shell, 1995, p.12). The tendency had been for state officials and oil companies to blame the problems on sabotage by local communities. For instance, Shell claimed that out of 87 instances of oil spillage in Ogoniland between 1985 and 1993, 60 (about 70 percent) were sabotage acts; the figure tallied with government claims that out of 11 incidents in Ogoniland in 1990, eight or 73 percent were due to sabotage (Okerenta, 2006).

Damages to the environment in Ogoniland went along with deprivation. Consequently, local leaders protested these injustices. The regime of Structural Adjustment Programme (SAP) reduced public spending, subsidies to goods such as petrol, which led to the rise of pump price of petroleum products from N0.75 per liter in 1986 to N11 per liter in 1996. These severely affected standards of living and hardship everywhere, which were more pronounced in the oil-producing areas. Evidence of conflicts began to show before 1980, but the situation worsened in the second half of the 1980s and 1990s.

However, because oil exploration by multi-national oil corporations had increased with the expanding space of squalor, the Niger Delta people began to hold oil companies and the government responsible for their deprivation. They lamented, for instance, the failure of the two institutions to construct new or at least rehabilitate existing roads, schools, hospitals, and provide opportunities for employment, support for farming, and indeed do everything to improve their livelihood. Oil companies and government insisted that these claims were exaggerated as they were sometimes outrageous and indecorously demanded (Rowell

& Kretzmann, 1999). In response, Shell, government, and seven other neighboring oil-producing communities like Asa-Ndoki, dismissed these claims (Shell, 1995; *Daily Champion*, 1994; *The News*, 1995). However, it was relative deprivation, the gap between expectation and actualization, like the one in the foregoing claims that explain why men rebel (Gurr, 1974), and more importantly, that explicates the Niger Delta conflicts. Osaghae (1995a) argues that the approach of minorities in their demand for better living hitherto were passive, namely by delegation and petitions to the state and oil firms. The failure of these means to engender meaningful changes may explain why the Ogonis decided on a different line of action in the early 1990s. Precisely in 1990, a non-political organization comprising Ogoni elite and traditional rulers, known as KAGOTE whose origin dates back to the 1970s, drew up and presented to the state the Ogoni Bill of Rights. Among other things earlier highlighted, they demanded political autonomy within Nigeria and a fair access to and use of oil revenue derived from Ogoniland to develop their homeland and language, as well as protection from Shell. As an instrument to pursue the actualization of the demands in the Bill of Rights, the Movement for the Survival of Ogoni People (MOSOP) was set up in 1990.

MOSOP followed the Bill of Rights up with intense campaigns at both the national and international levels with a view to publicizing the Ogoni predicament. In that effort, the Bill was presented to the United Nations Sub-Committee on Human Rights on the Prevention from Discrimination and Protection of Minorities, the African Human Rights, and several other non-state actors such as the General Assembly of the Unrepresented Nations and Peoples' Organization at the Hague in 1993 (Okonta, 2000). The government and Shell initially responded to the Bill with indifference. However, as MOSOP began to secure public and international support, the state reacted by banning ethnic and other similar organizations, such as MOSOP and the Ethnic Minority Rights Organization of Africa (EMIROAF), both led by Saro-Wiwa. These two organizations and the National Youth Council of Ogoni People were the three main organizations which spearheaded the Ogoni insurrection.

Attaching it to the Bill of Rights, MOSOP wrote to Shell, Chevron, and the Nigerian National Petroleum Corporation (NNPC) in December 1992, asking for a favorable disposition to Ogoni demands or evacuation from the land. Other demands included the payment of $6 billion in accumulated rents and royalties for oil exploited in Ogoni fields from 1958; reparation of $4 billion for soil, water, and air pollution; cessation of gas flaring; and commencement of negotiation with Ogoni people. According to Osaghae (1995b), the significance of the letter to the companies was that it showed the people's loss of confidence in the state. According to them, it was time for "the Ogoni to fight for their own salvation because there is no government to deliver us" (p. 46).

It is pertinent to note that in contemporary global politics, human rights and the environment are no longer issues of domestic concern. Because such issues may explode the international system, world leaders and states intervene positively and swiftly to put it asunder. This explains the limits of sovereignty in international organizations, particularly when states are contracting parties to some conventions on human and environmental issues. The defense by the then Nigerian Minister of External Affairs, Tom Ikimi, that the world had no business in the happenings in Nigeria and the government handling of the Ogoni crisis was, as such, a ruse.

Nigeria's handling of the Ogoni crisis was a clear violation of the Harare Declaration on Human Rights in 1991, to which Nigeria was a contracting party that compelled the Commonwealth to suspend Nigeria in 1995. Also, as a member of the UN, Nigeria was aware of existing treaties and conventions on fundamental human rights and freedoms to which it was bound by being a signatory. Perhaps the Ogoni issue might not have elicited much passion and concern if not for the fact that the problem of environmental pollution and degradation had become a global concern. The world had come to terms with the fact that the environment was the common heritage of mankind and that environmental degradation in any country could not be overlooked because it carried trans-border harm across nations. The focus on the environment thus brought the global searchlight on the activities of multinational oil corporations, whose relentless drive for oil exploration and the attendant unscrupulous drive for profit often culminated in environment abuse and unconcern for their host communities, especially in the developing countries. In the Niger Delta, the activities of the Royal Dutch Shell oil company had to come into sharp focus because it was the main culprit in Ogoniland (Okerenta, 2006).

Rather than take the necessary measures to assuage the wounded feelings of the Ogoni people, the Abacha regime embarked on a ruthless military pacification by establishing and deploying the notorious Rivers State Internal Security Task Force in Ogoniland. The regime took steps that further made it lose credibility in the international system. For instance, it set up in November 1995 a 50-man National Committee of Traditional Rulers and Leaders of Thought to advise it on sensitive diplomatic problems.

The timing of the execution of the Ogoni Nine which coincided with the Commonwealth Summit in Auckland, New Zealand, in 1995 was embarrassing to a global community that had pleaded for clemency so much and had been assured even by Ikimi at the Summit that the Abacha regime was redressing the issue. Nelson Mandela had even staked his personal integrity to persuade the Summit not to take a hard-line action against Nigeria, having been assured by General Abacha that all would end well (Fawole, 2004).

It was even more ridiculous that just when Ikimi had finished addressing the Summit and granted interviews to the world press that the Nigerian government was not going to and had not hanged the Ogoni leaders, he was confounded with the news that the nine activists had been hanged. The UN Commission on Human Rights at its 52nd session in Geneva in April 1996 condemned the regime for continued violation of human rights; the Commonwealth through its Commonwealth Ministerial Action Committee proposed the freezing of the personal assets of Nigerian rulers, imposition of a comprehensive ban on sporting activities, severance of air ties unless the regime took urgent measures towards speedy restoration of democratic rule and showed respect for human rights. The report of the Fact-Finding Mission of the UN Secretary General to Nigeria also severely indicted the regime for gross violations of Human Rights and the rule of law and recommended a quick return to democracy, among other things (Fawole, 1999).

The Nigerian government from this time, simply sacrificed Nigeria's age-long hard-earned international respect and goodwill on the altar of incompetence and inordinate ambition to crush all local and external challenges in his quest to consolidate his powers.

The Economics of the Niger Delta Conflicts

The cost of the Niger Delta struggle/conflicts in economic terms may not really be estimable. Every party in the conflicts (the oil MNCs, the Nigerian state, the people of the Niger Delta, and of course, the international community) appears to be mostly concerned with immediate benefits to interests represented. However, the overall adverse consequence of the situation is rarely considered by any. The people who have been in the struggle over the claim to a decent living as well as a decent environment have been abused, oppressed, and suppressed by the elite using the instrument of the state. The reason for this is quite obvious; the people are of little or no economic relevance to the government. This is because the government needs not depend on them for raising any significant revenue needed to run the state. The state thus over the years has misplaced its primary responsibility of protecting lives and property to that of protecting the multinationals at the very expense of the people it is meant to govern.

The multinationals who seek more profits at the expense of the region have over the years opted for the cheaper but immoral and criminal alternative of flaring and venting gas and have in the process messed up the environment and wasted so much resources even in the midst of hunger in the faces of so many around them. As earlier stated, it is on record that a financial loss to Nigeria of about \$2.5 billion annually is traceable to gas flaring. Besides, the associated loss of lives and failing health can never be sufficiently evaluated. The international community at large is also paying heavily as these MNCs contribute their unsolicited fair share of toxic emissions to the environment thereby increasing the problems of global warming and rising sea levels all over. Moreover, every disruption in the supply of crude from the Niger Delta has consistently had its adverse impact on the world prices of crude oil. What this means is that everybody all over has had to pay more for petroleum products. The international community has not done enough to stem the ugly tide. For example, the World Bank has been widely criticized over its inability to require the use of Associated Gas (AG) before approving its credit guarantees for the financing of the West African Gas Pipeline Project. Yet, the Bank has since November 2004 approved \$125 million in guarantees supporting the construction of a 678 kilometer gas pipeline to transport natural gas from Nigeria to Benin, Ghana, and Togo—the West African Gas Pipeline (WAGP).

Conclusion

This study has been able to review environmental issues central to the Niger Delta crisis. It adumbrated the issues and subsequent conflicts within the uncommon perspective of the effective impact of domestic policies on foreign policies or external relations of a state. More importantly, the study has looked at the different costs of the emergent militant nationalism in the Delta on national development and international relations of Nigeria. The study also discovered the fact that the successive regimes in Nigeria considered the oil TNCs, with which they had personal businesses, paramount in the hierarchy of Nigeria's national interest. This probably explains the disposition of the nation's foreign policies to protecting foreign business interests and securing their stakes in the Niger Delta.

The Abacha approach seemed to have reared its ugly head again in both Presidents Obasanjo and Yar'Adua eras. The continued neglect of the Delta areas despite increased exploration activities of many new foreign oil companies, a development prodded by an aggressive campaign by the Obasanjo administration for foreign investment, exacerbated the Delta crisis. Several other militant groups have emerged, with a more ferocious approach under the Yar'Adua dispensation. Their grievances include government's seeming overprotection of the exploitative oil companies, growing impoverishment of the people, emergence of more slum settlements, increased environmental degradation, and the recklessness of the current Yar'Adua administration in combating the multiple militant groups who have been further irked by government's insincerity in carrying out the Niger Delta clause of the Seven-Point Agenda. The MEND and NDPVF, among others in the struggle, have been abducting expatriates, holding MNCs and their home government to ransom and sometimes asking for ransom fees, and have been making the same old demands: good living for Deltans, social responsibility on the part of the oil companies, and government's attention by way of physical and economic development, meaningful allocation from the huge revenues coming from the oil-producing areas, as well as the control of activities capable of destroying the ecosystem in the Delta region. It is hoped that the initial Yar'Adua-Jonathan initiative on the Seven-Point Agenda to dialogue with all stakeholders and deploy resources to the Delta for social rehabilitation and structural development would be faithfully implemented.

It is pertinent to note that the oil companies need to be more perceptive of the plight of the people and be more socially responsible by contributing to their welfare, provide jobs for them, construct good roads, build decent low-cost housing for them, increase academic scholarship awards to their children, build schools and hospitals, provide water and electricity to the communities, etc. Put differently, the problem would be lessened when oil companies get more committed to their agreement with the government and the host communities by ensuring that they carry out their corporate social responsibility (CSR) to their host communities and avoid indulging in unethical activities.

Talking about CSR, companies and government should pay much attention to the problem of infrastructure (including roads, bridges, schools, hospitals, drinkable water, electricity, etc.) in the Niger Delta, which could experience a national emergency at any time. There is the need for both the governments at the various levels and the multinational oil companies to invest massively in infrastructure in this region just as it has been done in Lagos and Abuja. This will ensure that the environment is tidied up, made much more comfortable to live in, and that the economically idle but restive youths in the area are engaged in the mean time and of course provided some profitable means of livelihood. Further, the youth can be more profitably engaged if they are encouraged to go to school. This can be engendered by a policy of provision of scholarships (compulsory and free and qualitative education up to tertiary level) to the children from this area so as to empower them economically and make them much more useful to the state in the future.

Moreover, the question of who controls the natural resources located in a given region can be answered by the convocation of a national conference whose recommendations should first be subjected to a referendum. This will allow for a consensus by all stakeholders and a more enduring arrangement for the smooth operation of the oil industry which is urgently needed for the stability of the world market and the Nigerian economy. On the political frontier, there is the need to shift presidential power to the region so as to complete the cycle among all the geo-political regions in the country. This will allow for equity in the polity, give the people a sense of belonging, and douse some tension that is already mounting. This expectation has been partially satisfied now since the incumbent vice president of the country is from the region. However, it must be emphasized here that nothing short of the position of the President of Nigeria will adequately pacify the Niger Delta people in their quest for a taste of political office in the country.

References

Achiefe, M. (1994). Nigeria risks external image crisis on Ogoni. *Daily Champion* (Lagos).

Agbese, D. (2002). How to fix Nigeria: The Nigerian conundrum. *Newswatch Magazine,* Lagos, January 17.

Agbese, P. (2001). Managing ethnic relations in a heterogenous society: The case of Nigeria. In A. Mbaku, P. Agbese, & E. Kimenyi (Eds.), *Ethnicity and governance in the third world*. London: Ashgate Publishing.

Akpofure, E.A., Efere, M.L., & Ayawei, P. (2000). *The adverse effects of crude oil spills in the Niger delta*. Benin: Urhobo Historical Society.

Amanyie, V. (2001). *The Ogoni in the Niger delta*. Port Harcourt: Horizon Concepts.

Atlas R.M. (1981). Microbial degradation of petroleum hydrocarbons: An experimental perspective. *Microbial Rev.* 45(1), pp. 180-209.
Atlas R.M. & Bartha, R. (1992) Hydrocarbon biodegradation and oil spill bioremediation. In K.C. Marshall (Ed.), *Advances in Microbial Ecology*, 12, pp. 287-338. NY: Plenum Press.
Barnhart, R.K. (1996). *The world book dictionary*, Vol. 1. Chicago: World Bank Inc.
Dollard, J., Doob, L.I.N., Miller, N.E., et al. (1939). *Frustration and aggression*. New Haven: Yale University Press.
Earth Action. (1994). *The Nigeria brief: The Ogoni issue*. Lagos: Shell Petroleum Development Company of Nigeria.
Egberongbe, F.O.A., Nwilo, P. C., & Badejo, O. T. (2006). Oil spill disaster monitoring along Nigerian coastline. Paper presented at the XIII Fédération Internationale des Géomètre (FIG) Conference, Munich, Germany, October 8-13.
EIA. (2005 April). *Country analysis brief: Nigeria*. Retrieved July 15, 2007, from http://www.eia.doe.gov/emeu/cabs/nigeria.html
Environmental Rights Action/Friends of the Earth. (1993). *ERA annual report*. Retrieved July 24, 2006, from www.eraction.org.
Fawole, W.A. (1999). Diplomatic blunders: The Ogoni crisis and Nigeria's external relations. *Nigerian Journal of Politics*, 4(1&2).
Fawole, W.A. (2004). *Understanding Nigeria's foreign policy under civilian rule since 1999: Institution, structure, processes and performance*. Ibadan: College Press.
Folarin, S. (2006). MNCs, foreign contractors and Nigeria's economic development: An enquiry into 45 years of exploitation. *African Journal of International Affairs and Development*, 11(1), pp. 1-19.
Friends of the Earth (2005). *FOE reports*. Retrieved July 2006 from www.foe.org.
Greenpeace.org. (1995). Reports on the Ogoni crisis: 10th November 1996- 1st anniversary of the death of Ken Saro-Wiwa. Retrieved August 22, 2009 from http://greenpeace.org.
Gurr, T. (1974). *Why men rebel*. Princeton: Princeton University Press.
Ikpatt, C. (2001). Letter to Niger delta people in the diaspora. Amherst: Urhobo Historical Society/Niger Delta Coalition in the Diaspora.
Ikpatt, C., & Scot, G. (2001). The Niger delta problems and solutions: The equilateral resource control (ERC) model as an alternative resolution (ADR) concept. Retrieved July 23, 2006, from www.nigerdeltacongress.com/narticles/niger_delta_problems_and_solutio.htm.
Kristeva, J. (1980). *Pouvoirs de l'horreur*. Paris: Seuil.
Lea, J., & Young, J. (1984). *Social problem*. New York: Addison Incorporated.
Leahy J.G., & Colwell, R.R. (1990). Microbial degradation of hydrocarbons in the environment. *Microbial* Rev. 54, pp. 305-315
Maier, K. (2000). *This house has fallen: Nigeria in crisis*. London: Penguin.
Nairaland.net. (2006). Oil spills in Nigeria. Retrieved January 6, 2010, from http://www.nairaland.net/forum/viewtopic.php?t=140.
Nwilo, P.C., & Badejo, O.T. (2001). Impacts of oil spills along the Nigerian coast. Retrieved July 15, 2007, from The Association for Environmental Health and Sciences, http://www.aehs.com.
Nwilo, P.C., & Badejo, O.T. (2005). Oil spill problems and management in the Niger delta. Paper presented at the International Oil Spill Conference, Miami, Florida, United States.

Nwilo, P.C., & Badejo, O.T. (2006). Impacts and management of oil spill pollution along the Nigerian coastal areas. Frederiksberg, Denmark: FIG Publication No. 36. Retrieved July 15, 2007, from http://www.fig.net/pub/figpub/pub36/figpub36.htm.

Okerenta, K.H. (2006). International politics of the Ogoni crisis: Environmental issues and Nigeria's foreign policy. Unpublished Bachelor's research project, Covenant University, Ota, Nigeria.

Okonta, I. (2000, March). Lingering crisis in Nigeria's Niger delta and suggestions for a peaceful resolution. CDD Research and Advocacy Department. London: CDD.

Omoarelojie, E. (2006). Niger delta crisis changes course. *The News* (Lagos).

Onanuga, B. (1995). New twist to the Ogoni saga. *The News* (Lagos).

Osaghae, E.E. (1995a). The Ogoni uprising: Oil politics, minority agitation and the future of the Nigerian state. *Journal of African Affairs*, 94(376), pp. 325-344.

Osaghae, E.E. (1995b). *Structural adjustment and ethnicity in Nigeria.* (Research Report No. 98). Uppsala: Nordiska Afrikainstitutet.

Rowell, A., & Kretzmann, S. (1999). The cost of doing business: Transnational corporations and violence in Nigeria. *Security Dialogue,* PEGG 30, 5(2), pp. 13-36.

Seminitari, I. (1993). Oil: Delta explodes on degradation. *African Guardian.* Lagos.

Seminitari, I. (2006). Cries of foul play in the Oil Rivers. *The Guardian*, Lagos, September 3.

Shell. (1995). *Reports of activities in the Niger delta.* Port Harcourt: Shell.

Townsend, J. (1970). *Measure and explanations of poverty in high and low income countries.* London: Penguin.

Varma, S.P. (2005). *Modern political theory.* New Delhi: Vikas Pub. House Put Ltd.

World Bank. (2002). Reports of world summit on sustainable development. Retrieved January 2007 from http://www.mainaksworld.com/gasflaringpollution.html.

CHAPTER EIGHTEEN

OIL CONFLICT IN THE NIGER DELTA: REVISITING THE ODI GENOCIDE

ANDREW OSELOKA SAWYER

Official handling of conflicts in Nigeria is often characterized by inadequacies as well as problematic and questionable styles that are filled with various kinds of human rights abuses. The Ogoni case of the mid-1990s, Odi in 1999, and Zaki Biam of 2002 are salient examples. Cases of genocidal killings can no doubt easily be established against the Nigerian state in each of these conflicts. Focusing on the Odi case, this chapter poses many questions such as: Why is the military option the most frequently employed by the government in the age of liberal democracy? Why did the citizenry become militarized? The chapter examines the four scientific conflict-handling styles and proposes the best option for the Nigerian state.

Introduction

Odi is a small town located along the Nun River in Bayelsa state, Federal Republic of Nigeria. It is the second largest town in the state, having a pre-1999 population of 60,000 people (Human Rights and Civil Society Groups, 1999, p.1). In late 1999, a brigade of the Nigerian army invaded the town with a mandate to flush out local bandits in the aftermath of a treasonable act. Tragically, the town was completely wiped out, save for three buildings: an Anglican church, a bank (First Bank), and a public health center. The invasion which lasted from November 20-24, 1999, was led by one Lt. Col. Agbabiaka. Today,

Odi remains underdeveloped, impoverished, and a highly and grossly unplanned city. The current administration of President Yar'Adua has empowered the Joint Military Task Force (JTF) in the Niger Delta to attack the Gbaramatu Kingdom which led to more despair on the part of the indigenes of Odi (Onuorah and Ebiri, 2009, p.6). It is a ghost town in a region that is in desperate need of recovery.

Characteristically, the Nigerian state is known for the continued plunder of its land and people. Today, crude oil has taken over from palm oil as the major attraction. For the peoples of the Niger Delta area, however, oil represents the destruction of the natural environment upon which they depend for survival. Their communal order, long violated by colonialists, has been further distorted by the exploitation of crude oil.

To facilitate exploitation of oil and gas resources, the Land Use Act of 1978 vested ownership and control of all land and mineral resources in the central government. Government could give away communal lands and forests to transnational oil companies for exploration and exploitation of crude oil and gas at will. These transnational oil companies have in turn significantly reduced arable and productive land, and thus created avenues for both inter-ethnic and intra-ethnic dislocation and violence.

The Problems

The official handling of conflicts in Nigeria is usually inadequate. The conflict resolution styles adopted by the Nigerian government show its preference for an iron-fisted approach to conflict. Like in most societies of the world where gross human rights violations are wished away, the response of the Nigerian state to each of these problems has been in three categories: outright denial, partial acceptance of guilt, and total defiance. According to Albert (2003, p. 5) the government either denies their activities or they state that their actions were for the sake of national security, or total defiance.

The research questions therefore identified by this study are: What are the effects of the current approach to handling conflicts? What are the alternative options of solving these conflicts? In trying to explicate these, the research will focus on the oil conflict in the Niger Delta by adopting a systematic investigation into the nature and causes of Operation *Hakuri ll* as genocide in Odi. It will also investigate the various roles played by the federal government in the mismanagement of the resources and how these led to the eruption of violence among the youth and the subsequent genocide that ensued.

Using extant primary and secondary sources, the study will take an advocacy approach.

Genocide: A Definition

Although human history has witnessed many acts of genocide, the concept is relatively new. The term finds its origins in the work of the jurist Raphael Lemkin (1944), a primary proponent of an international convention on the subject. Lemkin's definition of the term centered on the requirement of a coordinated plan to destroy the "essential foundations" of the life of a group, with the aim of eliminating the group. In his words,

> The objectives of such a plan would be disintegration of the political and social institutions, of culture, language, national feelings, religion, and the economic existence of national groups, and the destruction of the personal security, liberty, health, dignity, and even the lives of the individual's belongings to such groups. Genocide is directed against the national group as an entity, and the actions involved are directed against individuals, not in their individual capacity, but as members of the national group. (Lemkin, 1944, p. 79)

The concept of "genocide" received its first formal, legal recognition in the context of the Nuremberg trials. Although the Charter of the Nuremberg Tribunal did not expressly use the term, the definition of crimes against humanity provided in Article 6(c) of the Charter covered many acts today constituting genocide; the indictment of the criminals tried before the Tribunal expressly charged the defendants with genocide, and the prosecution made reference to the term during the proceedings (Ratner et al., p.27). The UN General Assembly initiated the process of elaborating the genocide convention in 1946; hence we have what is known today as genocide.

Article II of the convention defines "genocide" as:

> [A]ny of the following acts committed with intent to destroy, in whole or in part, a national, ethnical, racial, or religious group, as such:
> a. Killing members of the group;
> b. Causing serious bodily or mental harm to members of the group;
> c. Deliberately inflicting on the group conditions of life calculated to bring about its physical destruction in whole or in part;
> d. Imposing measures to prevent births within the group; and
> e. Forcibly transferring children of the group to another group. (General Assembly Resolution 1946, 96(1) cited in Ratner et al., 2001, p.27)

Genocide, therefore, can be understood as a denial of the right of existence of entire human groups, as homicide is the denial of the right to life of individual human beings. Such denial of the right of existence shocks the conscience of mankind, results in great losses to humanity in the form of cultural and other contributions represented by these human groups, and is contrary to moral law and to the spirit and aims of the United Nations (Res. 96(1) cited in Ratner et al., p. 28).

Oil as the Issue in Conflict

The Niger Delta has remained the treasure base of the Nigerian state in the past four decades. The area harbors over 95 percent of Nigeria's crude oil and gas resources, which accounts for 90 percent of the country's foreign exchange earnings (Ogbogbo, 2005, p. 169). It is regarded to have a natural gas reserve of 160 trillion cubic feet, while the crude oil reserve stood at 33 billion barrels. (Onuoha, 2004, cited in Ogbogbo 2005, p. 169). The marginalization of the land-owning group and the wanton desiccation and destruction of their land have bred a serious move by the people to have a say in how the resources from their land are being managed. The struggle has become more virulent in recent times. Although the struggle for resource control dates back to pre-independence Nigeria, we shall be dwelling on the period of civilian rule from 1999.

Government officials have tended to explain away the Niger Delta crisis as an expected by-product of the country's difficult transition to democracy. With ten years of democratic rule, the country's democratic institutions have remained weak, and law enforcement structures are more prone than ever to manipulation by national and regional political figures. Legislation that prevents communities from having a legal stake in the oil pumped from their environments has remained intact, and the nation's security forces have often reacted to violence with the form of brutality reminiscent of military rule. Civilians bear the brunt of the crisis when they get caught variously between rival gangs, militias, and security forces (The International Crisis Group, 2006a, p. 6).

Historically, the Niger Delta area populated by the Urhobo, Ogoni, Ijo, Isoko, Itsekiri, and so on has engaged in serious struggles in response to the crisis within the Nigerian state. It is pertinent to note here that the Niger Delta question cannot be addressed outside of the Nigerian crisis. Suffice it to say that the crisis in the Nigerian Delta is a manifestation or an expression of a more fundamental Nigerian crisis, which manifests in the Sharia controversy, ethnic violence, one party dictatorship, corruption, massive impoverishment of the citizenry, and so on (Osuoka, 1999, p. 14).

Historically, the Niger Delta communities have suffered for and in defence of their resources. In the nineteenth century, local communities that attempted to assert their rights to the proceeds of palm produce suffered severe punishments in the hands of colonial forces. For instance, on February 22, 1895, a British naval force working for George Taubman Goldie's Royal Niger Company destroyed Brass and Fishtown, killing over 2,000 community people for daring to oppose unfair trading arrangement of British imperialists (Osuoka, 1999, p. 15). During that era, community leaders such as Jaja of Opobo, Dappa Pepple of Bonny, and Nana Olomu of Itsekiri were dethroned or exiled for daring to challenge the violence of the colonialists (Ikime, 1969, p. 2; Okonta & Douglas, 2001).

Just like in the days of imperial conquests, thousands of the Niger Delta people have been killed in the contemporary period. Several of them have also died in oil pipeline explosions because of over-aged and ill-maintained pipelines and other facilities that resulted in oil spills and blowouts. These oil spills have an inimical effect on human lives and the flora and fauna. Communities that depended solely on farming and fishing have seen their only source of livelihood destroyed by the transnational oil companies.

Unfortunately, the Nigerian state and its political leadership have at various times attempted to protect transnational oil companies and to brazenly expropriate the revenue from oil. In doing this, they have come to be seen as the problems of the people of the impoverished Niger Delta. This propelled the Ogoni to present their Bill of Rights to the Nigerian state in 1990. Parts of the Bill affirmed:

> The Ogoni people before the advent of British colonialism were not conquered or colonized by any other group in present day Nigeria. That in 1951 we were forcibly included in the Eastern Region of Nigeria where we suffered utter neglect. That we protested against this neglect. . . before the Willinks Commission of Inquiry into minority fears in 1958. That successive Federal administrations have trampled on every minority right enshrined in the Nigerian constitution to the detriment of the Ogoni and has by administrative structuring and other noxious acts transferred Ogoni wealth to other parts of the Republic. (Saro-Wiwa, 1990, pp. 6-8)

The Ogoni, under the leadership of their organization, the Movement for the Survival of Ogoni People (MOSOP) mobilized to peacefully challenge the partnership of oil and gas transnationals and the Nigerian State. In the process, the people expelled Shell oil company from their land and created a dual power situation in which people's power, for a moment, took primacy over the state. A defining moment had arrived in the history of Nigeria. The attempts by the minorities in Nigeria to redefine their positions within the Nigerian state would bring out of the government a renewed attempt to re-affirm its authority in the restive region. Odi provided this opportunity. The Odi invasion exemplified the kind of violent response from the Nigeria government in its attempt to regain control of the situation.

The Odi Example

Following the killing of seven police officers near Odi town in Kolokuma/Opokuma council area of Bayelsa State on November 4, 1999, and another five within the same council within a week (Chukwurah et al., 1999, p. 8), the stage was set for a reprisal by the Nigerian state. The federal government ordered the army to take control of the situation. Unofficial reports, quoting high casualty figures hinted of 'heavy bombardment' (Chukwurah et al., 1999, p. 8) of the Odi junction of the East-West Road. Many people were also said to have fled Odi town and the neighboring Kiama community. It was estimated that no fewer than 50 trucks with about two thousand (2,000) soldiers (Asoya, 1999, p. 4) were deployed to Odi. It was gathered that the military invasion and the subsequent reinforcements continued until the entire area had been captured and its rampaging youths humbled. Already the entire area had been declared a military zone and travelers turned back. The spokesperson for the Ijaw Youth Council (IYC), Isaac Osuoka claimed that about 200 persons including women and children who could not escape were killed (Osuoka, 1999, p. 17) by the invading soldiers. It was also gathered that people from nine neighboring communities also fled to towns not affected by the "war."

Analyzing Odi as Genocide: Evidence from Graffiti

The Niger Delta people have always complained of neglect. For the 20 million residents of the 70,000 square kilometer Niger Delta (see Fuelling the Niger Delta Crisis, Crisis Group Africa Report No. 118, 28 September 2006), a region of swamps, rivers, and tropical forests, alienation increased not only because civilian rule failed to bring about expected improvements in average standards of living, but also because many people continued to suffer the negative impacts of oil, violence, environmental degradation, and poverty. Nigeria's federal system indirectly encouraged violence in the Niger Delta by rewarding those who posed the greatest threats to oil facilities with juicy oil contracts and government positions (Fuelling the Niger Delta Crisis, Crisis Group Africa Report No. 118, 28 September 2006).

Odi allegedly served as haven for some of the hoodlums that killed the policemen. Notably, it would be recalled that the security situation in Bayelsa appeared to have deteriorated. Police reinforcement dispatched to the areas to control the situation were assaulted and forcibly turned back at illegal road blocks mounted by armed hoodlums (Oyeleye, 1999, p. 5). The Special Adviser to the president Doyin Okupe did not deny the fact that troops were deployed, but went further to stress that "an intervention is imperative to avert a total breakdown of law and order . . . and protect the lives and properties of ordinary citizens of the state" (Ali, 1999, p. 2). This position gives an insight into the power and spirit that powered the invasion.

It was also alleged that Ken Nneweira (an indigene of Odi) was instrumental in causing the mayhem. However, was Nneweira too powerful for the police to arrest? Why should truck loads of high-powered army personnel be the only option left to the government? Who is to be held responsible for this act of genocide? While some are of the view that the soldiers should be investigated and tried for overshooting their mandate, a U.S.-based Human Rights Watch opined that the Nigerian government should initiate criminal proceedings against the soldiers responsible for committing the Odi abuses (Ali, 1999, p. 3). Others are of the view that the Nigerian state lacks the moral right to set up such panels and should therefore be held responsible for their actions and inactions. One senator metaphorically described President Obasanjo as an "Abuja butcher," after visiting Odi with some members of the senate for firsthand information following the invasion of Odi. In his words:

> What I saw in Odi reminds me of a phrase in Latin: *horri willet wizzel,* meaning horrible sight, agonizing embarrassing, shameful. This was what I saw. I saw a degradation of human habitation and sadness written on the faces of hapless

> and helpless women faces that show mourning. Even the butcher of Abuja did not see this! I hope one day Obasanjo will be put on trial for this, the murder of Lady Kuti and other heinous crimes that apparently doesn't bother the conscience of this "Born Again Christian": How any human being can support this sort of thing, especially in a "democracy" is a way beyond my imagination. (Senator Durojaiye, quoted in *Tribune*, Tuesday, November 23, 1999, p. 12)

Another commentator was of the opinion that "the Federal government knew that the criminals they were looking for were not in Odi at the time that they went in . . . they were there to demonstrate that the Nigerian army had the capacity to kill. The whole area smelled of corpses after the army left" (Osuoka, cited in Ali, 1999, p. 3). Leaders of Human Rights and civil society groups who visited Odi, noted that they

> Saw no single livestock, poultry or other domestic animal except a stray cat . . . The Odi invasion by our investigation was premeditated . . .So ruthless, savage and thorough was the operation that it could only have been intended to achieve a genocide outcome. (Albert, 2003, p. 15)

No aspect of the community was spared. Places of worship and other sacred places, including sacred forests and groves, churches, ancestral shrines, and burial places were demolished. His Royal Highness J.P.B. Komonibo, the *Amananaowoi* of Odi noted, "all the records of *Ogori* . . . have been burnt and destroyed by the soldiers" (Ombe, cited in Albert, 2003, p. 15).

However, the Obasanjo administration cannot deny that something akin to genocide was carried out in Odi. This became more obvious with the graffiti left behind by rampaging soldiers. According to Albert, one of the soldiers who considered the objectives of Operation *Hakuri II* to have been perfectly accomplished wrote:

> We will kill all Ijaws. Bayelsa will be silent forever. Nobody can save you. Shame to the Ijaw people. We go (will) kill all Ijaw people with our gun. Ijaw face, monkey face. Odi where is your pride. Nigeria is Nigeria, Odi is dead. You are burnt. Odi is no more. Gone to the past. Pity. (Albert, 2003, p. 17)

Another graffiti said most incisively "Next time there will be no trees left" (Albert, 2003, p. 16). The effects of the genocide had such a negative impact on the socio-economic lifestyle of the people afterwards (UNDP, 2006, p. 125). The military sent to quell the crisis in Odi community became agents of human degradation. There were reported cases of rape in Odi by the soldiers sent to ensure "peace" in the community. Two years later, the community became filled with fatherless babies.

Theory and Knowledge of Conflict-Handling Styles as Ways of Tackling the Odi Genocide

Conflict is a social reality. It is a phenomenon that is widely known all over the world. It could be seen as an integral part of human existence. Consequently, some means or approaches are recommended for transforming such conflicts. There exists a spectrum of methods for resolving conflicts in a global age. There is no universally accepted and binding approach or procedures for dealing with conflicts. However, some of the following approaches are generically known: domination, avoidance, accommodation, collaboration, compromising, confrontation, and problem solving. However, for the purpose of this chapter, we will discuss avoidance, confrontation, problem solving, and collaboration in relation to the 1999 Odi genocide.

Avoidance

Avoidance is usually an unwise approach. It leaves the root causes of the conflict unaddressed. It usually occurs when one party in a potential conflict ignores the issue in the conflict or downplays the significance of such issues in the conflict. It is an unhealthy way of handling conflict because it is seen as a means of postponing the conflict. This is a dangerous style or approach to conflict, but most often than not, the Nigerian government adopts this destructive approach. As it were, the ongoing disturbances in the Niger Delta that resulted in the Odi genocide happened as a result of the avoidance by the government officials, before now, of the issues in the Niger Delta crisis left unattended to and ignored by the past governments. The adoption of conflict avoidance by the federal government of Nigeria no doubt led to lawlessness, banditry, and militarization of the Niger Delta.

Confrontation

Confrontation is the direct opposite of avoidance. It is a more deadly and destructive approach to resolving conflict. Its ‘lose-lose’ outcome leads to the intensification of a conflictual situation, since it employs the use of physical attacks on the parties involved. Generally, confrontation involves the use of violence. Ojiji opines that “there is a considerable degree or lack of understanding of each other’s position as each one tries to hold on to their views” (Ojiji, 2006, p. 124). This approach was used by the Nigerian government against the town of Odi. This conflict-handling style gave birth to the death of thousands of poverty stricken people and the destruction of Odi.

This approach is not appropriate. It offers no lasting resolution of the conflict; rather, it creates room for grudges and wounds in the minds of people, and it increases the intensity of the conflict as was the case in the Niger Delta today. The attack on Odi was a flawed strategy to stem militancy in the Niger Delta. The approach must change for peace to reign in the Niger Delta.

Joint Problem Solving

This is a conflict-handling style that leads to a win-win outcome. It deals with the underlying issues in the conflict as all parties involved in the conflict constructively listen to one another. The structural root causes of the conflict are addressed leading to their resolution. This appears to be the best option available for a lasting resolution of the conflict in the Niger Delta. This is so because the issues underpinning the crisis in that volatile region of the country can only be resolved when all parties are ready to shift grounds and tell themselves the truth. Only then will peace reign in the conflict-torn area. The recent amnesty granted to the militants can be considered a joint problem-solving strategy. Even then, it has to be more transparent without the gray areas which it possesses now (Ebiri, 2009, pp. 1-2).

Collaboration

This conflict-handling style is related to the disposition of being assertive and cooperative. It requires active listening and dialogue. And most importantly, the understanding will enable them come up with a better solution that will result in a win-win situation. This style is more socially adaptive, as whatever is reached after the horse trading is usually accepted by the parties in conflict. Most negotiations are of this nature (Ojiji, 2006, p. 123), such that even though getting to the final solution can be quite tedious, the outcome is usually binding to the parties. The Nigerian state can also adopt this approach, but prefers the iron-fist approach which shows the superiority of the government. Unless the state officials are ready to swallow their pride and the militants are ready to sheath their swords, the conflict may be far from over.

The Link between National Security, Global Capital, and Citizenship in the Odi Genocide

The concept, national security means different things to different people. In its ordinary sense, security is the state of being secured and free from apprehension, and having confidence of safety and freedom from danger or risk. National security as a concept has two perspectives: the traditional and the broader perspectives. Traditionally, national security is seen as the state of military preparedness to defend a country against external threats. From the broader perspective, national security covers not only the military preparedness of a country, but also includes political, social, economic, and environmental securities (Essien, 2008, p. 38). The conception of national security by John Mroz as "relative freedom from harmful threats" and that of Ian Bellany as "relative freedom from war coupled with a relatively high expectation that defeat will not be a consequence of any war that should occur" (Essien, 2008, p. 40) typify the cold-war era thinking about national security (Barry Buzzan, as cited in Nwolise, 2006). This is more so following Stalin's dictum that "everyone imposes his own system as far as his army has power to do so" (South Magazine, 1983, cited in Essien, 2008, p. 36).

National security from the Nigerian perspective is state centric and focuses on the military. It is within this broad context of national security that Nwolise (1985, p. 24) rightly argues,

> A country may have the best army in terms of training and equipment, the most efficient police force, the most efficient customs men, the most active secret service agents, and best quality prison, but yet be the most insecure nation in the world, as a result of defense and security problems from within—bad government, alienated and suffering masses, ignorance, hunger, unemployment, and even activities of foreign residents or companies.

In this same sense, Ujomu (2002, p. 34) argues that the consolidation of the nation's military capacities as a key approach to national security emphasizes the role of conventional military and paramilitary institutions in the maintenance of national security.

History has it that most of the crisis experienced in Nigeria since independence bordering on national security had their roots in the military and the paramilitary (especially the police). It is evident that following Nwolise's argument above, national security cannot be guaranteed by a large body of security or military forces, because, these organizations have perpetrated many atrocities leading to insecurity in the Nigerian society (Ujomu, 2002, p. 34). Examples of these atrocities include bloody coup d'état, dictatorship, corruption, oppression, human rights abuses, and state terrorism (Ujomu, 2000, pp. 38-39). The last three were exemplified in this discussion. All these untold hardships unleashed on Nigerians are the characteristics of the military regimes and their civilian collaborators. In linking this issue of national security to global capital and citizenship, three things readily come to mind: colonialism, clientelism, and prebendalism. These concepts ultimately lead to underdevelopment.

Colonialism simply means control by one power over a dependent area or people (*Webster's*, 1991, p. 261). This definition suggests superiority and inferiority. One power detects the pace the lower power will follow because that higher power is in control. The maintenance of national security has eluded the military because they have had to depend on their colonial masters for direction to enable them to handle their own domestic problems. This situation is a carry-over from their colonial origins, and these military institutions have continued to be notorious for coercion, intimidation, and oppression (Ujomu, 2002, p.35).

Thus they have been incapable of achieving operational efficiency and institutional solidarity and stability. They have engendered fractures and conflicts (Hutchful, 1998, p. 602) in the Nigerian socio-political systems and have failed to achieve any significant success in the task of national defense.

Clientelism is the very channel through which one joins the dominant class and a practice which is then seen as fundamental to the continued enjoyment of the perquisite of that class (Joseph, 1991, p. 55). The state in Nigeria is essentially comparable to the state in most developing countries which are minimally industrialized and in which the majority of the population is tied to agrarian pursuits often of marginal or precarious profitability. The state enjoys a pre-eminent position because the nation was created by foreign conquest and domination and not through a gradual process of aggregation or expansion of indigenous societies. Continued foreign penetration and domination of economy after political independence, together with the constraints to peripheral capitalist industrialization in the world economy (Joseph, 1991, p. 55), meant that access to the state remained disproportionately important in the struggle for resources for upward mobility. "Clientelism," "patronage systems," and "patron-client clusters," are terms used interchangeably to refer to the same phenomenon. It has an anthropological origin (Joseph, 1991, p. 56). According to James Scott (1972, p. 62):

> The patron-client relationship—an exchange relationship between roles—may be defined as a special case of dyadic (two-person) ties involving a largely instrumental friendship in which an individual of higher socio-economic status (patron) uses his own influence and resources to provide protection or benefits or both, for a person of lower status (client) who, for his part, reciprocates by offering general support and assistance, including personal services to the patron.

The study of clientelism as a crucial "mechanism of power" (Flynn, 1974, p. 133), especially in developing societies, proliferated very rapidly during the 1970s. Joseph (1991, p. 57) quoting Weingrod, saw a difference in the use of the notion of "patronage" by anthropologists and by political scientists. For the former, it is "a type of social relationship," while for the latter it is "a feature of government." In the case with Nigeria, it will be argued that this distinction is not a meaningful one. Patron-client ties reflect a social relationship which has also become a crucial element of the governmental process.

Nigeria, in the decades following independence, has never had a stable state-power, and the form of politics which operated at all levels including the current administration can be termed "prebendal politics." A "prebend" is an office or state, typical of feudal China and Europe, which an individual procures through examinations or as a reward for loyal service to a lord or ruler. Joseph (1991, p. 59) quoting Max Weber captures it thus:

> We wish to speak of *'prebends'* and of a *'prebendal'* organization of office wherever the lord assigns to the official rent payments for life, payments which

are somehow fixed to objects or which are essentially *economic* usufruct from lands or other sources. They must be compensations for the fulfillment of actual or fictitious office duties; they are goods permanently set aside for the economic assurance of the office.

The peculiar political and economic conditions of the post-colonial world have contributed to the entrenchment of a form of state organization, and of attitudes regarding the uses of state office, which are pre-modern. Instead of constitutional and legal systems, as well as the stated impersonal norms, determining the form of this state organization, such legal-rational features largely serve to camouflage extensive prebendal practices.

In agreement with Joseph (1991, p. 62), this work contends that clientelism and prebendalism are two of the fundamental principles of political organization and behavior in Nigeria. A person (man or woman) seeks the support of a "godfather" while trying to acquire the basic social and material goods—loans, scholarships, licenses, plots of urban land, oil blocks (as exemplified by developments in the Niger Delta), promotion and employment—and the main resource of the patron in meeting these requests is quite literally a piece of the state. One can pose such arguments in the nomination of ministers and other governmental appointments. For one to do business he/she would need an import and export license, building and other permits. There are so many other benefits accruable to political positions. Prebendalism, therefore, is a consequence of patrimonialism as northern Nigeria demonstrates with its traditional (patrimonial) emirates which have evolved in the contemporary context to embrace a prebendal use of state offices (Joseph, 1991, p. 63).

Having shown that national security is patriarchal in nature in the Nigerian case, and that colonialism, clientelism, and prebendalism are necessary ingredients for the linkage, it is pertinent to note that the multinational companies (MNCs) in the case of the Niger Delta are responsible for generating the global capital. This was evident in the recent imbroglio between the National Assembly, Movement for the Emancipation of the Niger Delta (MEND), a militant wing of the Ijaw Youth Council (IYC), and one of the multinational oil companies in laying accusations and counteraccusations on who arms the militants. It also explains the roles played by Shell, Mobil, and Chevron in the heydays of the crisis during the administrations of Generals Babangida, Abacha, Abubakar, and President Obasanjo. Fleshman (2002, p. 157) showed the role of Shell in coercing Babangida and Abacha to exterminate Saro-Wiwa and the structure of the Movement for the Survival of Ogoni People (MOSOP). He proved this by demonstrating through leaked company and Nigerian government documents how "Shell closely monitored Saro-Wiwa's foreign travels and instigated the Babangida and Abacha regimes to crush MOSOP's structures on the ground" (Fleshman, 2002, p. 157). He went on to show that Saro-Wiwa's arrest on murder charges in 1994 inaugurated an international campaign for his release and generated unwanted public scrutiny of Shell's Nigerian operations. Yet Shell's public relations strategy was to "deny MOSOP's charges of environmental degradation and to attack Saro-Wiwa's character and motives" (Fleshman, 2002, p. 157). Fleshman went on to prove that the oil companies and their owners (United States and the European Union) played a pivotal role in the "pauperization of the Niger Delta," Mobil as a "Partner in Oppression," (Fleshman, 2002, p. 158) and Chevron as mixing "Blood and Oil" (Fleshman, 2002, p.159).

Another example is the Halliburton bribe scandal where Albert "Jack" Stanley, an American national, pleaded guilty before a Houston Federal Court to serially bribing some unnamed Nigerian federal government officials to the tune of $182 million (Akanimo, 2008, p. 6). The bribes were given through two agents to win some contracts related to the $6 billion liquefied natural gas (LNG) plant in Bonny, Rivers State (Akanimo, 2008, p. 6). These "powerful" unnamed Nigerians would have made sure that whatever policy the government was going to make regarding that liquefied gas would have favored Halliburton and not any other multinational company because of their financial involvement. Therefore, whatever happens favors the metropolis, and the poor citizenry bear the brunt, just as the poor citizens of Odi had the genocidal act meted out on them without any qualms of mind on the part of both the MNCs and the Nigerian government.

Interpreting the Geneva Convention as a Further Strategy for Resolving the Odi Genocide

Following the Charter of the International Military Tribunal at Nuremberg, August 8, 1945, the attack on Odi can best be regarded as genocide. Specifically, the Statute of the International Tribunal for the prosecution of persons responsible for serious violations of International Humanitarian law committed in the territory of the former Yugoslavia since 1991, May 25, 1993, as amended should be meted out to all those who took part actively and those that handed down the orders. Everything under this statute, from Article 1 to 29 (Ratner et al., pp. 365-370), should be carried out as they are related to the protection of civilians in time of war otherwise known as the Geneva Convention IV. Emphasis will be laid here on some articles to buttress my point.

The crimes committed at Odi in 1999 fall within the ambit of Geneva Convention IV as related to treatment of civilians.

The Geneva Convention forbids:

a. Willful killing;
b. Torture or inhuman treatment;
c. Wilfully causing great suffering or serious injury to body or health;
d. Extensive destruction and appropriation of property, not justified by military necessity and carried out unlawfully and wantonly; (Article 2)
e. Wanton destruction of cities, towns or villages or devastation not justified by military necessity;

f. Attack or bombardment by whatever means of undefended towns, villages, dwellings, or buildings;
g. Seizure of destruction or willful damage done to institutions dedicated to religion, charity and education, arts and sciences, historic monuments, and works of arts and sciences; and
h. Plunder of public or private property. (Article 3)

Article 4 of the Geneva Convention condemns genocide in its entirety; it is a punishable crime against humanity. Hence, genocide means any of the following acts committed with intent to destroy, in whole or in part, a national, ethnical, racial, or religious group, as such;

a. Killing members of the group;
b. Causing serious bodily or mental harm to members of the group;
c. Deliberately inflicting on the group conditions of life calculated to bring about its physical destruction in whole or in part;
d. Imposing measures intended to prevent births within the group; and
e. Forcibly transferring children of the group to another group. (Article 4)

The following acts shall be punishable:

a. Genocide;
b. Conspiracy to commit genocide;
c. Direct and public incitement to commit genocide;
d. Attempt to commit genocide; and
e. Complicity in genocide. (Article 4) (Ratner et al., 2001, pp. 235-236).

Article 5 of the Geneva Convention condemns every act that can be classified as a crime against humanity—for example, murder, extermination, torture, rape, persecutions on political, racial, and religious grounds, and other inhumane acts.

Individual criminal responsibility as ascribed in Article 7 of the Geneva Convention should equally be considered:

1. A person who planned, instigated, ordered, committed or otherwise aided and abetted in planning, preparation or execution of a crime referred to in Articles 2 to 5 of the present statute, shall be individually responsible for the crime;
2. The official position of any accused person, whether as Head of State or Government, as responsible government officials, shall not relieve such person of criminal responsibility nor mitigate punishment; and
3. The fact that any of the acts referred to in Articles 2 to 5 of the present statute was committed by a subordinate [soldiers that executed the Odi genocide] does not relieve his superior of criminal responsibility if he knew or had reason to know that the subordinate was about to commit such acts or had done so and the superior failed to take the necessary and responsible measures to prevent such acts to punish the perpetrators thereof.

For the Nigerian state to move forward, it is important that broad-based negotiations with Niger Deltans be held. Such negotiations should involve ethnic councils from the region, religious groups, and other civil society organizations. Special reference should be made on expanded issues of local resource control as called for by Special Committee on Oil Producing Areas in 2002. In addition, the venue of the negotiation should be within Niger Delta to enhance greater transparency and local participation. It is equally important that the deliberations take into consideration the special needs of individual communities in the region, with the mind of proffering possible options for addressing them.

The Nigerian government should therefore be compelled to reform such legislations as the Petroleum Act and the Land Use Act that effectively deny local control of resources. Heavy-handed military operations should be discouraged both among the militants and the government, and negotiations between the federal government and the Niger Delta groups should be encouraged. Transparency in the administration of budget and expenditure should be made a prerequisite for aid grants to federal, state, and local governments as a means of ending the relationships between local and state administrative practices that have largely failed to address corruption.

Illicit and semi-illicit payment to the military and paramilitary security forces deployed to protect oil installations should be brought to an end. The joint venture partnerships should also be refashioned to reflect local participation and ownership. Thus, there is the need to encourage more talks (negotiation) between the government and local groups.

Environmental impact assessment (EIA), as defined by global best practices, should be carried out on individual companies' projects in the region. In collaboration with community groups (to make the study more transparent), the community's assent should be sought for and obtained before proceeding with infrastructure and other developments.

The rulings of independent arbitration and court decisions looking into environmental claims must be implemented. Both the federal government and companies should ensure that they pay this share of pollution compensation awards. More importantly, there is a need to implement these suggestions, and at the same time inaugurate a monitoring and evaluation team that will monitor their progress, setbacks, and any other issue that must be put into consideration to forestall future crises.

In conclusion, in interpreting the Geneva Convention as a further strategy for resolving the Odi genocide, this work aligns with the stipulations in Articles 2 to 5 of the present statute that if the crime was committed by a subordinate (soldiers that executed the act), that does not relieve his superior of criminal responsibility. If the superior knew or had reasons to know that his/her subordinate was about to commit such acts or had done so and the superior failed to take necessary and responsible measures to prevent such acts to punish the perpetrators thereof, he or she can be held responsible. There is no doubt that an approach such as collaboration and joint problem solving, if systematically implemented, will guarantee a gradual reduction of the incessant crisis in the

Niger Delta. Odi and the entire Niger Delta region which have remained volatile will then experience relative peace. Both the federal government and the rampaging youths should be encouraged to adopt an alternative to violence in their relations. However, the government should play a leading role in enabling the return of peace to the oil-rich but volatile region.

References

Agbo, E. (1999). Bayelsa and the Odi genocide. *Sunday Times*, December 5, p. 28.

Akanimo, S. (2008). Halliburton: How government officials were bribed with $182m. In *The Nation* Saturday, September 6, p. 6

Albert, I.O. (2001). *Introduction to third-party intervention in community conflicts*. Ibadan: John Archers Publishers Limited.

Albert, I.O. (2003). *The Odi massacre of 1999 in the context of the graffiti left by the invading Nigerian Army* (PEFS monograph, New Series No I). Ibadan: University of Ibadan, Department of Political Science.

Ali, B.A. (1999). Nigeria: Focus on the deployment of troops in Odi. Retrieved July 23, 2007, from http://www.africa.upenn.edu/Newsletters/irinw-123099.html.

Asoya, S. (1999). The Odi killings. *The News*. Vol. 29 (08), 04 December.

Best, G.S. (Ed.). (2006). *Introduction to peace and conflict studies in West Africa*. Ibadan: Spectrum Books Limited.

Chukwurah, H., Orimolade, A., & Ogoigbe, E. (1999). Bloody shoot-out in Bayelsa. *National Concord*. Tuesday, November 23.

Ebiri, K. (2009). Protests rage against JTF: Government links politicians with militants. In *The Guardian*. June 12, pp. 1-2.

Essien, F.E. (2008). Niger Delta conflict and Nigeria's national security. Unpublished Ph.D. thesis, Institute of African Studies, University of Ibadan, Nigeria.

Fleshman, M. (2001). The international community and the crisis in Nigeria's oil producing communities. Retrieved May 14, 2008, from ACAS Bulletin: It's About Oil! http://www.jstor.org/stable/4006874/articles/html.

Flynn, P. (1974). Class, clientelism, and coercion: Some mechanism of internal dependency and control. *Journal of Commonwealth and Comparative Politics,* 12(2), pp. 133-156.

Human Rights and Civil Society Groups. (1999). Genocide in Odi. Retrieved on July 6, 2007, from http://www.africaaction.org/resources/ejournals.php.

Hutchful, E. (1998). (Ed.) The military and militarism in Africa. Senegal: CODESRIA.

Ikime, O. (1969). *Niger Delta rivalry: Itsekiri-Urhobo relation and the European presence, 1884-1936*. London: Longman.

International Crisis Group. (2006a). Fuelling the Niger Delta crisis. (Crisis Group Africa Report No. 118). Retrieved June 15, 2008. from www.crisisgroup.org.

International Crisis Group. (2006b). The swamps of insurgency: Nigeria's Niger Delta unrest. (Crisis Group Briefing No. 115). Retrieved June 15, 2008, from www.crisisgroup.org.

Joseph, R. (1991). *Democracy and prebendal politics in Nigeria the rise and fall of the Second Republic*. Ibadan: Spectrum Books Limited.

Lemkin, R. (1944). Axis rule in occupied Europe. Washington: Carnegie Endowment for International Peace.

Nwolise, O.B.C. (1985). (Ed.). *Nigeria: The first 25 years*. Ibadan: Heinemann.

Nwolise, O.B.C. (2006). (Ed.). *Challenges of sustainable democracy*. Ibadan: John Achers Publishers Limited.

Ogbogbo, C.B.N. (2005). The Niger Delta people and the resource control conflict, 1960-1995: An assessment of conflict handling styles. In I.O. Albert (Ed.), *Perspective on peace and conflict in Africa*, pp. 169-180. Ibadan: John Archers Publishers Limited.

Ojiji, O. (2006). Conflict handling styles. In G.S. Best (Ed.), *Introduction to peace and conflict studies in West Africa*, pp. 116-129. Ibadan: Spectrum Books Limited.

Okonta, I, & Douglas, O. (1999). (Eds.). *Where the vultures feast*. Port Harcourt: ERA Publications.

Ombe, I. (2000). Royal Highness recounts experience on the invasion of Odi. *The Comet*, November 26.

Onuorah, M., and Ebiri, K. (2009). Niger Delta crisis: Over 60 feared dead. In *The Guardian*, May 17.

Osuoka, I. (1999). Killing spree in Bayelsa. Retrieved May 12, 2008, from http://www.earthrights.net/nigeria/eco.plan. html.

Oyeleye, D. (1999). The occupation of Bayelsa. *Tribune*, Tuesday, November, 23.

Ratner, S.R., & Abrams, J.S. (2001). (Eds.). *Accountability for human rights atrocities in international law*. London: Oxford University Press.

Roberts, N.F.O. (1998). Managing the minorities and development problem in Nigerian federalism: The OMPADEC Initiative. (NISER Monograph Series No. 11). Ibadan: NISER.

Saro-Wiwa, K. (1990). *Ogoni bill of rights*. Port Harcourt: Saros International Publishers.

Scott, J. (1972). Patron-client politics and political change in Southeast Asia. *American Political Science Review*. 66(1), pp. 91-113.

Ujomu, P. (2000). Ethics and national security in Nigeria: Critical issues in the search for sustainable development. *The Voice*. Millennial Edition (No. 39), pp. 38-40.

Ujomu, P. (2002). In S.O.O. Amali et al. (Ed.), *Consolidation and sustenance of democracy The United States of America and Nigeria*. Ibadan: Hope Publications Ltd.

UNDP. (2006). Niger Delta human development report. Ikeja: Perfect Printers Ltd.

Washington, James M. (Ed.). *A testament of hope*. San Francisco: Harper.

Webster's Ninth New Collegiate Dictionary. (1991). Markham, Ontario: Merriam-Webster Inc.

SECTION V

CONCLUSION

CHAPTER NINETEEN

CONCLUSION

OLUTAYO C. ADESINA, AKANMU G. ADEBAYO, AND RASHEED O. OLANIYI

Two dissimilar forces at work in contemporary Africa—homogenization and hegemonization, both of which are offshoots of the globalization process—have compounded the continent's problems in the global age. Globalization and global forces have moved significantly to affect national cultures and have gone ahead to negate cultural boundaries (Akoh, 2008, pp. 163-175) in ways previously unknown. In a world in which there are no longer definable frontiers geographically and where the spread of ideas has gone unhindered, marginality and crisis are the symptoms of a much deeper malaise unleashed by globalization. The reasons are obvious. Globalization has become a new way of legitimizing the ideas and practices of relations of superiority and inferiority. In other words, it has become an effective instrument of not only socio-economic but also political domination. In the process, all much older principles of domination such as gender, religion, region, race, ethnicity, etc. have acquired new meanings. In several locales, globalization has also developed, defined, or redefined the society's structure of power, complete with all forms of control, appropriation, and exploitation. The changing conditions created by globalization has therefore led not only to deep contestations, but has also altered patterns of existence and reasoning. Thus, while many assumptions and positions have attended the effects of globalization, several positions have also emphasized certain aspects such as development, equity, and social justice, and how these orient the dynamics of thinking in the global age (Stiglitz, 2002; Chomsky, 2003; Wolf,

2004). The consequences these offer for action in Africa have been assessed by several authors in this volume.

While contemporary globalization has coincided with the triumph of global capitalism and neo-liberal democracy (Amuwo, 2009, p. 37), the African condition in the age of globalization on the other hand has been rooted in acts of political brigandage, ethnic rivalry and hegemony, leadership struggles, economic slavery, under-development, brain drain, corruption, reprisal and revenge attacks, and inordinate ambitions (Abaagye & Bah, 2005, p. 281; Oche, 1998, p. 117). Any political progress in the last 30 years has been irrelevant to most Africans (Calderisi, 2006, p. 60). From this perspective, it is therefore easy to accept Mamdani's position (2004, p. 3) that "the modern political sensibility sees most political violence as necessary to historical process."

Several policies enthroned and entrenched by globalization have at the end of the day compounded the African problem. Specifically, the World Trade Organization (WTO) has served primarily the U.S. government and corporate interests over developing country and civil society interests (Cavanagh & Mander, 2004, p. 66). Also, the debt crisis sucked the vitality out of African economies. Rather than working to help reduce the problems associated with this, the International Monetary Fund (IMF) and the governments of the creditor nations did what they could to make sure the poverty-stricken countries of Africa and other developing countries fulfilled their debt obligations, whatever the costs to their people (Stiglitz, 2007, p. 220). What this meant for underdeveloped countries has been amplified by Collier (2007, p. 91): "The lack of capital inflows is only half the story of why global capital markets are not working for the bottom billion. The other half is that their own capital flows out of them." The privatization strategy, also an essential component of globalization, has succinctly been described as "a means of taking over enterprises and penetrating markets so much as it is a means of eliminating structures of production which could compete or challenge an imperially dominated world" (Petras & Veltmeyer, 2001, p. 93). This has been amplified by Hoogvelt (2001, p. 121) when he asserted that globalization is nothing more than the deepening phase of capitalist integration. This deepened the exploitation and subjugation of the African continent. Thus, like the earlier phases, poverty and unemployment on the African continent began to reach an intolerable level. Indeed, inadequate income is a strong predisposing condition for an impoverished life (Sen, 2000, p. 87). The implications were clear and far-reaching. Africans began to move out of the continent in droves, with at least 70,000 skilled graduates abandoning the continent every year (Calderisi, p. 5). People also began to revolt and resist government policies. Others took out their anger and frustration on fellow Africans: migrants from sister African countries. A salient example of such transferred aggression was the case of acute xenophobia in South Africa. As noted by Amuwo (2009, p. 57):

> The immediate cause of the virulent xenophobia that gripped several townships in South African major cities of Johannesburg, Durban, and Cape Town in May

> and June 2008 was displaced and misplaced aggression spurred by unprecedented rising costs of living occasioned by a series of price and interest rare shocks, galloping inflation and high gasoline prices. As life became more and more unbearable for ordinary South Africans, reinforcing failed government policies and lack of social delivery, less skilled foreigners who live amongst them became easy targets of senseless attacks, looting, rape and murder.

There is no gainsaying the fact that wars, civil wars, ethnic rivalries, and complex emergencies have punctuated the last 40 years of African history (Nwolise, 1997, p. 39), but the history of the continent in the last two decades has been that of acute and unprecedented strife. According to Chris Garba (1998), "[a]s recently as 1998, people in about 14 of Africa's 53 countries [were] engaged in armed conflicts simultaneously. These violent conflicts have taken severe economic and social tolls on the continent, seriously undermining development efforts in many countries" (p. 149). An estimated 20 million people are known to have been displaced by conflict in the Great Lakes region countries of Rwanda, Burundi, and the Democratic Republic of Congo; Somalia, Sudan, Sierra Leone, Liberia, and Cote D'Ivoire. But if the crisis of the early periods were symptomatic of changing conditions such as decolonization and the Cold War, the crises witnessed in recent years were the results of the post-Cold War era and the overweening effects of globalization. The continent cannot but remain prostrate as the forces of globalization and tyranny have combined to hold on tightly to the continent's jugular.

The unending cycle of catastrophe, tyranny, economic problems, and civil wars have not sent a good signal for the future. The continent is experiencing a failure of its structures and systems. This has led to pertinent questions: Is Africa imploding and fragmenting? Is the state really becoming more corrupt, oppressive, and inefficient? Or is the continent rejuvenating itself? How much of this was really a problem of the global disorder created by globalization? The process of rolling back the nation-state in Africa has assumed a frenetic dimension. African youths are now growing up in a world highly dissimilar to that of their fathers and grandfathers. It is a brave new world where the aspirations of a new generation can no longer be taken for granted. The problematic nation-state, which had become the primary defining entity of African nations in the contemporary world, is being forced to reassess itself. The movement of the planet into unipolarity and multi-civilizational world order also has significance for Africa as these have affected the equilibrium built in the days of the Cold War.

The African continent has a plurality of systems that has made it to be identified as the new Tower of Babel. The crises and conflict on the African continent have had monumental economic, political, social, and psychological consequences. The relative decline of the continent and the rise of the developing countries of Asia have brought into bold relief the polar opposite effects of globalization on different parts of the world. While China, India, and the Asian Tigers are on the same trajectory of focused development, the countries of Africa are still battling with the problems of ethnicity and underdevelopment. The younger African generation is growing up to love American culture and ways of life. The passion for consumption and an urbane life has opened a new battlefront, one in which new questions are being asked and new values are being constructed. In the process, the world has come to taint Africa as the land of conflict, corruption, and crisis.

However, from the depth of marginality and crisis comes a glimpse of hope. The crisis situation has allowed the continent to adopt new paradigms and strategies. The new strategy ranged from Nigeria's rapprochement with the Niger Delta militants to East Africa's use of Swahili as a tool of integration. For Barkawi (2006), in his incisive study of the variable processes of interconnectedness and how this has affected the nation-state in the contemporary world, he affirmed that war does not just tear nations apart; it brings people and places together, providing a new lens on globalization. He has therefore conceived war as a form of interconnection between home and abroad, and as an occasion for circulation and interchange. This perspective has ennobled the impulses of integration and interconnectedness. This has been amply demonstrated by Noordin (in this volume) who asserted that Kiswahili was used not only as a liberation language in Mozambique, Zimbabwe, and South Africa during apartheid, but also recently played a crucial role in the expansion of the East African Community (EAC), which was expanded in 2007 to include Rwanda and Burundi, two countries wracked by unremitting civil war and genocide. The expansion of the EAC as a tool of integration immediately posed the fundamental question of the role of Kiswahili in relation to other languages in the process of identity formation in the EAC. This arose from the fact that many citizens of Rwanda and Burundi who lived in Tanzania over an extended period as political refugees not only speak Kiswahili but have also adopted it and institutionalized it through use of the Swahili culture (Kawoya & Makokha, 2009).

Sachs' (2005, p. 360) assertion seems to offer some inspiration and guidance to Africans in the present age. He reiterated: "As global prosperity has accelerated in the past two centuries, each generation has been called upon to meet new challenges in extending the possibilities of human well-being" (p. 360). The challenges of marginality, crises, and underdevelopment have continuously stared Africa in the face. The continent has no reason not to meet such new challenges head-on. Thus, as Africans look forward to sustained development, therefore, the building of strong people-centered institutions and structures, and good governance have become the new mantra. Building a better world and future together based on equality is sine qua non to peace and development. The construction of the nation-state in Africa on a structure based and organized on the dominance of a particular group and a feeling of cultural superiority has become anachronistic in the age of globalization. The acute dependence on the rentier state and the deeply rooted attitude of keeping the other groups down have also gone with the Cold War. The world is now witnessing a rapid configuration of the world based on mobility of peoples and the waning of the global dominance of the Western powers. The state is having its powers curbed by non-state actors who have also sought to impose a redefinition of reality and by a generation that has begun to entertain other ambitions beyond the restrictive embrace of the state. Globalization has left an indelible impression on the minds of the brave and younger generation of Africans. Although we still live in a world that conforms to a Western template, Africa, like Asia, has to begin to recognize the plurality of its structure and the need to reinvent the continent.

References

Abaagye, F., & Bah, M.S. (2005). *Tortuous road to peace: The dynamics of regional, United Nations and international humanitarian interventions in Liberia.* Pretoria: ISS Press,

Akoh, A.D. (2008). What is globalization to post-colonialism? An apologia for African literature. *Journal of Global Initiatives: Policy, Pedagogy, Perspective*, 3(2), pp. 163-176.

Amuwo, K. (2009). Politics, identity and citizenship in diasporic spaces: Skilled African migrants in France and South Africa. In A. G. Adebayo & O. C. Adesina (Eds.), *Globalization and transnational migrations. Africa and Africans in the contemporary global system*, pp. 36-63. Newcastle upon Tyne: Cambridge Scholars Publishing.

Barkawi, T. (2006). *Globalization and war.* Lanham: Rowman & Littlefield.

Calderisi, R. (2006). *The trouble with Africa. Why foreign aid isn't working.* New York: Palgrave Macmillan.

Cavanagh, J., & Mander, J. (Eds.). (2004). *Alternatives to economic globalization: A better world is possible.* San Francisco: Berrett-Koehler Publishers, Inc.

Chomsky, N. (2003). *Hegemony or survival: America's quest for global dominance.* New York: Metropolitan Books

Collier, P. (2007). *The bottom billion.* Oxford: Oxford University Press.

Garba, C.A. (1998). *Capacity building for crisis management in Africa.* Lagos: Gabumo Publishing Limited.

Hoogvelt, A. (2001). *Globalization and the post-colonial world: The new political economy of development.* Baltimore: Johns Hopkins University Press.

Kawoya, V., & Makokha, M. (2009). The case of Kiswahili as a regional broadcasting language in east Africa. *Journal of Pan African Studies* 2(8), pp. 11-37.

Mamdani, M. (2004). *Good Muslim, bad Muslim. America, the cold war, and the roots of terror.* New York: Pantheon Books.

Noordin, M.M. (2010). Kiswahili language and the future of the East African integration in the age of globalization. (Chapter 5 in this volume).

Nwolise, O.B.C. (1997). ECOMOG peace-keeping operations in Liberia: Effects on political stability in the west African sub-region. *Africa Peace Review* 1(1), p. 39.

Oche, D.O. (1998). *Africa and the United Nations system: The first fifty years.* Lagos: Nigerian Institute of International Affairs, Printing Press Division.

Petras, J., & Veltmeyer, H. (2001). *Globalization unmasked: Imperialism in the 21st century,* Halifax, NS: Fernwood Publishing Limited.

Sachs, J.D. (2005). *The end of poverty.* New York: Penguin Books.

Sen, A. (2000). *Development as freedom.* Oxford: Oxford University Press.

Stiglitz, J.E. (2002). *Globalization and its discontents.* New York: W.W. Norton.

Stiglitz, J.E. (2007). *Making globalization work.* New York: W.W. Norton.

Wolf, M. (2004). *Why globalization works.* New Haven: Yale University Press.

INDEX

Abuja, 22
Accra, 22
Acheulian, 32
Addis Ababa, 66
Adebayo, Akanmu G., xvi
Adesina, Olutayo C., xvi
Afghanistan, 6, 22, 93
Africa, xv, xvi, 3, 4, 5, 7, 10, 13, 15, 16, 19, 21, 22, 26, 37, 38, 39, 40, 65, 90, 106, 118, 121, 125, 127, 128, 168, 169, 170, 175, 181, 192, 213; African Rural Women Day, 77; African Union (AU), 64, 65, 66, 68; sub-Saharan African States, 122, 125
Afro-Brazilians, 35
Aguda, 35
ajobi, 53, 54; *alajobi*, 43, 44, 52, 54
ajogbe, 53, 54; *alajogbe*, 53, 54
Ake, 9, 81, 82, 83, 87
American, 4; citizens, 4; Indians, 34; occupation, 6
Americo-Liberians, 184, 185
Anan, Kofi, 93
anti-globalization, 5, 6
Arab, 22, 23, 189; Arabic, 66; Arabic script, 64
Argentina, 35, 36
Aristotle, 33, 48
Asante, 34
Asia, 7, 26, 32, 65, 121, 168, 169; Asian Tigers, 261; South, 89; Southeast, 40
Association of South East Asian Nations (ASEAN), 168
Australia, 15, 33
Awolowo, Obafemi, 210

Bakweri women, 72
Baptist missionaries, 73
Bauchi, 94
Bello, Ahmadu, 210
Benin, 24, 33, 34, 77
Boko Haram, 5
brain drain, 21
Brazil, 32, 35, 36, 40
Brazilian architecture, 36
Bretton Woods institutions, 6, 169
British Consul, 91
Burundi, 9, 61, 63, 65, 66, 262

Cable News Network (CNN), 226
Cairo, 4
Calabar, 4
Cameroon, 4, 71, 72, 74, 76, 78; National Union (CNU), 77
Canada, 5
Cancun, 25
capitalism, 16, 17; unbridled, 27
capitalist, 6
Casablanca, 4
cassava, 34

Central Bank of Nigeria (CBN), 113, 156
Chile, 32, 35, 40, 169
China, 5, 10, 21, 167, 261
choiceless democracies, 24
Cicero, 49
citizenship, 9
clientelism, 8, 249, 250
Cold War, 16
communism, 16
community based organizations (CBOs), 8, 133, 135, 136, 137, 139, 140, 142, 143, 144, 145
compatriotism, 43, 46, 47, 50, 52
Congo, Democratic Republic of, 64, 261
cosmopolitanism, 43, 46, 47, 49, 50
Cote d'Ivoire, 174, 261
crisis, 3
Cuba, 35, 36, 40
cultural, 6, 83, 84; hybridity, 82; imperialism, 6
cyber cafe, 4

Dahomey, 35
Daniel, Isioma, 95
Danish, 92, 93, 95
Darfur, 7, 182, 187, 189
Das Kapital, 16
Dasuki, Ibrahim, Sultan of Sokoto, 92
Davos, 25
de Sousa, F.F., 35
developing, 20; world, 20, 122; countries, 23, 125, 169
diaspora, 7, 35, 36, 202
Doe, Samuel, 185
Doha, 25
Douala, 73, 77

East Africa, 9, 61, 67, 262
East African, 9; Community (EAC), 9, 61, 63, 68, 262; Integration Taskforce, 67; Kiswahili Commission, 66
Economic Commission of West African States (ECOWAS), 128, 168
Egypt, 33, 40; Egyptian pyramids, 33
El-Zakzaky, 91
Environmental Impact Assessment (EIA), 253
Ethiopia, 173, 174, 175
ethnic conflict, 211, 212
EU-ACP (European Union–Africa, Caribbean, and Pacific), 20
Europe, 15, 16, 21, 32, 65, 92, 93, 168, 174; European, 4, 16; European Union (EU), 126, 127, 128
Ewe, 34, 35

fair trade, 10
fatwa, 92
Federal Office of Statistics (FOS), 113, 139
female circumcision, 7
Fernando Po, 35
foreign direct investment (FDI), 20, 21, 120, 125, 127, 152
free market ideology, 4
free trade, 8
Friedman, T., xvi
Friends of the Earth, 230

Galtung, Johan, 17
gari, 34, 35
General Agreement on Trade and Tariffs (GATT), 20, 119
genocide, 182, 190, 240, 241
Ghana, 32, 77; Ghanaians, 22, 34
global, 3; capital, 7, 8; economy, 7, 18; governance, 7, 15, 18; identity, 3; issues, 7; media, 10; politics, 22; processes and interconnections, 3; restructuring of capitalism, 3; South, 4, 6, 8; trade, 163; village, 10, 20, 54, 55

globalization, xv, xvi, 3, 4, 5, 6, 7, 8, 9, 10, 13, 15, 16, 18, 20, 21, 22, 23, 24, 26, 31, 32, 34, 35, 37, 39, 40, 43, 44, 45, 46, 54, 55, 83, 84, 89, 90, 97, 103, 104, 105, 107, 118, 122, 149, 150, 167, 168, 169, 170, 182, 220, 259, 263; of development, 26; glocalization, 84; and transnational migrations, xvi; and the unending frontier, xvi; of world economy, 26
globe, 45
Gothenburg, 5, 6
grassroots, 24; resistance, 24
Great Lakes, region, 261
Greeks, 33, 40, 49
Group of Eight (G8), 25
Gumi, Shaikh, 90

Haiti, 35
Harare Declaration on Human Rights, 233
Hausa, 66
highly industrialized economies, 164
hijab, 95
HIV/AIDS, 6, 122, 134
Hobson, J.A., 17
hometown associations, 7
homo erectus, 31
homo sapiens, 33
Human Development Index (HDI), 113
Huntington, S., 22
Hutu, 183

Ibadan, xv, 96; Government College, 82; University of, xv, 4, 24
Ifa, 36
Ife Descendants Union, 202
Ife-Modakeke crisis, 7, 197, 198, 201, 206
Igala, 37
Igbo, 34, 37
Ijaw Youth Council (IYC), 234, 244
Imhotep, 33
imperialism, 16
India, 5, 10, 21, 167, 169, 170, 261
industrial capital, 15
industrialized nations, 9, 13
Information and Communication Technologies (ICT), 7, 20
Intellectual Property Rights, 23
International Bank for Reconstruction and Development (IBRD), 108
International Finance Corporation (IFC), 109
International Labour Organization (ILO), 153
International Monetary Fund (IMF), 25, 26, 38, 39, 40, 105, 107, 260
International NGOs, 6
Internet, 6, 10, 45, 93, 97
Iran, 91
Iraq, 6, 22
isakole, 203
Isara, 82
Islam, 10, 23, 90
ivory tower, 5
Izala, 90

Jamaatul Izalat al-Bid'ah wa Iqama as Sunnah, 90
Janjaweed, 188
Japan, 21
Joint Military Task Fore (JTF), 240
joint-stock companies, 15
Jyllands Posten, 92

Kabba, 10, 71, 72, 73, 74, 75, 76, 77, 78; *onikaba,* 85
Kaduna, 91, 95
Kano, 4, 95
Kant, Immanuel, 49, 50
kenke, 34

Kennesaw, xv, 24; University, xv, 24
Kenya, 4, 9, 32, 62, 64, 67
Khomeini, Ayatollah, 91, 92
Kinyarwanda, 64
Kiswahili, 61, 62, 63, 64, 65, 66, 67, 262
Kuwait, 95
Kyoto Protocol, 176

Lagos, 36, 94
Land Use Act; 240, 253; Land Use Decree, 200
Latin America, 7, 121, 168, 169, 170
Lebanon, 93
left-wing student unionism, 5
Lenin, V.I., 17
liberalization, 9, 18, 83, 119, 149
Liberia, 174
Low Income Countries Under Stress (LICUS), 175

Madagasar, 124
Magubane, Zine, xv
Maiduguri, 94
Malawi, 24, 124
Malaysia, 167, 169
Mamdani, Mahmood, 22
Mandela, Nelson, 233
Mano River area, 7, 181, 193; conflict, 184
marginality, 3, 192; marginalization, xv, 3, 9, 16
Marx, Karl, 16, 17
Mau Mau, 65
Mazrui rebellion, 65
Mexico, 170
Middle East, 22, 23, 90, 91, 97, 174
military dictatorship, 6
Millennium Development Goals (MDG), 129
Modakeke Progressive International, 202
Mohammad, Prophet, 92, 95
Movement for the Emancipation of the Niger Delta (MEND), 226, 250
Movement for the Survival of Ogoni Peoples (MOSOP), 232, 243, 250
Mozambique, 65, 126, 262
Muna, Madam Ama Tutu, 78

Nasrullahi-Fathi Society of Nigeria (NASFAT), 93
National Patriotic Front of Liberia (NPFL), 187
National Population Commission (NPC), 139
neo-bipolarism, 16
neo-Marxism, 17
New International Economic Order (NIEO), 24
New Partnership for African Development (NEPAD), 128, 129
Niger, 174; Niger Delta, 6, 8, 163, 225, 226, 230, 234, 235, 236, 239, 240, 246, 247, 250, 254, 262
Niger Delta Peoples Volunteer Force (NDPVF), 226
Niger Republic, 174, 175
Nigeria, 4, 5, 7, 8, 10, 32, 35, 91, 93, 94, 97, 104, 106, 113, 114, 124, 175, 210, 230, 240,248, 262; NIGCOMSAT, 26; northern, 6; Television Authority (NTA), 26
Nigerian Muslims, 89, 92
non-governmental organizations (NGOs), 4, 7, 134
North, 13, 14, 15, 16, 18, 24; America, 15
Norway, 5

Obasanjo, Olusegun, 108, 214, 235
Odi, 8
Ogboni cult, 85, 86
Ogoni, 6; Ogoniland, 231

Onitsha, 94
Organization for Economic Cooperation and Development (OECD), 23, 167
Organization of Islamic Conference (OIC), 93
orisas, 36
Oslo, 5
outsourcing, 4

Pakistan, 22, 93
Palestinian Territory, 22
patriotism, 48
Pentecostal, 5
Plato, 33, 48
polio, 6
Pope John Paul II, 96
popular culture, 9
poverty, 120, 122, 167, 170, 172, 173, 174; alleviation, 117, 118; alleviation programs, 6; reduction, 169
privatization, 104, 106, 108, 113, 114, 124
Puerto Rico, 40

Quebec, 5
Qur'an, 90, 95

Ransome-Kuti, Rev and Mrs., 82, 85
Revolutionary United Front (RUF), 186
Rushdie, Salman, 91, 92
Rwanda, 7, 9, 61, 64, 66, 175, 181, 190, 261, 262

Saker, Rev Alfred, 73, 74
Sankoh, Foday, 186
Santeria, 35, 40
Sao Tome, 35
Saro-Wiwa, Ken, 226
Satanic Verses, The, 91, 92
Saudi Arabia, 95, 96
Sawa women, 71, 73, 75, 77, 78
Seattle, 5, 25
sekete, 34
Shiite, 91
Sierra Leone, 173, 174, 175, 186, 261
slave trade, 15; trans-Atlantic, 35
Somalia, 173, 261; Somalis, 4
Sotho, 66
South, 5, 9, 13, 14, 16, 18, 20, 24, 26, 27
South Africa, 65, 262; African Preferential Treatment Trade Area (PTA), 168
South America, 26
Southern Hemisphere, 5
Soyinka, Wole, 81, 83, 84, 92
state-owned enterprises (SOEs), 107, 108, 114
Stiglitz, J., xvi
Stone Age, 31
structural adjustment program (SAP), 20, 24
Sudan, 4, 175, 189, 261; Sudan Federal Democratic Alliance (SFDA), 190; Sudan People's Liberation Movement (SPLM), 187
Swahili, 66, 262
Sweden, 5

Taiwan, 5
Tanzania, 62, 63, 64, 66
Technical Committee on Privatization and Commercialization (TCPC), 114
Thatcher, Margaret, 105
Tiv-Jukun ethnic crisis, 7, 209, 211, 218, 219, 222; conflict, 221
Togo, 32, 34
Tolbert, William, 185
transnational, 15, 77; corporations, 15, 19; interconnections, 37
Trilateral Commission, 25
Trinidad, 35, 40

Tswana, 66
Tunisia, 124
Turkey, 93
Tutsi, 183, 190, 191, 192

Uganda, 62, 63, 66
underdevelopment, 26
United Kingdom, 38
United Nations (U.N), 24; Development Programme (UNDP), 113, 121, 134, 140
United States, 16, 21, 22, 23, 35, 38, 65, 91, 127, 170; Agency for International Development (USAID), 174; Environmental Protection Agency, 230
Unity Party of Nigeria (UPN), 200
Uruguay Round, 20
USSR, 16

Victoria, Queen 1, 73

Washington, D.C., 25
West, 5, 16, 20, 22, 26, 27, 37
West Africa, 33, 34; African Gas Pipeline (WAGP), 235
Western values, 36
Whitman, A.R., 72
Wild Christian, 82
witchcraft, 4
World Bank, 5, 24, 25, 26, 121, 140, 230; Conference, 5; Policy Research Report, 169; Report, 168
World Economic Forum, 25
World Trade Organization (WTO), 5, 19, 20, 24, 25, 26, 38, 39, 40, 105, 109, 119, 124, 125, 176, 260

xenophobia, 183, 260

Yoruba, 34, 35, 37, 52, 66, 84; cosmology, 44; cosmo-morality, 52
Yorubaland, 34

Zambia, 24
Zanzibar, 77
Zeleza, Paul, xv, xvi
Zimbabwe, 65, 262
Zulu, 66

About the Editors

Akanmu G. Adebayo is professor of history at Kennesaw State University, Georgia, USA. He earned his Ph.D. from Obafemi Awolowo University, Ile-Ife, Nigeria. He is author of *Embattled Federalism: A History of Revenue Allocation in Nigeria* (New York, 1993), co-author of *Culture, Politics and Money Among the Yoruba* (New Brunswick, 2000), co-editor of *Instructional Technology for Basic Education in Ghana* (Cape Coast, 2003), and co-editor of *Globalization and Transnational Migrations* (London, 2009). He is currently working on a book-length study of African economic history since 1900.

Olutayo C. Adesina obtained his doctorate from Obafemi Awolowo University, Ile-Ife, Nigeria. He is currently Associate Professor of History at the University of Ibadan, Nigeria, where he teaches courses on Nigerian history, Economic history of West Africa, and History of Development. Dr. Adesina is Guest Editor of *Journal of Global Initiatives* (Special Edition, Vol. 3 No. 2, 2008), and also co-editor of *Globalization and Transnational Migrations: Africa and Africans in the Contemporary Global System* (2009). He is currently working on a book-length study of Indians in Nigerian History, Economy, and Society.

Rasheed O. Olaniyi is a lecturer in the Department of History, University of Ibadan and Sub-Dean (General) Faculty of Arts (2007-2009). He earned his Ph.D. from Bayero University, Kano, Nigeria. He is the author of *Diaspora Is Not Like Home: A Social and Economic History of Yoruba in Kano, 1912-1999* (Muenchen: Lincom Europa-www.lincom-europa.com, 2008); and *Community Vigilantes in Metropolitan Kano, 1985-2005* (Ibadan, 2005). He is currently working on post-doctoral research on Yoruba migrants' identity in Ghana.

About the Contributors

Olajide O. Akanji holds a doctorate degree in Political Science from the University of Ibadan, Nigeria. He currently teaches political science in the Department of Political Science of the same university. His areas of specialization include conflict and security issues, human rights, citizenship, and governance studies. His latest publication is "Group Rights and Conflicts in Africa: A Critical Reflection on Ife-Modakeke, Nigeria," *International Journal on Minority and Group Rights* (Volume 16, No 1, 2009).

Osita Agbu is an Associate Research Professor at the Nigerian Institute of International Affairs, Lagos, Nigeria. He earned his Ph.D. in Political Science from the University of Nigeria, Nsukka. He is the editor of *Children and Youth in the Labour Process in Africa* (CODESRIA, 2009); and author of *The Iron and Steel Industry and Nigeria's Industrialization: Exploring Cooperation with Japan* (Institute of Developing Economies, IDE-JETRO, 2007), *West Africa's Trouble Spots and the Imperative for Peace-Building* (CODESRIA, 2006), and *Ethnic Militias and the Threat to Democracy in Post-Transition Nigeria* (Nordic Africa Institute, 2004).

Moses T. Aluaigba is a Research Fellow at the Aminu Kano Centre for Democratic Research and Training, Mambayya House, Bayero University, Kano, Nigeria. He is currently a doctoral candidate in Political Economy and Development Studies at the University of Abuja, Nigeria. He was a Fulbright Visiting Scholar in African Studies at Ohio University Athens from August 2008 to May 2009. His contributions on various areas of political economy are published as book chapters and articles in national and international journals. His research interests include democracy, democratization in Nigeria, ethnic conflicts, conflict resolution, and research methods

Ronald Olufemi Badru is a doctoral candidate in the Department of Philosophy, University of Ibadan, Nigeria. He is a lecturer in philosophy at the Department of Politics and International Relations, Lead City University, Ibadan, Nigeria, and at the Saints Peter & Paul Major Seminary, New Bodija, Ibadan, an affiliate of the University of Ibadan, Nigeria. He has published in both local and international journals. He has also attended and presented papers at local and international conferences. His areas of research interest include African metaphysics and epistemology, global justice, democracy and governance, peace and conflict.

H. O. Danmole, Ph.D., is currently Professor and Head, Department of History, Lagos State University, Ojo. Formerly Professor of History at the University of Ilorin, he was at various times the Head of the Department of History. A seasoned scholar, Professor Danmole has contributed extensively to books as well as local and international journals. He is currently working on a book-length study entitled "Between Ilorin and Lagos: Studies in Islamic Cultural History of Yorubaland."

Sheriff Folarin lectures in the Department of Political Science & International Relations at Covenant University, Ota, Ogun State, Nigeria. He is also currently the International Students Officer of the university. A member of the U.S. State Alumni and IVLP, Folarin won the Fulbright Scholarship grant for the Study of the United States Institute on Foreign Policy in 2007, which took him and 18 others from across the world to the Walker Institute of International & Area Studies (WIIAS)/Department of Political Science, University of South Carolina, USA. Folarin is well published in the areas of foreign policy and diplomatic history.

Agbo Uchechukwu Johnson is lecturer of Political Science at Taraba State University, Jalingo, Nigeria. He earned his Ph.D. from Ahmadu Bello University, Zaria, Nigeria. He is co-author of *Communication for Health and Sustainable Development in Nigeria* (2008), co-author of *Parties and Politics in Nigeria, 1999-2009* (2009). He has numerous journal publications. He is currently working on a book, *Early Warning Study of Socio-economic and Political Issues in Africa in the Post Cold War Era.*

Olayinka Idowu Kareem is a research fellow at the Centre for Public-Private Cooperation and a Ph.D. candidate of the Department of Economics, University of Ibadan, Nigeria. He has worked on diverse areas such as the application of econometrics in trade and development, pension and social protection as well as economic governance. He has authored a number of articles in both local and international journals. He is currently doing a study on Nigeria's trade relations with China and the European Union.

Eamon Lenihan is the Director, Centre for Sustainable Livelihoods, University College Cork, Ireland. His main areas of expertise include exploring the two-way linkages between HIV/AIDS, nutrition, and food/agricultural production;

rural livelihoods and food security; small-scale rural enterprises; small-scale/co-operative dairy enterprises; rural credit and rural financial institutions; rural resource management; economic analysis of small-scale farming systems and project analysis.

Flavius Mayoa Mokake is a graduate student in the Department of History, University of Buea, Cameroon. He has a chapter in an edited book, *Cameroon: The Stakes and Challenges for Governance and Development* (2009). He is currently involved in a project on "Street Children and Lumpen Youth: Childhood and Youth Livelihood at the Margins."

David Omeiza Moveh is a doctoral candidate and an assistant lecturer in the Department of Political Science, Ahmadu Bello University, Zaria. His M.Sc. research (2007) was on the Political Economy of Privatization in Nigeria. Moveh has authored several articles in books and journals, including the *African Journal of Social Policy and Administration.*

Mwanakombo Mohammed Noordin is a lecturer of Kiswahili language and literature at Moi University, Eldoret, Kenya. She has recently submitted a Ph.D. thesis at Moi University, Kenya. She is the co-editor of *Kiswahili: A Tool for Development: The Multidisciplinary Approach* (Moi University Press, 2001). She is currently working on a study of Islamic feminism on the culture of Swahili women.

Olalekan Emmanuel Obademi is a lecturer with the Department of Financial Studies, Redeemer's University, Nigeria. He is about completing a Ph.D. in Finance having already obtained an M.Sc. in Economics from University of Ado-Ekiti, M.Sc. in Agric-economics from University of Ibadan, postgraduate diploma in Financial Management from Obafemi Awolowo University, Ile-Ife, and a bachelor's degree in Agric-economics from Obafemi Awolowo University, Nigeria. He is the author of "Money, Banking and the Economy." He has published extensively in several academic journals.

Samuel Oluwole Ogundele is Associate Professor of Anthropological Archaeology at the University of Ibadan, Ibadan, Nigeria. He obtained his doctorate from the University of Ibadan. He has been Visiting Professor at the University of Ghana, Legon, and University of the Witwatersrand, Johannesburg, South Africa, during which he served on the archaeological research team on the Mapungubwe Hill Complex in the Limpopo Valley region of South Africa. He is author and/or co-author of several books on aspects of African archaeology and anthropology.

Ayo Ogunsiji, a senior lecturer at the Department of English, University of Ibadan, Nigeria, obtained his Ph.D. from the University of Ibadan. His research interests cover applied English linguistics and discourse stylistics as demonstrated in many of his publications such as "Attitudinal Meaning in Soyinka's Ake, Isara and Ibadan," *Le Linguiste,* Antewerp; "Utilitarian Dimensions of Language in the Multilingual Nigerian Context," *Journal of Social Sciences,* Faisalabad; "Aspects of the Phono-Graphological Design in Soyinka's 'Faction'" *NEBULA*, Australia. He is currently co-editing a book on *Language, Literature and Discourse.*

Henry Okodua teaches economics in the Department of Economics and Development Studies, Covenant University, Ota, Nigeria, where he is also a doctoral candidate. He is an active member of the Development Research Group in his university and also a member of the Nigerian Economic Society (NES). He earned his B.Sc. degree in economics from the University of Ilorin, Ilorin, Nigeria, and an M.Sc. degree in economics from the University of Benin, Benin City, Nigeria.

Aloysius-Michaels Okolie is a senior lecturer in the Department of Political Science, University of Nigeria, Nsukka. He earned his Ph.D. from the University of Nigeria, Nsukka. A 2004 Fulbright scholar on U.S. foreign policy, Aloysius-Michaels has authored several peer-reviewed journal articles and book chapters. He is the author of *Political Behaviour* (Nigeria, 2004), *Statistics for Political Data Analysis* (Nigeria, 2005); co-author of *Law, Politics and Mass Media in Nigeria* (Nigeria, 2004); and co-editor of *State and Economy* (Nigeria, 2005). He is currently working on a book-length study of contemporary readings in foreign policy making and implementation in Nigeria.

Stephen Onakuse received his B.Agric. degree from the University of Agriculture, Abeokuta; M.Sc. degree from the University of Ibadan in Environmental Biology; and Ph.D. in Food Science and Technology from University College, Cork, Ireland. He is currently a lecturer in the Department of Food Business & Development and a Research Fellow with the Centre for Sustainable Livelihoods at the University College Cork. His areas of research include the use of indigenous knowledge within communities.

Andrew Oseloka Sawyer is a doctoral candidate of Peace and Conflict Studies Program, University of Ibadan. He was a visiting scholar at Kennesaw State University, Kennesaw, Georgia, USA, in 2008. His research interests are military disarmament, resource conflicts, inter-/intra-religious conflicts and strategic studies. He has presented a number of academic papers in Nigeria and in the United States of America.

Breinigsville, PA USA
07 May 2010
237528BV00005B/2/P

9 780739 145562